CLARENDON

CLARENDON

POLITICS, HISTORIOGRAPHY AND RELIGION

1640–1660

B. H. G. WORMALD

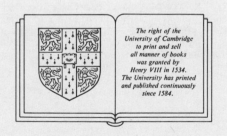

The right of the
University of Cambridge
to print and sell
all manner of books
was granted by
Henry VIII in 1534.
The University has printed
and published continuously
since 1584.

CAMBRIDGE UNIVERSITY PRESS

CAMBRIDGE
NEW YORK   NEW ROCHELLE
MELBOURNE   SYDNEY

Published by the Press Syndicate of the University of Cambridge
The Pitt Building, Trumpington Street, Cambridge CB2 1RP
32 East 57th Street, New York, NY 10022, USA
10 Stamford Road, Oakleigh, Melbourne 3166, Australia

First published 1951
This edition first published 1989

Printed in Great Britain by the University Press, Cambridge

British Library cataloguing in publication data
Wormald, B. H. G. (Brian Harvey Goodwin)
Clarendon: politics, history and religion 1640–1660
1. England. Politics. Clarendon, Edward Hyde, Earl of
1. Title
942.06′092′4

Library of Congress cataloguing in publication data
Wormald, B. H. G.
Clarendon – politics, history, and religion, 1640–1660/B.H.G. Wormald.
p. cm.
Originally published 1951; reissued 1989 with the 1976 Torchbook
ed. introduction and a new introduction.
Includes bibliographical references and index.
ISBN 0 521 37084 1. – ISBN 0 521 37953 9 (pbk)
1. Clarendon, Edward Hyde, Earl of, 1609–1674. 2. Great Britain –
History – Puritan Revolution, 1642–1660 – Historiography.
3. Great Britain – History – Early Stuarts, 1603–1649 – Historiography.
4. Great Britain – Politics and government – 1642–1660.
5. Great Britain – Church history – 17th century. 6. Statesmen –
Great Britain – Biography. 7. Historians – Great Britain – Biography.
1. Title.
DA447.c6w6 1989
941.06′092′4 – dc19 88–34680 CIP

ISBN 0 521 37084 1 hard covers
ISBN 0 521 37953 9 paperback

To
HERBERT BUTTERFIELD

CONTENTS

FOREWORD, 1989

HUGH KEARNEY

Brian Wormald's penetrating study of Clarendon, which has been reprinted several times since its first publication in 1951, enjoys wide recognition as a work of original scholarship. There are, I think, three reasons which explain its high reputation. In the first place, it is a successful attempt to get inside the mind of a man who was both a politician of great influence and a historian of genius. Edward Hyde, Earl of Clarendon, has not fared well at the hands of English historians since Macaulay. Mr Wormald attempts to redress the balance by a sympathetic re-assessment of Clarendon's political and religious attitudes during a period of revolution and civil war.

In the second place, this book is written by a scholar who has thought long and hard about the theological crosscurrents within the Church of England during a formative period of its history. In the years since 1945, Puritanism has tended to capture the attention of historians of the seventeenth century. Here, Mr Wormald explores the beliefs of the 'Erasmians' of Great Tew, showing Clarendon as one of a circle of Anglican intellectuals who were seeking an alternative to the high church school of Laud and to its Calvinist opponents. As Mr Wormald reminds us, it was not the Puritans who finally won the day, but Clarendon and his followers at the Restoration.

Finally, *Clarendon* is important for students of historiography. In his Introduction to the 1976 reprint Mr Wormald provides his readers with a powerful critique of 'Whiggish' history from Macaulay to certain contemporary proponents of a 'social interpretation' of the 'English Revolution'. Wormald's challenging book deservedly takes a place beside Herbert Butterfield's *The*

Englishman and his History (1944) and John Pocock's *The Ancient Constitution and the Feudal Law* (1957, 2nd edn, 1987) as a key text for those interested in how English history has come to be written. Wormald's own hero is David Hume, whose *History of England* is now experiencing a widespread revival of interest after many years of neglect.

PREFACE, 1976

I

Edward Hyde, historian, political philosopher and statesman, was born in 1609 and died in 1674. He became Earl of
Clarendon in 1661. This book is not his biography; nor, as
should be evident from reflexions in this preface, is it a comprehensive study of his place in history. But the period covered
is self-contained and can be read as such. Moreover, the argument, I hope, can be followed without the aid of information
beyond what is supplied. When Renaissance humanists used
to say that history is easy, they meant that it is easy compared
with scholastic theology, for example, or natural science.

In this book, first published twenty-five years ago, I have attempted to penetrate the period which is covered by the earliest
portion of Clarendon's own historical writing and to discover
his mind as it unfolded in relation to events. It has been assumed, for reasons which I hope may become clear, that his attitude before the outbreak of civil war can hardly have been
what he later implied it was. I have proceeded to try to
answer the question what in fact was this earlier attitude of
his; and then to deal with the further question how did an
earlier attitude turn into a later one? The work of Part I of
this book tells the story from the point at which the action of
the Long Parliament ceased to be successful in achieving clear
and agreed aims—that is to say, Part I starts with the beginning
of the second session (October 1641). It concludes with the
ending of the first civil war (1646).

Part II is concerned with the period from 1646 to 1660. It is
marked off from the preceding period because in it Clarendon
started to write history and thus added to himself, and with
striking consequences for his politics, the dimension of histori-

cal thinking. Part III contains a discussion of Clarendon's views on religion and on the relations of church and state. It constitutes to some extent a departure from a hitherto mainly narrative treatment. But the change has seemed to be necessary in order to round off an interpretation given in Part I and Part II.

II

Clarendon was member for Saltash in the Long Parliament (November 1640). Pym and Hampden are more famous, but Clarendon was prominent in the planned devastating assault of the first session upon the persons and institutions of Charles I's government. He was chairman of committees set up by the commons to investigate the prerogative jurisdictions of the Council of the North and Council of Wales, making a name for himself with a speech attacking the former. 'What', he had asked, 'hath the good northern people done that they only must be disfranchised of all their privileges by Magna Carta and the Petition of Right?' He took a leading part in proceedings against the judges and presented to the lords the charge against the barons of the Exchequer who had ruled against Hampden in the case of ship money. He assisted in preparing the articles to impeach the Earl of Strafford and took part in expediting his trial. Nor does Clarendon's name appear in the list of members who voted against Strafford's attainder. More important, when the monarchy was restored in 1660 Clarendon was lord chancellor and chief minister. He became, as Leopold von Ranke put it, 'one of the chief founders of that system in church and state on which the English constitution thenceforward rested'.

But save as author of *The History of the Rebellion and Civil Wars in England* his reputation has not been secure in his own land. His beliefs and achievements have been hard to square with the conventional framework created by prevalent preoccupations and obsessions about English history. He has had unsympathetic treatment from historians under Whig leadership all the way from Thomas Babington Lord Macaulay.

Macaulay stated that it is to the favourable comparison between Clarendon and the baseness and profligacy of Restoration times that he is principally indebted for his high reputation, and though ready to admire the *History*, Macaulay could write—'We suffer ourselves to be delighted by the keenness of Clarendon's observations and by the sober majesty of his style till we forget the oppressor and the bigot in the historian'. G. M. Trevelyan (Macaulay's great-nephew) reproached the man in a different way: the Restoration, he wrote in *The English Revolution, 1688–9* (1938) set up equilibrium between crown and parliament. This 'postponed the ultimate trial of strength between the monarchical and representative principle. That equilibrium was believed by Clarendon to be the summit of political wisdom, the true and final balance of our constitution. No more Strafford and no more Pym! It was a lawyer's idea of politics, with all the merits and defects of a lawyer's idea'.

According to a framework of notions seemingly indestructible, English constitutional history has consisted of a perennial and necessary conflict between kings and parliaments. Kings were always seeking to encroach on the rights and liberties of the people and parliaments always resisting. The constitution, defended by parliaments, and attacked by kings, was an embodiment of rights and liberties—civil, political, ecclesiastical —and it was taken for granted that it had always existed or at least that it ought to have done. The seventeenth century is the classic age because kings, four of them, furnished with a novel engine of autocracy, the Divine Right of Kings, spent that century in an attempt more determined than any made before to overthrow the constitution, and parliaments for their part were occupied with intensity unprecedented in struggling, even fighting with arms in hand, to preserve it. By the end of the century parliaments succeeded in beating kings. In 1688–89 Divine Right monarchy was suppressed and a parliamentary puppet set up. Rights and liberties were finally secured by vindicating parliamentary government.

Within such a framework, sovereignty, defined to mean a recognised possession of supreme unlimited authority in the state, has tended to be an obsession. If kings and parliaments were at odds, surely it must have been sovereignty they were at odds about? Who is sovereign, king or people?

The shortcomings of these beliefs have often been noticed. It has been stressed that rule lay always rightfully with kings not parliaments; and that since this was recognised, government by kings was government by consent. (No rulers save Oliver Cromwell and James II had large standing forces.) It has been shown that struggle and rivalry between kings and parliaments were exception not rule, the rule in theory and also in practice being cooperation, healthy tension and interchange: that in regard to seventeenth-century conflicts, parliaments were the innovators and aggressors, that such constitutional rights as existed backed the kings, and that this, again, was widely recognized. It has been pointed out that sovereignty as defined above was eccentric to matters at issue and objectives pursued. The revolution of 1688–89 did not resolve the issue of sovereignty in favour of 'the representative principle', and it did not liquidate the monarchy. William III was no puppet. The mixture was as before.

The ideas thus challenged have continued to live. They have persisted in the form of assertion or counter-assertion. They have also survived by implication in seeming indifference to anything better. History like nature abhors a vacuum. Powerful correctives have been offered in the eighteenth century and again in the twentieth, the first by David Hume, the second by writers in the United States, preeminent among them Charles Howard McIlwain. In each case the moves came from abroad: in each instance for understandable reasons.

Hume, a Scot, intervened because for better or worse his country was tied to the southern kingdom and affected by its factious politics. He aimed through his writings to dampen and rationalise faction. For McIlwain and the Americans, on the other hand, seventeenth-century England presents the mediaeval history of their own constitution. Scotland is bound to England in space. The United States of America is tied to it by time.

These eighteenth-century and twentieth-century corrections have had different and opposite fates. While the former was much attacked the latter has been largely ignored. In the event, however, the effect has been the same. The myth has lived on. The publication of Hume's *History of Great Britain—the Reigns of James I and Charles I* met at once with fierce opposition. The book was even complained of in the House of Lords by the Earl of Chatham. It was not the case that Hume had written with the object merely of vindicating in a constitutional sense the claims of James and Charles. Hume's aim was to correct, as he said, 'the misrepresentations of faction which had begun chiefly to take place at that time'. He hoped to do this by providing an account which should be impartial, and fair to all parties. Indeed, he had hard things to say of these monarchs and also, in the next volume, of Charles II and James II. Hume was charged all the same with having produced an apology for tyranny. By virtue of excellence his book before long began to sell steadily. Macaulay admitted that it became the narrative from which the great mass of the reading public were content to take their opinions. Nevertheless for more than half a century, *The History of Great Britain* was under continued attack from Whigs and radicals. Whole histories were written to confute its positions.

In the end these positions of Hume were overthrown. This happened not as a result of scholarly discussion and debate, with truth triumphing—*magna est veritas et praevalet;* but because the myth, having always been cherished, had doses of strong fresh life injected into it. Henry Hallam with his *Con-*

stitutional History of England, Henry VII to George II had a
hand in this. It seems, however, that the re-Whigification of
English history which took place in the nineteenth century
should be counted as the achievement of Macaulay. This is not
because what he said about Hume as historian is correct.

Macaulay classed Hume with modern historians 'who have
been seduced from truth not by their imagination, but by their
reason.' These writers he condemned in terms nearly identical
with those used long before by Pierre Bayle when attacking
historians in general: 'in every human character and transaction there is a mixture of good and evil: a little exaggeration,
a little suppression, a judicious use of epithets, a watchful and
searching scepticism with respect to the evidence on one side, a
convenient credulity with respect to every report or tradition
on the other, may easily make a saint of Laud, or tyrant of
Henry the Fourth'. Hume, wrote Macaulay, 'is an accomplished advocate': he displays an 'insidious candour' and this
'increases the effect of the vast mass of sophistry:' he has
'pleaded the cause of tyranny with the dexterity of an advocate,
while affecting the impartiality of a judge'. If this, as one
writer has remarked, is perhaps the most severe criticism ever
passed by one historian on another, conceivably it is also the
most unjust. Nor was Macaulay's version superior to Hume's
as history. Macaulay owed his success to the power of his style
of writing: also to the fact that what men read in him was what
many of them liked to be told.

The hubbub which had attended the *critique* of Whig doctrine delivered from over the Border was not repeated when
the revision arrived from across the Ocean some thirty years ago.
The general climate of opinion had changed. Hume and Macaulay had written at times when interest in the issues they
discussed in historical terms was vigorous. Both authors addressed themselves with success to an eager audience. Not only
was the twentieth-century public less excitable; in addition the
historians had become more professional. History had become

heavily academic, its practitioners self-enclosed. Moreover, their attention was directed in many cases to questions which were neither political nor constitutional. Historical interest, like much else of importance, is subject to fashion. Political and constitutional history had become unfashionable. In any case, if history is a science, narrow concentration upon the political and legal aspects of the past might be putting brakes on the progress of historical understanding. It could be argued that the neglect of political and constitutional history was a matter not so much of fashion as of scientific imperatives. Both Hume and Macaulay knew that there is much in history besides politics and the constitution: more than that—they taught that study of other aspects of the past would be likely to add to the intelligibility and utility of historical knowledge.

In the mid-twentieth-century there has been much concentration by scholars in England on social and economic history. They have devoted themselves to these studies for their own sake, and also because it has been believed likely that from such investigations explanations of political and constitutional changes might emerge. It became common, for instance, to assume that the upheavals of 1640–1660 are only to be understood in the light of social and economic factors.

However, to concede that Sir John Seeley was wrong, or at least that he was too close to common sense to have been scientific when he stated that history is past politics, is not the same as agreeing that history is little more than past social structure and economics. Such a doctrine seems to part company not only with sense but with science. Politics and its consequences do not and did not go away merely by being ignored.

Furthermore, it is not clear that investigation of social and economic factors has caused the politics of 1640–1660 to be understood with new intelligibility. 'The Storm over the Gentry', for example, generated more heat than light. A result of the persisting attraction of social and economic studies, whether for their own sake or as helping to explain the other aspects of the past, has been that even inside the profession the ancient myth has tended to linger. An interpretation of some sort is needed to do service in an area which even if ignored is allowed to have had an existence. It is all the more necessary to have an interpretation if it is hoped that what went on in that area can be explained by what went on outside it.

Within the historians' profession, there has been a lingering of the old mythical frame. There has also been the invention of a new myth. This is quite different and is not a mere stubborn residuum. It is the offspring of creative enthusiasm. I refer to the determination to promote 1640–1660 to a new status by calling it The English Revolution.

III

Ranke asked himself a question about the great French Revolution of 1789: 'has it a general interest which gains the support of the mind and heart and claims a complete sympathy, or is it only an ordinary event, which has its origin in certain particular facts, and which was the result of a concurrence of circumstances which might have been different? While recognizing its universal importance and what it was for each one of us in particular, yet I deliberately took my stand among those who opposed it'. Now it is clear that for the English nation the occurrence which has had this general interest gaining the sympathetic support of mind and heart is the Glorious Revolution of 1688–89. It is 1688–89 which has been the English Revolution. In addition to holding a key position in the mythological framework, it has had an equal importance in the reality. As Hume put it, 1688–89 erected the more uniform edifice in which 'to their mutual felicity king and people were finally taught to know their proper boundaries'. A decisive event, it was also relatively unrevolutionary.

As for the upheavals which had occurred between 1640 and 1660, these were rebellion, civil wars, a regicide, a time of rule by a victorious army, a restoration; or, if all would not have accepted that there had been rebellion, at least none could have denied civil wars, regicide, army rule and restoration. Both the rebellion and the first civil war could be called 'great'; so also could Oliver Cromwell (whether men said so or only thought so). There were men and events for many families to remember with emotion. Thomas Hobbes wrote, 'If in time, as in place, there were degrees of high and low I verily believe that the highest of time would be that which passed between the years of 1640 and 1660'. Yet the events were hardly of the kind to gain among large sections of men that intellectual and emotional discipleship which Ranke described in the devotees of 1789.

Before the middle of the twentieth century it has not been usual to call this great time of troubles the English Revolution —at least, it was unusual for English historians to speak in that way. A Frenchman might do so. François Guizot spoke of three Anglo-Saxon revolutions: 1640–1660, 1688–89 and the American Revolution, and he wrote about the first. An exception among the English is Thomas Hill Green. Philosopher and political radical, Green delivered *Four Lectures on the English Revolution* (1640–1660) before the Edinburgh Philosophical Society in 1867.

It will not be forgotten that historians, Samuel Rawson Gardiner and many others, have called what took place in the middle years of the seventeenth century the Puritan Revolution. They have descried in those events religious explosions and ecclesiastical upheavals of such greatness that they merit the title of revolution. The times were moved, it is assumed, by motives and objectives largely religious, these carrying political and constitutional concomitants and results. It was a time of flourishing religious genius and spiritual giants—Cromwell, Milton. There was a hurricane of passions and convictions. R. H. Tawney once suggested that a better way to define the period would be to see it as the true English Reformation. The

Reformation in the sixteenth century had been an act of state. A hundred years later religion threw off its shackles and took revenge. It broke the state. Moreover, what emerged was a church for England in a decisive lasting form. The Act of Uniformity of 1662 with much justification had its political aspect —the maintenance of order—but essentially it represented England's choice of a church by its ruling classes. But the English Reformation has remained in the sixteenth century. As for the Puritan Revolution, that notion is not now so fashionable. Even when it was much in vogue it was not intended that it should usurp the place so long allotted to 1688–89.

The fact of the matter is that until recently one reason for the fame of England, both at home and abroad, has been that it has not had a revolutionary tradition. At home, 1688–89 was often prized for having been neat, brief and unsanguinary. When Guizot considered the Anglo-Saxon Revolutions, he suggested somewhat enviously that they were not, even the first of them (1640–60), truly revolutionary when compared with 1789. However, in our day English historians in a different frame of mind have attempted to rescue a country unjustly deprived, as they seem to think, of a revolutionary tradition. Though decisive, 1688–89 makes a poor showing: it was bloodless and over in a month or two: it should be disqualified. Ingredients required are three-fold: emergencies, violence and overturnings sufficiently intense in quality and occurring in many departments of life: next, that proceedings of that kind must extend over a sufficiently protracted period: lastly, that as a consquence things are never the same again. These are in a mounting order of importance. It is the last requirement that most matters. The new English revolution must be as decisive as 1789.

Surely enough that was sudden, violent and unprecedented took place in most aspects of national existence after 1640? Surely the proceedings lasted long enough? Compared with the period 1789–1815 in France, the English revolution falls only a few years short. Surely it is the case that when all was over things could not be the same again? Prompted by dispositions of heart and mind which Ranke saw in others but rejected for himself when he contemplated the French Revolution, the questions are affirmatively answered. Since the qualifying events fall precisely in its middle, the seventeenth century is denominated 'The Century of Revolution'. Given this sufficiently catastrophic central complex, search is made for causes of comparable magnitude—causes suitably great in themselves, suitably great enough also in variety, and stretching suitably far back into preceding time. In addition to causes religious, political and constitutional, there must be causes of all other kinds: economic, social, cultural, intellectual. In all departments causes stretch themselves back into the Tudor age. Having assessed them retrospectively, investigators turn round and trace them prospectively, running over the ground again till they reach 1640. The upshot of many extended perambulations is that the events of 1640–60 no longer have their 'origin in particular facts' and cease to be 'the result of a concurrence of circumstances which might have been different'; instead, they present themselves as inevitable.

This English Revolution of 1640–1660 is a colonizing venture conducted from the twentieth century back into the seventeenth. But the foothold it maintains seems precarious. Excellent work has been done. There is much to be grateful for. But—changing the metaphor—the definition of a mirage is 'an illusory image produced by atmospheric conditions'. This English Revolution is a mirage projected by the atmospherics of our time. It is the twentieth century which is the Century of Revolution. In 1917 another great revolution occurred which has decisively altered the world. Trailing the historical dogmatics of a materialised Hegel, it claims to have added itself to 1789 as the next step in the revolutionary emancipation of mankind. The English Revolution can pass the first two tests. There were overturnings in many departments, and undoubtedly these extended themselves over a protracted time. What of the third criterion, the most important? Is it the case that as consequence of all this England was never the same again and that there occurred great permanent alterations?

Because of the presiding analogies of 1789 and 1917 much attention has been devoted to social phenomena not only in the realm of causes but also in that of results. It looks as if the work it has been inspiring is establishing the mirage character of the English Revolution. In terms of the social system and the distribution of wealth and power between groups or classes, changes resulting from the mid-century turmoils, according to what appear to be the present findings, were small.

The keynote in the crucial area is not revolution. Oliver Cromwell himself spoke for the fact, musing aloud before parliament in 1654; 'the ranks and orders of men,—whereby England hath been known for hundreds of years—A nobleman, a gentleman, a yeoman; the distinction of these: that is a good interest of the nation, and a great one!' The natural magistracy of the nation had been threatened, he said, but it had not been trampled underfoot.

IV

By resolution of the upper house of the Convention Parliament in Spring 1660 it was declared that in conformity with the ancient and fundamental laws of this kingdom, the government is and ought to be by king, lords and commons. Much of what was said and done by the men who made the settlement of 1660 seems like an echo in the political and constitutional spheres of the findings of Oliver and twentieth-century historians regarding the distribution of property and power in society.

Men who make history are not less subject to myths and mirages than those who write it. Cromwell in the matter of the ranks and orders appears to have been free of them. Were the men who made the political and constitutional settlement, above all Clarendon who was chief, free? Was he right that what was done was restoration and establishment of continuity? He was both right and wrong. The continuity was great; it was no myth: but so likewise was the breach. That was also great and no myth. In one respect Clarendon was subject to myth. He shared nothing else with Whig politicians and Whig historians, but he appears to have believed as they did that the way the king had governed before the meeting of the Long Parliament had been against the law. It was this belief that made him exaggerate a continuity which was real and to ignore a break equally real. The bills which had been sent to Charles I by lords and commons in that first session, in which Clarendon himself had sat, became acts when Charles accepted them. These statutes did not state or allow it to be assumed that what had been done by prerogative courts and declared by judges had been legal but were legal no longer. They pronounced these proceedings to have been illegal from the start. Arbitrary conduct was condemned for the past and prohibited for the future, the constitution thus emerging cleansed and restored to purity.

Before the lords in July 1641 at the impeachment of the barons of the Exchequer, Clarendon said, 'My Lords, there cannot be a greater instance of a sick and languishing commonwealth than the business of this day. Good God, how hath the guilty these late years been punished, when the judges themselves have been such delinquents? Tis no marvel that an irregular, extravagant, arbitrary power, like a torrent, hath broke in upon us when our banks and our bulwarks, the laws, were in the custody of such persons'.

In the Act for Regulating the Privy Council and for taking away the Court commonly called the Star Chamber it was stated that the 'proceedings, censures, and decrees of that court have by experience been found to be an intolerable burden on the subjects and the means to introduce an arbitrary power and government'. Again, by the act for the declaring void the late proceedings touching ship money, it was 'declared and enacted by the King's Most Excellent Majesty and the Lords and Commons in this Parliament assembled and by the authority of the same that the said charge imposed upon the subject for the providing and furnishing of ships commonly called Ship Money . . . and the said judgment given against the said John Hampden were and are contrary to and against the laws and statutes of this realm, the right of property, the liberty of the subjects, former resolutions in parliament and the Petition of Right.'

The assumption was that under the king's ministers of law and of state 'an irregular, extravagant, arbitrary power, like a torrent, hath broke in upon us . . .'; in short, that they had been proceeding, as we should say, unconstitutionally. Were the lords and commons right, Clarendon among them?

It is true that to adopt a clear concept of a constitution when dealing with the year 1600, is anachronistic. On the other hand, there were, as McIlwain said, quite evidently substantive principles deducible from institutions: 'a set of principles embodied in the institutions of a nation and neither external to these nor in existence prior to them'. Such principles are not discernible only by the historian looking back—they were accepted by the men operating the institutions. The principles were the upshot of utility and consent, the interaction between the two making rules of practice.

Taking the times before and after 1600, it was generally held that certain transcendent prerogatives were vested in the crown. When Lord Chancellor Bacon and Sir Edward Coke C.J. are in agreement, it is hardly likely that anybody else is better qualified to speak. They agreed that the transcendent prerogatives were legal, and that it was part of the law that the crown could not be divested of them: they were inherent—inseparable. The crown could not be divested of them even by an act of parliament which expressly asserted that it was doing such a thing. A king could not self-divest himself of them when he turned a bill into an act by accepting it—or, at least, he could self-divest himself only, not his successors. It was agreed that these prerogatives were not only inherent and inseparable they were indisputable too: indisputable save when the king granted permission for them to be disputed in courts of law or in parliament.

These prerogatives made the king of England an Absolute King: he was described as such, and he would call himself such. Queen Elizabeth had King Philip of Spain reminded that she was every bit as absolute as he. She was absolute because in the exercise of these prerogatives there was no one above to control her, save God Almighty, and no one below or coordinate who shared them or by whom she could be called to account. She was absolute also because in the exercise of these prerogatives the queen was not bound by formalities as in common law procedure and in parliament but acted according to free discretion. On the other hand, though an absolute monarch, the queen of England was no despot—she had no legal right to all property and goods in the kingdom.

With characteristic perspicacity, Hume noticed that the term 'absolute' might have had a meaning in those times which differed from the later one. 'We may infer either that the word absolute bore a different sense from what it does at present or that men's ideas of the English government were then different'. He seems himself to have favoured the latter possibility. It has remained for the Americans to adopt the former.

McIlwain has urged that Seneca's aphorism sums up the facts of the case: *Ad Reges enim potestas omnium pertinet: ad singulos proprietas*—to kings belongs authority over all: to private persons, property. Just as the former could not be shared or disputed by subjects save with the ruler's consent, so the latter, property, could not be shared or disputed by the king save with the consent of its owners. It followed that the monarch though an absolute ruler was also limited. It is easy to suppose that these principles must necessarily have been anti-parliamentary in tendency. That is not the case. Parliament was part of the principles: if the king needed taxes he must summon it. Furthermore, as Bacon argued, it is parliament which must be a sorting shop in cases of overlap. Speaking in the Commons in 1610 he stated that the king could prohibit debate on an essential matter which concerned the prerogative of the crown, and that upon receiving his inhibition the house always had obeyed. But if the matter of prerogative involved the right of the subject the house ought to inform the king of its liberties and proceed.

Again, though the monarch was called sovereign he was no sovereign according to Hobbes's doctrine. It was not the case that everything that the ruler might do would be legal in virtue of the fact that he had done it, though there might be no redress unless he agreed to grant it. Actions of the king could be illegal. 'The King's acts that grieve the subject are either against law and so void', said Bacon, 'or according to strictness of law, and yet grievous'.

V

Such a constitutional situation may seem crazy; but it is incorrect to suppose that a system with a king who was legally absolute but who yet was neither despot nor sovereign, could never have worked in terms of its own principles, or that it must necessarily soon have fallen apart. It worked. Above all it did so under the Tudors, who are not normally viewed as rulers under whom measures were ineffectual. Bacon wrote, 'let no one weakly conceive that just laws and true policy have any antipathy: for they are like the spirit and sinews that one moves with the other'.

The principles were not novel and they stretched back behind the Tudors. However, after 1600 there were two novel developments. The first was a movement into the realm of theory. This took place mainly in the reign of James. The second was a change in the realm of practice. This occurred chiefly in the reign of Charles.

In the reign of James, the attempt was made to extract and put forth into positive logical coherence principles which had been, as McIlwain said, neither external to the working of institutions nor in existence prior to them. Bacon and Coke were in agreement on these fundamental matters, but they stated an agreed view about them in different ways. Coke put all in terms of the common law. Bacon considered it better to class the king's transcendent prerogatives as 'being matter of government and not of law'. But there was a dilemma. On the one hand, without new definitions, men were left in a situation in which a deed could be at the same time both legal and illegal. On the other hand, new definitions seemed to imply principles themselves new and therefore unacceptable.

Secondly, in the reign of Charles, principles were misapplied in practice. The crown misused prerogatives which were designed for defence of the realm in emergency. The first misuse was in the arrest of the Five Knights, 1626, the second in the levy of Ship Money. The judges in Hampden's case found for the crown since it was for the crown alone to decide whether there was an emergency. There was none. The judgment also illustrated the need for definition. The judges defended the transcendent prerogatives in terms of the law of the land, following Coke's way of thinking, not Bacon's. According to Clarendon, this was a fact which caused consternation.

Clarendon described in the *History* how Ship Money became 'a word of lasting sound in the memory of this kingdom.' When Ship Money was transacted at the Council-Board, he wrote, men 'looked upon it as a work of that power they were always obliged to trust and an effect of that foresight they were naturally to rely upon. Imminent necessity and public safety were convincing persuasions; and it might not seem of apparent ill consequence to them that upon an emergent occasion the regal power should fill up an hiatus, or supply an impotency in the law. But when they saw in a court of law, (that law that gave them title and possession of all that they had) apophthegms of state urged as elements of law; judges as sharp-sighted as Secretaries of State and in the mysteries of state; judgment of law grounded upon matter of fact of which there was neither inquiry nor proof; and no reason given for the payment of the thirty shillings in question but what concluded the estates of all the standers-by; they had no reason to hope that that doctrine or the preachers of it would be contained within any bounds'. Here, it appeared, was 'a spring and magazine that should have no bottom, and for an everlasting supply of all occasions'.

The Long Parliament in its first session achieved a true revolution, a sharp break humanly speaking unthinkable in normal times. It was a surgical operation inflicted upon Charles I, the reluctant patient. Though the method was itself constitutional (acts of parliament) the deed was possible only through application of intense pressure, the king having allowed himself to be manoeuvred into a *cul-de-sac*. 'In Europe', declared James Madison in 1792, 'charters of liberty have been granted by power'. This was a European charter of liberty, and after it had been granted things, as it turned out, were not the same again.

Why? If 'no act', as Sir Edward Coke said, 'can bind the king from any prerogative which is sole and inseparable to his person', why did these, and others later, succeed in binding him? If 'this royal power cannot be restrained by any act of parliament, neither *in thesi* nor *in hypothesi,* but that the king by his royal prerogative may dispense with it', why did these, and others later, succeed in restraining it?

The answer is that just as principles of government operating before 1640 had needed time and events past for their establishment, similarly the principles of 1641 needed time and events future. Whether 1641 proved decisive would be a question of fact, of history. In 1643 Charles I had it in mind to dissolve the Long Parliament by proclamation in virtue of inseparable

prerogative, despite the fact that he had in 1641 accepted the
bill according to which parliament could not be dissolved except with its own consent. He was dissuaded by Clarendon. The
constitutional settlement of the Restoration clinched the revolution of 1641 because of the presiding presence in 1660 of the
same man.

In 1662 Charles II had it in mind to suspend the execution
of the act of Uniformity, thus giving relief to dissenters, both
Catholic and Protestant, in virtue of prerogative; despite the
fact that he accepted the bill of Uniformity, which forbade
all dissent. Clarendon told him that a promise was a promise
and must be kept but that in law he could not do it.

What had happened with appropriate irony is that an engine
which in the sixteenth century the crown had used against the
faith, jurisdiction and property of the universal church, was
turned in the seventeenth against the crown. The Tudors
asserted the competence of statute to legislate on the territory
of Holy Church. By the Long Parliament the competence of
statutes was extended to legislate upon that of the Prerogative
Royal.

Hallam stated that Clarendon showed unfitness for the government of a free country: he took him to task for having
written: 'He [Clarendon] did never dissemble from the time of
his return with the king, that the late rebellion could never be
extirpated and pulled up by the roots till the king's regal and
inherent power and prerogative should be fully avowed and
vindicated, and till the usurpations in both houses of parliament, since the year 1640, were disclaimed and made odious;
and many other excesses, which had been affected by both
before that time under the name of privileges, should be restrained or explained. For all which reformation the kingdom
in general was very well disposed, when it pleased God to restore the king to it. The present parliament had done much,
and would willingly have prosecuted the same method, if they
had had the same advice and encouragement.' Could this
mean, Hallam asked, that they might have been led to repeal

other statutes of the Long Parliament, besides the Triennial Act, and that excluding the bishops from the House of Peers; but more especially, to have restored 'the two great levers of prerogative, the courts of star chamber and high commission?' Clarendon's choice of words seemed sinister; 'regal' and 'inherent' had been descriptions of the *Potestas Absoluta*.

But Clarendon did not press for more to be undertaken than was achieved: also it is clear that the line he took as chancellor was the same as that adopted by Bishop Stephen Gardiner who was chancellor to Queen Mary I. The bishop had told the queen that the statutes offending against the church could not be put aside in virtue of having overstepped competence. Unless they were repealed they stood; she must wait for repeal. It was the same with the statutes offensive to prerogative. In 1664 there was an act which repealed that of 1641 on the ground that it was 'in derogation of His Majesty's just rights and prerogative inherent to the Imperial Crown . . . for the calling and assembling of parliaments'; enacting nevertheless 'that hereafter the sitting and holding of parliaments shall not be intermitted or discontinued above three years at the most'.

The act for the safety and preservation of His Majesty's person and government declared there to be no legislative power in either or both houses of parliament without the king and that orders or ordinances of both or either house were void. In the same year an act affirmed that the sole right of the militia lay in the king and that neither or both houses could or should pretend to the same. The result of these proceedings for the crown was statutory prerogatives; plainly not the restoration of the regal and inherent power. The essence of this had been that it was supra-statutory because pre-statutory.

VI

An old Whig charge against Clarendon is that he was authoritarian. Hallam having noted that he was unfit to rule a free nation, Macaulay asserted that he was oppressor and bigot. With regard to the imputation of bigotry, it is certainly the case that Clarendon embraced and supported the Restoration settlement of the Church of England when it was completed. This hardly helps to substantiate his authoritarianism. The anglican establishment of the church was made by parliament alone. The severity of its imposition was contrary to the wishes of both king and chancellor.

The Parliament of 1661 was left free to inherit all that parliaments had aspired to in the years before 1640, including that greatest prize of all—control over the character of the English church. Henry VIII's church, Elizabeth I's church, Charles II's church—these are a progression from one extreme to the other. Luther described the first, 'Whatever pleases Harry becomes an article of faith for life and death'. The prayer-book of 1559 was a compromise between the queen's wishes and those of the commons. That of 1662 represented exclusively the will of parliament. The fact that this was no longer a puritan will but an anglican will was parliament's own affair. This is not the end of the matter. The chancellor's parliamentarism in the matter of the church seems actually to have over-ridden ideas of his own for a more comprehensive, less 'bigoted' settlement.

Whig estimates of Clarendon seem astray. It is a singular fact for instance that whereas Gardiner writing of the pre-civil war period, made of his mythical Clarendon a figure to be sharply criticised, the real man whom he missed seems to have embodied Gardiner's own notions of what should have been done. Even when judgment comes nearer the mark, as in the case of Trevelyan writing of the Restoration (equilibrium between king and parliament), the man is still blamed. With the English Revolution school, Clarendon seems to fare no better. 'In 1640–41', writes the Master of Balliol, 'he thought he could make an omelette without breaking any eggs. . . . After 1660 Clarendon repeated his mistake. . . . blood, iron and

"fanaticism" go to the making of a revolution as well as reason.'
But all those necessary commodities had been employed in the
destruction of Strafford.

It is Hume who was right about Clarendon. Indeed there is
more than a little similarity between the two men. They both
stood for both authority and liberty—authority meaning a
strong executive: they had in common a justifiable anxiety
that authority might be too greatly diminished—Clarendon,
the statesman, looking back upon years of turmoil lying just
behind; Hume, the historian, looking forward, and judging
that perhaps the revolution of 1688–89 had too much diminished the crown's discretionary reserve. In common they incur
the hostility of the Whigs. But in each case liberty balanced
evenly with authority. Hume was himself a 'Revolution Whig',
though in his own special way. And this is Hume describing
Clarendon: he 'was always a friend to the liberty and constitution of his country. At the commencement of the civil wars he
had entered into the late king's service, and was honored with
a great share in the esteem and friendship of that monarch: he
was pursued with unrelenting hostility by the Long Parliament:
he had shared all the fortunes, and directed all the counsels, of
the present king during his exile: he had been advanced to the
highest trust and office after the restoration; yet all these circumstances, which might naturally operate with such force,
either on resentment, gratitude or ambition, had no influence
on his uncorrupted mind'.

The constitutional future was certainly not decided by the
Restoration settlement alone. But it is sometimes necessary
to take two bites at a cherry. The English Reformation needed
two bites, and if 1662 was more decisive for a stable Church
of England than Queen Elizabeth I's settlement, it has not
been usual on that account to deny the queen her credit.

Royal autocracy was still a possibility in the years after
Charles II came home. There was nothing inevitable about the
survival of a regime with an entrenched parliament. Charles II

possessed what his father had lacked, a standing army (though small) and a taxation system (though this took time to work well). He was not only his father's heir; he was Cromwell's too. These latter inheritances, if developed, might give the crown power in addition to its authority from the law: indeed the crown might more than recoup with such power what it had lost in terms of the constitution. The crown could perhaps become independent with the consequent opening for autocracy. The possibility occurred under James II. His army was large, his revenue great. In those circumstances the next step might have been reversal of the constitutional revolution and restoration of pre-statutory prerogative. Charles II, however, conducted himself on the whole as a limited king both in law and in fact. He was not independent. Even after Clarendon's fall he endeavoured to cooperate with parliament for as long as possible.

The events occurring in 1688–89 were able to clinch those of the 60's because of two outstanding historical circumstances: the indolence, extravagance and (perhaps) prudence of Charles II; and the imprudence or (perhaps) misfortune of James II, resulting in the collapse of all his efforts. These are the two cardinal negative facts which followed the cardinal positive fact—Clarendon.

There is thus one sphere in which the seventeenth century is truly the Century of Revolution. In an age when much, as in most times, moved in the evolutionary way, strictly in the matter of the constitution there was a succession of sharp turns. The full century was needed: the Petition of Right of 1628 (revealing that dispute had broken out over the fundamental principles of the government and that Sir Edward Coke had apparently changed his mind); the Long Parliament's first session; the Restoration; the Glorious Revolution. Here is a considerable constitutional omelette. It had required the breaking of a sizeable egg, Black Tom. Thomas Wentworth, Earl of Strafford, was the one formidably capable man of action in the king's service in the last times of the pre-1640 regime.

Francis Bacon had been the most penetrating of its thinkers. The revolution was the transition from a Baconian to a Clarendonian constitution—Bacon and Clarendon, both men of the law and of letters, readers and writers of histories for instruction, parliament-men and counsellors of kings.

Parliament and statute had been parts of the Baconian constitution, but Restoration statute, like Restoration parliament, was an instrument with extended competence—competence stretched beyond the extension made by the Tudors for the purpose of destroying the church. Restoration statute was stretched to omnicompetence, so that everything, without limit, which statute stated was law. Provided the judges would see matters that way, Hobbes's sovereignty had arrived. The doctrine was not promulgated by statute: it was established by judges from 1660 onwards. The King in Parliament under the Clarendonian constitution would be sovereign in a way the Absolute King under the Baconian had never been.

Doctrine that here there is absolute authority, the word carrying the new and to us more familiar meaning—such would be the antithesis of a constitution. But no such outcome had been or was now the aim. It was by-product of the performance of specific tasks—the removal in 1641 of alleged usurpations by the crown and the reversal after 1660 of actual usurpations by parliament.

VII

What had happened over the centuries to produce the Baconian constitution was this: the crown was the fount of justice and order; therefore it was the fount of institutions to provide them. The common law flowed out of the crown. There is utility, there is consent, the two together producing rules of practice. There had been no officials in the localities wholly dependent on the crown—the king's officers were the local landholders. Parliament, too, had flowed out of the

crown. 'By the positive law', wrote one of the Jacobean theorists, 'the King was pleased to limit and stint his absolute
power and to tie himself to the ordinary rules of the law, in
common and ordinary cases . . . retaining and reserving notwithstanding in many points that absolute and unlimited
power which was given unto him . . .' That must be so—emergencies always come. There would be defects in the common
law and fresh problems of order, and so new institutions, extraordinary prerogative courts parallel with ordinary courts.
There would also be greater, more sudden emergencies—rebellion, invasion—demanding suspension of institutions.

There is continuity between the Baconian and Restoration
constitutions which Clarendon correctly perceived. He remembered that there had been no local royal officials dependent
only on the crown, and no standing army to buttress the authority of the monarch, that instead there had been parliaments.

Also there was breach with the past to which he was blind.
What happened in the Restoration settlement was that the
creative freedom of the crown was estopped. Its liberty was
crystallized as in amber. The Jacobean theorists had argued for
a difference between an absolute and an ordinary prerogative
in order to safeguard the constructive freedom the crown had
exercised throughout history. In the Restoration settlement
that distinction disappeared. From henceforward the king had
prerogatives defined by statute. The Restoration was the moment at which the secretion of institutions by the crown turned
into the secretion of a constitution. The crown in terms of the
law imprisoned itself within its creations.

'Clarendon', Ranke wrote, 'belongs to those who have essentially fixed the circle of ideas for the English nation'. He
did not impose ideas. If he had done so they would not have
lasted. He fixed what was there already. A king and a parliament, both were wanted. The ideal war aim of both sides in
the first and great civil war would have been an uncoerced king
and an unforced parliament each agreeing about the other's

rights and cooperating: a true king and a free parliament—
each strong, because each was indispensable. The Baconian
constitution had worked. So, after the eventual discovery of
necessary conventions, did the Clarendonian. Equilibrium:
Montesquieu's Separation of Powers: the Constitution of the
United States of America: all contrary to logic, no doubt. But
Clarendon had argued that point with Hobbes. It is not, he
had said, logic but history which is the proper science for
statesmen.

VIII

The History of the Rebellion and Civil Wars in England
was not made in one piece. In fact, Clarendon wrote history at
intervals between helping to make it. Having left England at
the end of the first civil war, he wrote an original *History* between 1646 and 1648 which carried the story up to March 1644.
Between 1668 and 1670, after his fall and during the last exile
in France, he wrote the *Life*. In 1671 the final *History* was composed by dovetailing the original *History* and the *Life,* so that,
when there was an overlap, sometimes the one account and
sometimes the other prevailed. For the period following that
covered by the original *History,* Clarendon supplemented the
Life with sections written for the occasion. The Revd. W. D.
Macray, whose edition is conclusive, marks the points of transition and includes in footnotes those portions of the original
History or the *Life* which Clarendon decided to jettison. It is
thus possible not only to follow the process of composition, but
also to distinguish the original *History* in its original form.
This cannot be done in the case of the *Life,* however. Clarendon omitted so much of the latter that enough remained of it
to constitute a preliminary section to the *Continuation* of the
Life, the work which covers the period from the Restoration onwards.

The original *History* was reflective and didactic for Charles
I's benefit: an account of what had happened with reflections

on what could and should have been done and on courses which might have been avoided. The *Life,* on the other hand, was a vindication of his own part in events, which the original *History* was not. The *Life* was more outspokenly critical of the king even than the original *History* had been, though Clarendon suppressed for the purposes of the final *History* some of the more outspoken passages. The original *History* is altogether more reliable for chronology and the details of events than the *Life.* The latter work, it must be understood, was written entirely from memory in France. In the present book when I refer to the *History* in the text I mean the original *History,* not the final one. *Life* means the portion of that work which was not incorporated in the final *History* but eventually published separately. All references in the footnotes are to the edition of Macray (1888) and to the 1857 edition of the separated *Life.* I thank the Delegates of the Clarendon Press for allowing me to make extracts from Clarendon's works.

PETERHOUSE   **B. H. G. W.**
CAMBRIDGE

PART I

POLITICS

§ 1. *From the Opening of the Second Session of the Long Parliament to the Attempt on the Five Members*

THE EDITOR of the portion of D'Ewes's *Journal*[1] that covers the period from the first recess of the Long Parliament to the withdrawal of the King from London in January 1642 has added one more tribute to the historical work of S. R. Gardiner. Fresh from the study of the sources for the four months with which he is concerned, he declares, 'Gardiner's narrative[2] for this period is on the whole unassailable'.[3] In noting, however, that the biographers of Pym and of Hyde have neglected the analysis of their parliamentary tactics, Professor Coates suggests that 'such an investigation would reveal in Hyde a statesmanship, albeit unavailing, somewhat superior to that with which Gardiner credits him'.[4] In making the suggestion, he defines Hyde's aim as follows: 'to mould Royalist sentiment out of the conservative spirit which emerged in Parliament after ten months of unremitting activity and a few weeks of religious disorders'.[4] It is clear, therefore, that, though he thinks Gardiner has underestimated Hyde's political ability, he does not question Gardiner's interpretation of his political objectives.

Gardiner's formula, a formula reinforced by the authority of the late Sir Charles Firth,[5] is well known and has become

---

[1] [*The Journal of Sir Simonds*] *D'Ewes* [*from the First Recess of the Long Parliament to the withdrawal of King Charles from London*, edited by Willson Havelock] Coates. [Newhaven: Yale University Press, 1942.]

[2] [S. R.] Gardiner, *History* [*of England from the Accession of James I to the Outbreak of the Civil War*. 1884].

[3] *D'Ewes*, Coates, p. xxv.   [4] Ibid. p. xxix.

[5] D[*ictionary of*] N[*ational*] B[*iography*], XXVIII, p. 371.

I

the basis of modern interpretation. The original unity of the Long Parliament was shattered by the ecclesiastical dispute. The Episcopalians under Hyde deserted the main line of the parliamentary cause as represented by the leadership of Pym and became Royalists in order to save the Church. As the first session drew to its close in the summer of 1641 with the King absent in Scotland, 'there was', says Gardiner, 'an episcopalian party in the House, but there was no Royalist party as yet'.[1] Then came the Commons' orders on Laudian 'innovations' in the Church, and the House adjourned for the recess in a condition of division which was never to be remedied. The language of Hyde and of Lord Falkland in the first days of the new session, Gardiner goes on, 'was sufficient evidence that the episcopalian party was in process of conversion into a Royalist party'.[2] But the conversion was not as yet fully effected. The signal for 'the final conversion of the episcopalian party into a Royalist party'[3] was Pym's revolutionary Additional Instruction to the committee which attended the King in Scotland to the effect that unless he would remove evil counsellors and 'take such as might be approved by Parliament' they would not hold themselves obliged to help him in Ireland. This was carried, though admittedly in a modified form, on 8 November. From then on, the chief object of Hyde's party was 'to baffle the Puritans'.[3] 'For the sake of that it was ready to trust the King, and to take its chance of what the Irish campaign might bring forth.'[3] Henceforth those who dissented from the parliamentary cause were to show the effect of their earlier views and to betray their political ancestry only in the fact that they did not at once leave the House but, as can be seen for instance in the fierce debate on the Grand Remonstrance on 22 November, remained to conduct a stubborn rearguard action for the Church and the King's rights; they showed it perhaps, also,

[1] Gardiner, *History*, x, p. 2.   [2] Ibid. p. 32.
[3] Ibid. p. 59.

in the fact that they carried with them into the King's camp a moderation of policy and a comprehensiveness of ideals which justifies the application to them of the title of Constitutional Royalists.

One of the possibilities opened up by this admirable edition of the *Journal* is precisely that of following the editor's suggestion and analysing the parliamentary tactics of Hyde. But the process of analysing and its results are bound to involve the question: what were the policy and aims these tactics were calculated to serve? The interpretation of Gardiner and Firth rests in large part upon the assumption that Hyde's own statements in his historical and autobiographical writing are by themselves a sufficient guide to the interpretation of his past conduct, an assumption which involves the further one that his opinions and purposes underwent no development, but were constant throughout his life, and that the experience of the events he describes played no part in creating his views. That is the picture painted by the *History* and the *Life*. But such a picture is intrinsically improbable. It may be conceded that loyalty to the Church was a fact and a consideration with him from the beginning, and that the discrepancy between an earlier attitude and a later one was not so great that it was impossible for an honest man to say that later experience had confirmed the earlier attitude. Hyde did indeed display episcopalian opinions, and it is possible to make them, as Gardiner and Firth have done, the explanation of his policy. But it is also true and, in addition, significant (if we bear in mind the likelihood of development in his outlook and the connexion between his opinions and his experience) that, did we not possess his own writings, it would never have occurred to a historian to regard him as the most outstanding partisan of the episcopalian interest. That part was played by Falkland. Hyde was the most influential of the politicians who happened to agree with Falkland in this matter, and he carried greater weight than the latter in the general proceedings of the House. In this sense he was the leading Episcopalian. But judging by the contemporary sources alone, and even taking those relating to the second session, it is by no means obvious that he was the leader of the Episcopalians in the sense that it was his predominant aim to lead them to victory against their ecclesiastical opponents. Hyde was a common lawyer and was chiefly distinguished for the part he played in the destruction of the agents and institutions of prerogative rule. That work sufficed to keep him in the forefront of the parliamentary reformers far into the summer of 1641. The ecclesiastical dispute was already some months old by July, but it was not a central issue, and Hyde, though he took part in that dispute, was concerned with central issues. This, and only this, is congruent both with his own later testimony and with the contemporary sources.

In approaching the politics of the second session and Hyde's part in them, it is necessary to bear in mind an aspect of the history of the period which has probably been underestimated by modern historians, namely the projects which implied that the reforming leaders should take the place of the royal servants who had fallen before the wrath of the Parliament. These projects have been underestimated partly because of their obscurity and the difficulty of saying anything definite about them, and partly because they failed. But it is difficult to doubt that they were regarded as of great consequence at the time, and it is a serious question whether they ought not to be looked upon as representing something like the addition of a constructive side to the programme of the Long Parliament. Against this it can be urged that the situation should be understood as a race for life between the Commons' leaders and the Earl of Strafford, or as a duel in which the penalties for treason were the weapons, and that after Strafford had lost, the King himself entered the contest and maintained it in the same spirit. But this aspect of the matter, true as it is, only explains why the projects failed. It does not detract

4

from the importance of them, which resides in the fact that they were the only way of consolidating the achievements of the Revolution and of envisaging a political future that would be anything short of disastrous. Nor need it follow that they were not regarded as such by many people at the time, nor that Pym was in principle opposed to them.

What Hyde has to say on this topic in the final *History* is, on the face of it, confusing. He criticizes the King's appointment of the opposition or 'popular' councillors in February 1641 on the ground that they held themselves to be primarily the servants of the Houses of Parliament and so rendered the Council-table 'useless to the King'.[1] At a later point in the narrative[2] he is describing the scheme of 'the Great Patriots', whereby having overthrown Strafford and Archbishop Laud, they would themselves succeed to places and preferments at Court. The chief of these patriots was the Earl of Bedford, who was to be Treasurer, Bishop Juxon having already resigned. Pym was to be Chancellor of the Exchequer, Cottington having expressed his willingness to vacate that office, and the lawyer St John was actually made Solicitor-General as a first instalment of the scheme, only, according to Hyde, 'by his fast and rooted malignity'[3] to demonstrate how useless and indeed dangerous such projects were from the King's point of view. However, Hyde went on to say, despite what he had written about the first instalment of popular councillors, that it was to be regretted the plan had not been fully acted upon 'that the King might have had some able men to have advised him or assisted; which probably these very men would have done after they had been so thoroughly engaged: whereas the King had none left about him in any immediate trust in business...who either did not betray or sink under the reproach of it'.[3] At a later point still in his account, he

---

[1] Clarendon, *History*, i, p. 258.
[2] Ibid. pp. 333 and 280 (from the *Life*).
[3] Ibid. p. 281 (from the *Life*).

was stressing the disadvantage to the King arising from the fact that he had no reliable servant in the House of Commons: 'sure the raging and fanatic distempers of the House of Commons (to which all other distempers are to be imputed) must most properly be attributed to the want of good ministers of the Crown in that assembly...'[1] In these circumstances, as can indeed be easily understood, the King and the Commons, even had the issue between them been less acute, must have gone different ways. Had the link existed, even with things as bad as they had become, the final rupture, Hyde thought, might have been avoided. In this connexion, he refers again[1] to 'the stratagem of winning men by places': this was 'none of the best', he considered, but if it had been practised as soon as it was resolved at York to call a Parliament, and if Pym, Hampden and Holles and St John had been at that time preferred 'before they were desperately embarked...and had innocence enough about them to trust the King and be trusted by him', they might have been the means to much good or at least have been restrained from doing so much harm. Unfortunately, Hyde explains, the King acted upon the wrong rule, the rule of favouring only those who had already done some service. It was unfortunate because the service that above all required performing and upon which the safety of the kingdom depended could not have been done unless these men were first established as councillors. Nor could they desert their own party without an unmistakable gesture from the King: and so the King waited for service, and the popular leaders 'did all the hurt they could to show the power they had of doing good' until the gulf of mutual suspicion was so wide that it could not be bridged. The King was thus blamed by Hyde for being too slow in preferring his enemies. In a passage[2] struck out of the manuscript of the *Life*, however, the King was blamed for being too slow in

---

[1] Clarendon, *History*, I, p. 431.
[2] Ibid. p. 447 (from the *Life*).

giving preferment to those who were showing themselves to be his friends.

The obscurity of these remarks is not due to the conflated and synthetic character of the final *History*, but to another cause. Whether writing the original *History* or the later *Life*, Hyde was writing from the King's point of view. He was explaining that it was in the King's interest to heal the breach from his end. But at the time, in 1641, of course, he had looked at the matter from the other side of the chasm. In a sense which he could have brought out only if he had not ended by fighting on the King's side in the Civil War, Hyde had originally been one of the King's enemies. When Charles first made contact with him in the summer of 1641 he was clearly an enemy from the royal standpoint. He had just played a leading part in the destruction of conciliar jurisdiction. The King, fearful for the Church, interviewed the most influential of the men who had opposed the Root-and-Branch Bill, but he made no offer of preferment to him. Of his eventual resolution to call Falkland, Culpepper and Hyde to his service, the 'friends', as they eventually became, of whom Hyde spoke in the erased passage in the manuscript of the *Life*, Hyde said[1] that it would have been better had he more punctually acted upon it. The distinction between friends and enemies meant something at the time he was writing which it could not have meant at the time of which he was writing and therefore presented the writer with difficulties in telling the story. All Hyde's comments on this subject are reducible to coherence on the assumption, which is not in other respects ill-founded, that his own position and that of Pym were very similar in the early stages of the Long Parliament, that not only was he himself, of course, a reformer, but, further, that he did not question that Pym was a man who, though bent on radical reforms, was yet constructive in his attitude and clear that everything depended in the end upon mutual

[1] Ibid.

7   2-2

collaboration between the Commons and the King, and that in this respect the King's conciliar policy was critical. Even when writing as an enemy of Pym, he allowed the accents of appreciation to emerge from his accounts.

The drift of Hyde's argument is that the appointment of opposition councillors early in 1641 proved abortive because it did not go far enough to affect the vital problem, which was the linking together of the King and the House of Commons. It left out Pym and the others, and by so doing ensured that the appointment of the 'popular' Lords would aggravate rather than improve the prospects. When the matter came to the fore again during the onslaught upon Strafford, and in a more definite form since it was now a question of ministerial office for the patriots, it did so, according to Hyde, because Bedford and his party wished to succeed Strafford in power at Court, and to obtain preferment for the leading members of the party in the Commons. Bedford, also, was a man of whom Hyde speaks highly in the *History*. With Pym as Chancellor of the Exchequer he would have put the finances of the State on a new footing. However, there was delay and final failure. Bedford would not take office unless the Tonnage and Poundage Bill were first passed, an end towards which Pym himself worked. Those already provided for in the scheme were reluctant to go forward unless 'the rest of their chief companions' were also found places, to secure that these, when left behind, did not fall away from their leaders. The main impediment, however, was that in the King's eyes the plan was a method of saving Strafford and of preserving the Church. There was relatively little difficulty about the Church. Bedford, as an ecclesiastical moderate, was content to limit the ecclesiastical revolution and so were Essex and Pym. Moreover, Bedford was willing that Strafford's life should be saved. But the other leaders demanded the death penalty. Hyde says[1] he was employed by Bedford to try and dissuade Essex from this

[1] Clarendon, *History*, I, p. 320 (from the *Life*).

view. Firth writes that the story contains 'manifest impossibilities', but it would appear at least to show that Hyde was a party to such schemes. Firth himself admits that Hyde 'may ultimately have joined the party who were contented with Strafford's exclusion from affairs of State'.[1] Pym, however, was unwilling to yield, unable, as Hyde says, to feel safe so long as Strafford was alive. The project was brought to an end when Charles gave way on the Bill of Attainder, and when Bedford himself died on 9 May.

It is not wildly hypothetical to suppose that Hyde looked upon such plans as Bedford's with something more than passive interest. To do so has the advantage of enabling us to abandon the assumption that his views and policy underwent any great change in the summer. The only assumptions we have to make are, first, that projects of this sort were normally regarded as important by the 'popular' leaders, and more so, perhaps, by them than by the King (the latter, as we have seen, was blamed in the *History* for his inactivity in the matter); and, secondly, that Hyde's main concern was to save and to consolidate the legislative work of the Parliament. This latter assumption is supported by the importance of his known contribution to that work and by the praise he bestows upon it in the *History*. In support of the hypothesis that he was in favour of the projects, we may adduce the interest displayed in them in the *History* and also his own story to the effect that he was deputed to win round Essex to Bedford's plan.[2]

The question, therefore, arises whether the event which is usually relied upon as indicating the decisive inception by Hyde of a royalist policy ultimately explicable in terms of the Church dispute, does not after all fall into place in a story of general consistency, and whether the changes we see in the second session are not tactical ones dictated by Hyde's opportunities and by the development of the situation as

[1] *D.N.B.* xxviii, p. 371.
[2] Clarendon, *History*, i, p. 320.

a whole. What is usually adduced is the interview with the King, already mentioned, which took place in the summer before the Scottish visit, when Charles thanked him for his services and, in particular, encouraged him to continue in defence of the Church.[1] But we have no right to regard this as necessarily different in principle from the contacts the King had made, and was to make, with Pym, or as indicating that Hyde felt himself henceforward to have been commissioned by the King to defend the Church. If on other grounds it is reasonable to suppose him still predominantly interested in the Common Law reformation of the State and consequently anxious for any project of reconciliation (the one is a consequence of the other because hardly anyone, despite the fact that the reformation had had to be carried against the King, and despite the deep mistrust which he inspired, could conceive of the future without him), the interview would remain of great significance, but its meaning would be that, to hopes entertained as a matter of course all along, there was now added an opportunity for action to implement them. This would imply not a change of view, but, instead, an inspiration for a course of action which in reality was based on pre-existing views. It is not necessary to deny that he deplored the policy of Root-and-Branch; but that he was able by his chairmanship of the committee on that Bill to frustrate it is merely his own story,[2] and it is to be noted that his first and last serious biographer, T. H. Lister,[3] rejects it. Even if the story be true, it does not conflict with the view that Root-and-Branch was objectionable precisely because, as a deepening of ecclesiastical radicalism, it widened the gulf which was already so great after Bedford's death and Strafford's execution and so jeopardized what the Parliament had so far achieved. Was he guided by the conviction that Root-and-Branch was

---

[1] [Clarendon], *Life*, [Part] 1, p. 77.   [2] Clarendon, *History*, 1, p. 363.
[3] [T. H.] Lister, [*Life and Administration of Edward, First Earl of Clarendon*, (1838),] 1, p. 113.

obnoxious simply as an ecclesiastical measure? Did he act, as Shaw says,[1] simply as the 'most blindly thorough-going of the episcopal party', or did he deplore the policy because it menaced, as indeed it did, the whole parliamentary cause, not only splitting the Commons, but rendering relations with the King hopeless? Was 'to baffle the puritans' the real aim of his policy, as Gardiner says, or was even this only a means to an end? Against the former view there is the fact that he does not emerge as a mainly ecclesiastical statesman in the first session, or even, as will be seen, in the second. In favour of the alternative there is the whole trend of his known activity up to and beyond the full emergence of the ecclesiastical issue.

Lister did not even discuss the possibility that the explanation of Hyde's 'change of sides' might have been an ecclesiastical one, and we may attribute this omission to a deeper penetration into the mind of the man who wrote the *History of the Rebellion* than many later scholars have been able to achieve. But he does presuppose a change of sides and he explains it by reference to the theory of the balanced constitution. Having set himself with the Commons to rectify the recent excesses of the monarchy, Hyde proceeded to throw himself into the other scale when he saw that the balance was now threatened from the side of the Commons. This theory of balance was to remain until the nineteenth century the classical theory of the constitution, and it was natural to interpret the actions of the most constitutional statesman of the classical age of the constitution in terms of it. But the difficulty with this explanation is that there is not as there is with the ecclesiastical theory even the sanction for it of Hyde's own matured reflexions on his past conduct. He does, indeed, testify in the *Life*[2] to his reverence for the constitution, believing it 'so equally poised, that if the least branch of the

---

[1] [W. A.] Shaw, [*A History of the English Church during the Civil Wars, etc.* 1900,] I, p. 91.
[2] *Life*, II, p. 89.

prerogative was torn off, or parted with, the subject suffered by it, and that his right was impaired: and he was as much troubled when the crown exceeded its just limits, and thought its prerogative hurt by it'. But it is doubtful whether such a statement can be regarded as sufficient sanction for Lister's explanation. As a doctrine it sounds more like a consequence than a cause of Hyde's action. Moreover, though on the face of it Hyde here propounds a theory of balance, he does so only in a metaphorical sense. A true theory which, though in the main adequate only to a later fashion of thinking, was emerging in his time, conceived the constitution literally in terms of a balance between King, Lords and Commons, the three estates of the realm, a system which would maintain itself through check and counter-check. Not only is there no indication that he ever supported such a theory; he took exception to it[1] when Falkland and Culpepper expounded it in the answer to the Nineteen Propositions. While it looks as if it was the constitutional position of the bishops, whose exclusion from the House of Lords he and Selden opposed in 1641 on the ground that they were the third estate, which had led his thought in this direction in the first instance, in 1642 he regarded the doctrine of Falkland and Culpepper as involving in respect of the King 'in truth a mistake in point of right'. The King was not an estate of the realm but 'head and sovereign of the whole'. Falkland and Culpepper were propounding an erroneous novelty that should not be allowed to supersede the true doctrine: the doctrine which indeed envisaged the State as a corpus of institutions with spheres of function, including that of the King, defined by law, but which assumed above all a mutual co-operation between the King and the three estates.

It was Thomas Hobbes,[2] it seems, who was the first to put forward this balance theory to explain a change of sides on

---

[1] *Life*, II, p. 131.
[2] *Behemoth* [*or the Long Parliament*, ed. F. Tönnies, 1889,] p. 116.

the part of Hyde and those 'in love with mixarchy', who 'when they saw the parliament grow higher in their demands than they thought they would have done, went over to the King's party'. But Hobbes, even if he had been able to discriminate between the authorship of the answer to the Nineteen Propositions and most of the other papers put out in the King's name in 1642, was describing the politics of other people in terms of his own political philosophy and explaining what such politics amounted to when tried by what he held to be the true criteria. He can hardly be relied upon to give a decisive ruling in this matter.

The Hobbesian solution, like the ecclesiastical one, is the solution to a problem the existence of which is itself a hypothesis. Did Hyde change sides at all? Lister mentions 'mediation',[1] but only as a course which could not be considered at a time when parties were already so far crystallized that it was right to accept their existence as a fact. But that is a diagnosis of the situation to which it is possible to demur. As 1641 wore on, it was much more a case of a process of disintegration, a situation where each of the decisive elements, Pym, the King, the Lords, and the City moved in a chaos of potential alinements. In regard at least to the whole of 1641 it is necessary to protest against the assumption that parties created events. It is truer to say that events created parties. Looking at the whole picture in this light, and leaving the solution of the problem why Hyde changed sides to those who can prove that it exists, it may well be found that 'mediation' is a formula far more fruitful than Lister could suppose.[2]

Of the need for mediation in the late summer and early autumn of 1641 there could be no doubt in the mind of anyone who valued the legislative work of the first session and saw with dismay the increasing political disintegration and the

---

[1] Lister, I, pp. 118–19.

[2] In this connexion it may be noted that Hyde claims to have tried to mediate between the King and the Commons in the Short Parliament. *D.N.B.* xxviii, p. 371, and *Life*, I, pp. 68–9.

progress of actual disorder. The history of the ecclesiastical dispute must not be allowed to obscure the fact that it was only in the summer that the victory of Parliament and the Common Law over the late instruments of prerogative government was completed.[1] To anyone who had had a pre-eminent part in the architecture of that victory, as Hyde had, the time must have seemed a time of achievement. To such a one, any course that promised to abate the political confusion would strongly recommend itself.[2]

Regarding the possibility of reconciliation, the main hindrances inside the House of Commons were the ecclesiastical radicalism and the fear of the King. This fear, always present, was brought to a head by his determination to visit Scotland, and actually operated to restrain the radicalism. The visit to the north served to keep the Commons united up to the end of the first session, and probably in the end led to the dropping altogether of the Root-and-Branch Bill.[3] In the Ten Propositions of the end of June, adopted without a dissentient voice, the King had been desired to delay his journey to Scotland and to effect the disbanding of the army.

The existence of the English army had been a natural corollary of the existence of the Scottish one and of its residence on English territory pending the conclusion of peace between the two nations. The presence in England of the Scots had been the decisive element in Pym's political strategy. The King could not dissolve the Parliament so long as the Scots required to be paid the contributions that had been agreed upon. But this was an expensive weapon, and the burden of taxation, the heaviest ever known, was turning the people against the Parliament. Moreover, the discontent of

---

[1] On 5 July the King assented to the Bills for the abolition of the Courts of Star Chamber and High Commission, and on 7 August to that annulling the proceedings relating to ship-money, and to that limiting the bounds of the forests.

[2] Cf. Clarendon, *History*, III, p. 344.

[3] Gardiner, *History*, X, p. 1.

14

the English army, whose needs were placed second to those of the Scots, put at the King's disposal a weapon against the Parliament which there was no guarantee he would not use. A definitive treaty of peace with the Scots was completed in the summer,[1] and it was now a main object with the Commons to hasten the disbandment of both armies. It was a matter of anxiety that the King should be in the north before this should have been completed. It contributed, therefore, not a little to relieve apprehension, as Gardiner admits, when it was known that the King had passed through both armies 'without causing any stir amongst them'.[2] Moreover, the withdrawal of the Scots to their own country and the break-up of the English army were proceeding without undue delay or difficulty and were completed by the end of September.

Following, as it did, the sealing by the King of the legislative work of the first session, the disbandment of the army should have contributed to an easing of tension.[3] It would not work in this way, however, save as it was allowed to do so, and there was still the King's absence in Scotland where he was to stay until November. This absence inevitably fostered pre-existing suspicions. The parliamentary investigations of army plots protracted the psychological consequences of events long after the time that they had taken place, and what was discovered tended to be related to the circumstances of the after-period. As Gardiner says, speaking of the examination of Captain Chudleigh, 'that such a plan [the first army plot] should have been talked of in March was enough to increase the alarm of those who heard of it in August'.[4] But to anyone able and willing to discriminate, the consideration that the King had disbanded his army must have carried weight.

[1] Ibid. IX, p. 417.   [2] Ibid. X, p. 5.
[3] See Cal[endar of] S[tate] P[apers] Venet[ian], 1640–2, pp. 212, 215, 223
[4] Gardiner, History, x, p. 2.

In the ability to discriminate, Hyde had an advantage over many of the others. What made many susceptible to intense alarm was not so much the King's previous action as the background into which every incident was fitted, namely the conviction that the country was the victim of a popish plot of European dimensions. 'The alarm of popish plots', wrote Nicholas, 'amuse and fright the people here more than anything.'[1] Now Hyde was always thoroughly anti-papal. But he had been a member of Falkland's circle, and had imbibed there the dispassionate and highly critical ideals for which it was distinguished. Moreover, he had known Archbishop Laud well enough to realize that he was not a Papist in disguise. In the *History* his contempt for the feverish misconceptions which prevailed in these matters is marked, and there is little reason to doubt that he was personally free from the irrational fears that made the tension in 1641 so acute. This meant the difference between something like the scrutiny of events on their merits and a state of mind which, believing anything, was clay in the hands of Pym.

It would be incorrect to say that Hyde henceforth trusted the King. The interview of the summer was not followed up by any further action on Charles's part until Hyde received a message from him through Nicholas in November.[2] It is reasonable to suppose that Hyde, in describing it, made the most of what passed at his interview with the King. But it would be necessary to suppose that he minimized it before we could assume that he could have had a personal reason for trusting him now to any greater extent than he had done in

[1] Nicholas to the King, 27 October 1641. [John] Evelyn, [*Diary*, edited by William Bray (1879),] IV, p. 113.

[2] Nicholas reported that certain members, including Hyde, had supported the prerogative in the matter of the appointment of councillors on 28 October, and advised the King to take some notice of this service 'for their encouragement'. The King replied: 'I command you to do it in my name, telling them that I will do it myself at my return', Evelyn, IV, p. 116. Hyde refers to the episode (*Life*, I, p. 77–8) but states, incorrectly, that Nicholas sent for him in the summer.

the past. He must have shared the general opinion of the Commons about the prevalence of evil counsel in the past, and he had no reason for certainty that the future would be any better. Nicholas was acting as observer for the King, watching events in London and sending to the north confidential information and advice. But it is clear from his correspondence that there was no concerted action between him and Hyde during the recess in preparation for the forthcoming session, in spite of the fact that he reported such activities amongst Pym's men, and in spite of the fact that the King urged him to make contact with any members who might be sympathetic.[1] All it is possible to say is that Hyde may have been among those members of Parliament who, on the first day of the new session, addressed alarmed inquiries to Nicholas regarding the significance of the 'Incident'. This had been an unsuccessful attempt by rival factions in Scotland to seize Argyle and Hamilton, and it naturally became a matter of anxiety whether Charles himself had been implicated and had been trying to overthrow the leadership of Scottish parliamentarism. Nicholas, no doubt, did his best to reassure his inquirers.[2]

In order to get Hyde's position and aims at the outset of the second session into focus, it is necessary to understand the position and aims of Pym. It is not so much that Hyde trusted the King in a new way, or more than before, as that Pym's distrust of him had entered upon a new phase. He was now in a weaker position than before. The King was without the army, but Pym had lost that hold over him which the presence of the Scots had given him. The ecclesiastical dispute had affected the strength of his position in the Commons and there was reaction outside the House against his leadership. He had no doubt feared for his own safety at the King's hands and his view of his own position coloured his estimate of the prospects of the cause. It was now no longer a question for

[1] Evelyn, IV, pp. 93, 97, 101, 105.   [2] Ibid. p. 107.

him whether the existing degree of suspicion of the King was justified. That suspicion was an instrument to be used creatively to buttress an imperilled position.[1] It is of immense significance that whereas there are no indications of Hyde plotting an initiative before the session, there is evidence that Pym had done so.[2] There is indeed no need to postulate more in Hyde's case than a heightened sense of the need for settlement, and the sense of opportunity springing from the interview with the King. From such a basis, all he did was to react to the steps taken by Pym in ways and for purposes which are intelligible enough. To suppose that he was any less 'parliamentarian' or any more 'royalist' is to introduce categories that are both irrelevant and misleading.

The first thing that is clear about the politics of the second session is the partisanship on the ecclesiastical issue. There was much ecclesiastical disorder, and that disorder had been encouraged by the Commons' orders on Laudian 'innovations'. The validity of these orders was hotly disputed by a section of the House. Root-and-Branch was indeed not reintroduced, but the fact that it had once been entertained made it hard for those who had opposed it to believe that the exclusion of the bishops from the Upper House, now provided for in a second bill introduced on 21 October, was the limit of what their opponents desired. It seemed that the abolition of the bishops' votes was preparatory to the abolition of their function. On 25 October Nicholas was circulating amongst the Lords a note written in the margin of a letter in which the King declared he would live and die in the maintenance of the discipline and doctrine of the Church.[3] Simultaneously the King took action to fill five vacant sees, a proceeding which stung the radicals and rallied their opponents. There was now a sharp division in the House on the matter of

[1] E.g. *D'Ewes*, Coates, p. 58. [2] Evelyn, IV, p. 93.
[3] Ibid. p. 111.

18

Church order, which showed itself especially in the debates on the ecclesiastical clauses in the draft of the Grand Remonstrance. D'Ewes begins to speak of 'the party for episcopacy', a party formidable enough to affect the tactics of their opponents. In fact, the orders on 'innovations' were dropped.

But we shall not find Hyde leaving his mark on the evidence at our disposal as having been one of the foremost fighters for the Church in these debates. He spoke, indeed, against the second Bishops' Exclusion Bill. This we should expect. He had opposed the first Bill. He first moved that it was unfitting to read the Bill 'by reason of the thinness of the House'.[1] Holles replied, carrying the House with him, that the Commonwealth must not suffer through men's neglect of their duties. The Bill was passed and sent up to the Lords. Hyde's point in his speech seems to have been that the Bill was an unjustifiable interference with the constitution of the Upper House. He himself claims to have spoken in the violent debate arising out of the King's determination to fill the vacant sees,[2] but the only contribution of a positively ecclesiastical nature which has left a mark upon contemporary sources was a speech of his in the debate of 16 November on the clause relating to the Book of Common Prayer in the draft of the Grand Remonstrance. The 'episcopal party' had secured that the objectionable clause be omitted and they went on to move, unsuccessfully, that a clause be added 'to justify the use of the Common Prayer Book till the law had otherwise provided'.[3] In this connexion, apparently, Hyde made the point 'that many sober good men were afraid the Common Prayer Book should be taken away'.[3] But we ought to note that this debate presented the Church issue in its widest possible implications. To attack the Prayer Book was a more fundamental matter than to attack the bishops and up to this point little disposition to make such an attack had manifested itself in the

[1] D'Ewes, Coates, p. 30.   [2] Clarendon, History, 1, pp. 402–3.
[3] D'Ewes, Coates, p. 151.

Commons. The question of the validity of the Prayer Book was connected much more directly and much more obviously with actual disorder in the City and in the country. Concern on this score in the House of Commons at this time was wider and deeper than the interest in ecclesiastical points as such. It affected such men as Grimstone and Maynard, neither of whom were especially 'episcopal' men.

Hyde's main preoccupation at this time is sufficiently clear. The House had reassembled in a suspicious mood, and Pym's handling of the 'Incident' served only to aggravate it. From the first, though he can have had no certain reason for holding that the Commons had no grounds for alarm, Hyde set himself against the inclination displayed by the House to succumb to an atmosphere swollen with rumours, and strove to moderate the interpretation put upon events by Pym. The House should not, he said, 'take up fears and suspicions without very certain and undoubted grounds'.[1] Scottish business should be left to the Scottish Parliament. It was politically possible and politically desirable to regard the King's absence and the 'Incident' as balancing, but not cancelling, the disbandment of the army.

On 28 October Strode seconded, very violently, an extremist motion of Robert Goodwin respecting evil counsellors. Strode said that 'all we had done this parliament was nothing unless we had a negative voice in the placing of the great officers of the King'.[2] There might be truth in this, but a measure proposed in that vein gave Hyde his chance. D'Ewes confesses that 'it was so extreme a strain as Mr Hyde did upon a sudden confute most of it'. There could be no question but that the King's councillors were his own concern. Hyde went on that the passing of the three Bills (concerning, that is, Star Chamber, High Commission, and Ship-money) was a great achievement, 'and', he thought, 'all particulars were in a good condition if we could but preserve them as they were'.[2]

[1] *D'Ewes*, Coates, p. 15.   [2] Ibid. p. 45.

It is noteworthy that this line of thought converted D'Ewes, a safe register of moderate left-wing opinion, save that he did not agree that in regard to the Church 'all was well settled and constituted if we could but keep them as they were'. But unless the content of the speech as given by D'Ewes is incorrect, it would appear that Hyde had omitted to refer to the Church. Just as in speaking about the Prayer Book it was possible to touch opinion wider than that which was definitely episcopalian, so in this case to have introduced the view that even in regard to the Church 'all particulars were in good condition' would have limited the appeal of what he was saying. It would appear that both Pym and Hyde were playing down the ecclesiastical issue, each in the interest of a wider purpose; Pym for the sake of widening the issue on which the Commons were at odds with the King, Hyde for the sake of broadening the backing for an attitude that would give Charles the benefit of the doubt. From that point of view, it would have been impolitic to make himself prominent as the leader of the episcopal party as such. On the other hand, the King's attitude in matters of the Church was well known. Furthermore, the Episcopalians were the core of the moderate body. Both facts, apart from any views of his own, made conservatism on the Church question on Hyde's part desirable in relation to his general objective, that is, a retrieving of the situation by an easing of the tension between the Commons and the King. It was a difficult position. This was illustrated the next day in the heated debate whether a conference be sought with the Lords to stay the investiture of the five new bishops, especially in that he himself, as we have seen, claims to have taken part in it. But the King's action made the debate inevitable and we do not know what Hyde said.

The outbreak of the Irish rebellion made the policy which Hyde had adopted a great deal harder to conduct. The House was henceforward much more susceptible to Pym's alarmism and he exploited the advantage up to the hilt. But when Pym suggested in the Additional Instruction to the committee in Scotland that they should insist that the help of the Commons in the Irish business must turn upon the King's agreement to the removal of evil counsellors and the appointment of men of whom Parliament could approve, Hyde was the first to object. Threatening bargains could only worsen the relations between the King and the House, even if he yielded (which was improbable) and Ireland did not suffer.[1] Any action required should proceed from free agreement between them and that could only be on the basis of the constitution exactly and only as it had been modified by recent legislation. To use the emergency to demand more from the King could not possibly improve relations with him. Nor did Hyde's effort to minimize the sense of danger and distrust, rather than to maximize it as Pym was doing, fall on deaf ears. There was a large element in the Commons that, having gone so far with conviction, was now disposed to be alarmed by the proposals to go further in constitutional matters. Hyde's main hope, may be supposed, was that a majority could thus be acquired which would swallow up the violent party. Nor, until the fatality of the Remonstrance, was his course unsuccessful. Pym could secure a majority for his Additional Instruction to the Committee in Scotland only by moderating the wording.[2] Even then, the Lords were unaccommodating, rallied by Bristol and Digby. Eventually, though Pym reported back a compromise proposal to the Commons, the matter was dropped even there.[3]

But the point was involved in the Remonstrance, and the Remonstrance was the real trial of strength between Hyde and Pym. One of Hyde's circle of friends,[4] Thomas May, writing as the contemporary historian of the Long Parliament,

---

[1] '...Mr Hyde stood up and first opposed it and said amongst other things that by such an addition we should as it were prevail the King.' *D'Ewes*, Coates, pp. 94–5.

[2] Ibid. p. 104.   [3] Ibid. pp. 140–1.

[4] *Life*, I, p. 32–3.

was not without insight when he commented as follows on the policy of the opponents of the Remonstrance. They 'held it fitter at such a time, when the King's affections were dubious toward the parliament, to win him by the sweeter way of concealing his errors, than by publishing of them, to hazard the provocation of him, with whom it was not behoveful to contest, unless they were in hope to change his disposition for the future, or ascertained of their own power, and resolved to make full use of it'.[1] The modifications effected prior to 22 November in the draft of the Remonstrance could not alter the fact that the assumption on which that document was based and the intentions which it embodied were precisely those against the acceptance of which (as the basis for the policy of the House of Commons) Hyde, whatever his private opinions, had decided to range himself: namely, the view that the King was still governed by evil counsel which did not accept the constitutional reformation, and the determination that the Commons themselves should make further substantial changes. The Remonstrants, according to their own accounts, aimed to make plain both to the King and to the world what they had done, were doing, and intended to do, in vindication of themselves against the slanders of malicious persons who said that they had not been working for the King and kingdom but only for themselves. They intended to make it clear that malicious persons of this kind had influence with the King. The King, therefore, was to be asked to dismiss them and to appoint councillors in whom the Commons could confide. If the Remonstrance in its existing form was carried and presented to the King, it would constitute a calculated provocation. Its publication to the world would multiply its evil consequences and stir up popular partisanship.

In the early afternoon of 22 November, when the House at last fell to debating the passing of the Remonstrance, Hyde 'stood first up' and desired the Sergeant might go with his

---

[1] [Thomas] May, [The] History [of the Parliament of England, 1854,] p. 135.

mace and call the members walking in Westminster Hall.
This, D'Ewes says, 'was much debated', but was carried.
The House was presumably not as thin as on 23 October and
Hyde now addressed himself more insistently and more successfully to this vital matter than he had done on that date.[1]
'The Serjeant being returned & the mace laid upon the table
where also lay the said declaration or remonstrance ready
engrossed', Hyde opened the debate. D'Ewes says he spoke
'very vehemently against the Remonstrance', but the speech
seems to have been carefully constructed. The labour spent
in the preparation of the Remonstrance would not, he said,
be lost if it were not published, and in his view it was not
necessary to publish it; 'we may desire to see, but not divulge
our own infirmities, no more than a general the defects of his
army to his enemy'. Whether it were published or not, however, he objected to it in its present form. He took exception
to one point as constitutionally incorrect, and to the manner
in which several other points were expressed: there were
'some unfit expressions of more sharpness than we do intend';
and some particulars which it had been agreed to leave out
had been included. Next, he seized upon a major ambiguity:
what was the relation of the Remonstrance to the House of
Lords? Much of it touched the Lords and if the Commons did
not act jointly with them, there was the danger of a counter-
Remonstrance from them. 'The end of this Remonstrance is
peace.' It aimed to show that what malicious persons said
about the selfishness and aggressiveness of the Commons was
untrue. But in its present form it contradicted this aim. He
agreed to a part of it as a vindication of, or apology for, the
Parliament in the face of slanders, but he argued against
'looking too far back': 'the narrative part he disliketh'. 'We
stand upon our liberties for the King's sake, lest he should be
King of mean subjects and we subjects of a mean King.'
Statements to the effect that the Commons' actions had been

[1] *D'Ewes*, Coates, pp. 30, 183.

24

self-interested were slanders. For that very reason there ought to be some consideration of the King in the framing of the Remonstrance.

The above reconstruction is necessarily partly conjectural, but there is no doubt that the keynote of the speech is the phrase, 'the end of this Remonstrance is peace'.[1] From this point of view, he disputed the necessity of the publication of the Remonstrance. From the same point of view, if it were to be published, it must be altered, and it must be altered even if only presented to the King. What he said no doubt represented what he thought, but apart from this fact, the speech represented a good piece of tactics. If we can believe D'Ewes, who is emphatic on the point, Pym was determined to accept no alterations,[2] and we may assume that the whole point of the Remonstrance in his eyes was its challenging character. But it was hardly possible for the upholders of the document as it stood to repudiate the contention that its purpose was peace; therefore, to urge changes for the sake of peace was a telling line of attack. D'Ewes himself could not swallow some of the wording and was in such a quandary that he withdrew altogether in the course of the afternoon pleading a cold in the head.[2] Furthermore, the point about the House of Lords was unanswerable from a parliamentary point of view. All the success achieved so far had been achieved in concert with the Upper House. Hyde avoided the ecclesiastical

[1] There are two contemporary versions of Hyde's speech: Holland, fos. 45 b–46 a (see *D'Ewes*, Coates, p. 183), and Verney, [*Notes of Proceedings in the Long Parliament,* Camden Society, 1845,] p. 121. The account given above is a conflation of the two versions. The two accounts have little in common save the words, 'the end of this remonstrance is (public) peace'. Gardiner, *History*, x, p. 75, appears only to have used Verney, and writes: 'Hyde positively declared that the narrative part of the Remonstrance was true, and in his opinion, modestly expressed.' But comparing the two versions, it is not clear whether the words, 'all is true and expressed modestly', reported by Verney alone, refer to the narrative part or to the part Hyde allowed 'for satisfaction'. It should be noted that Holland, unlike Verney, reports the words, 'the narrative part he disliketh'. With the contemporary versions, cf. Hyde's own. (Clarendon, *History*, I, pp. 417–18.)

[2] *D'Ewes*, Coates, p. 185.

issue altogether,[1] leaving it to Falkland and Dering to urge less abusive language in respect of the Church.[2]

After a debate of a length and a vehemence famous in the history of the House of Commons, the Remonstrance was carried by a very narrow majority. The Remonstrants relinquished their decision not to allow alterations, and the modifications conceded may have turned the scale in their favour. But the modifications were not such as to alter the character of the document as a manifesto of Pym's group, or affect the fact that its passing was a triumph for Pym's policy. It is true that the triumph went no further that night. The minority were able to force the Remonstrants to reserve the question of printing.[3] When the motion for printing was put, the threat of protestation led by Hyde sufficed to kill it. It can be seen, indeed, that apart from the political victory in the matter of publication, the whole debate had something of the character of a moral victory for Hyde. The narrowness of the division and the absence of many members who were out of reach of the Sergeant and who would probably, as Hyde maintains,[4] have voted as he did, demonstrated that his policy could have succeeded. But we must miss none of the signi-

[1] There is an obscure reference in Holland's version to the question of a national synod.

[2] *D'Ewes*, Coates, p. 183; Verney, pp. 121–2.

[3] Coates says that Pym showed himself sensitive to the vehemence of the opposition to the idea of an appeal to the people: 'The defence for an appeal to the people became weak; and the final vote on the Grand Remonstrance did not imply that the declaration was directed to the people. It was only after the Remonstrance had been passed that its supporters took heart to propose that it should be printed. Hyde and Culpepper promptly retaliated that they would enter their protestations, and the matter was dropped.' ('Some Observations on the Grand Remonstrance', *Journal of Modern History*, IV, p. 7.) The Venetian ambassador reported that the Remonstrance probably would not be published. (*Cal. S.P. Venet.* 1640–2, p. 258.)

[4] Clarendon, *History*, I, p. 429. The thinness of the House in the second session was commented on (*Cal. S.P. Venet.* 1640–2, p. 242). Nicholas advised the King to issue a proclamation calling upon all members to attend the House (*D'Ewes*, Coates, p. 287). It is to be noticed, however, that as usual there was a fatal delay. The proclamation was issued on 12 December. In any case, we cannot be sure that Hyde would have approved such a step.

ficance of what had happened. Pym's boldest throw up to date had succeeded. Small as was his majority, it had a decisive significance. A member who had been absent from fear or disapproval on 22 November was unlikely to change his habits now that the Remonstrance had been carried. The Remonstrance was of such a nature that it must create, and having created, sustain, a stronger and bitterer partisanship in the House than had existed before. Plots and incidents which had existed (or, more important, were thought to have existed) between the King and the Commons, were now to be thought to exist between the members of the House of Commons themselves. Further, it was certain that the mere passing of the Remonstrance would worsen relations between the House of Commons and the King. It would also encourage the junction between the latter and members of the minority. Pym must have known and intended this before the debate and his success was the signal for the prosecution of the advance along the lines laid out in the Remonstrance—he profited from the graver conditions created by its passing. Pym had willed the means as much as the end, and his achievement in the realm of means was a resounding defeat for Hyde who had worked to hold the Commons together in a firm assertion of the position they had achieved, but without the aggressiveness that would perpetuate the hostility of the King. It is true that the ends laid down in the Remonstrance were far from being achieved, and even the question of publication was still undecided. Hyde said[1] that the Remonstrants were out of heart at the narrowness of their majority and that they trod warily in the succeeding phase: but that was precisely because the partisanship had now reached so deadly a stage. Even if the ends were never achieved, the bitterness of the partisanship and the sharpness of the constitutional and ecclesiastical issues behind it represented an appalling aggravation of the situation.

[1] Clarendon, *History*, I, pp. 420, 443.

27

During the small hours of 23 November the Parliamentarians as a party which fought the Civil War were born. Hyde, in regard to status and success, though not in conviction, now ceased to be a Parliamentarian in the sense of one of the chief of those who were carrying through a great constitutional revolution. Hyde's own keen consciousness of this shines clearly through the bitterness of his comments on the absence of so many members from their places in the House.[1] Thenceforward, there was no hope of making the House the instrument of his policy: the leaders of the minority, as he says, 'grew...cast down and dejected'.[2] That this was so, was due not only to the defeat on the night of 22–23 November, but also to the victory. For what had caused the motion for printing to be dropped was the threat of protestation. A protestation offended the parliamentary sense of the House, a sense well represented by 'the Northern men' with whom up to then Hyde had worked so closely and effectively.[3] In offering to protest, he put himself in the wrong in the parliamentary sense in the very same way as those members whom he castigated in the *History* for staying away on the ground that they could not approve of what was taking place. The life and work of the Commons as a corporate body was dependent upon the willingness of a defeated minority to give way before the majority. Hyde's defence when the general question of protestations was debated on 20 December was to admit the essential point: 'clearly no man ought to protest when the vote of the House was passed: wherein he must needs be involved'.[4] However, it was right, he contended, for a member to ask to have a dissentient voice recorded as was permitted in the House of Lords: ''tis no more than if the Clerk should

---

[1] Clarendon, *History*, pp. 427–9.   [2] Ibid. p. 432.
[3] *D'Ewes*, Coates, p. 192. Hyde claims that 'the Northern men', out of consideration for his services in the destruction of the Council of the North, diverted the Commons' wrath against the protesters from himself to Palmer. Clarendon, *History*, I, pp. 421–4.
[4] There are three versions of this speech: *D'Ewes*, Coates, p. 320; Peyton (*D'Ewes*, Coates, p. 320); Verney, p. 136.

set down all the Assents and Dissents, the Yeas and Noes...'.
He went on to say that if this was unprecedented in the Commons, the printing of the Remonstrance was equally so. That
was true, in that it was in a general sense unconstitutional.
But though the publication of a Remonstrance contravened
the constitution, as indeed did several other measures against
which Hyde himself had desired to record no protest (save
later as a historian), it did not stab at the life of Parliament
itself, which in the circumstances of the day was the effect of
the threat to register protestations against the publication of
the Remonstrance. If the defeat on the night of 22 November
partook of the character of a moral victory, the victory in the
matter of printing was itself a moral defeat. Hyde's own action
completed the defeat of his hopes that the body which had
taken the initiative in the reform of the State might begin
the consolidation of its work by taking the initiative in
conciliation.[1]

But to assume that Hyde now became a stern unbending
Royalist even in regard to the Church is still to beg the only
question we should ask: what, in the light of the evidence at
our disposal, did Hyde now do and what may most reasonably
be supposed to have been his intentions? He did not leave the
House, though he seems to have moved to the rear, and to
have remained from that time more in the background. The
leadership of Pym's opponents passed to Culpepper. He had
always been prominent, speaking forcefully and lucidly at the
close of debates.[2] Hyde himself usually opened debates during
the period of his leadership. But that phase was over. He
spoke in defence of Geoffrey Palmer, the scapegoat protester,
on 24 November.[3] On 30 November he insisted that the
London mob which had jostled Sir John Strangeways on his

---

[1] *Life*, II, p. 83: 'and from the night of the protestation, he [Hyde] was as
much in their [the governing party's] detestation as any man'.
[2] Clarendon, *History*, I, p. 457.   [3] Verney, p. 126.

way to the House was armed and urged that means be found of preventing 'the confluence of the citizens'.[1] He claims to have spoken in the militia debate on 7 December.[2]

On 15 December the House of Commons passed the order for the printing of the Remonstrance. That event enables us to pick out the thread of the development of what we may call the second phase of Hyde's policy, the phase during which he remained in the Commons, but had no more hope of using them as an instrument for peace. He tells us in the *Life*[3] that as soon as the Remonstrance was printed he made, merely as an exercise, a draft of an answer, 'such...as the subject would have enabled any man to have done who had thought of it'. He explains that in the course of political discussion with Digby, with whom he was well acquainted, he read him the draft, and that Digby asked that he might take it to the King to serve as the answer to the Remonstrance. Hyde declares that he refused on the ground that he would be ruined if the House suspected that he exercised himself in such offices, but that after Digby had consulted the King, he yielded on condition that secrecy was maintained about the authorship, and on condition that it was communicated to the Council and issued expressly with the advice of that body.

By the time the Commons passed the Remonstrance, it was evident that they and the Lords were no longer marching in step, and by the latter part of November relations between them had become strained. They differed about Ireland, they differed about a guard for the Parliament, and over policy in regard to the mob, and they differed over ecclesiastical matters, the Lords, for their part, desiring to enforce conformity. Moreover, the Lords did not pass Bills sent up to them from the Commons, in particular the Bishops' Exclusion Bill. Bristol and Digby were leading them in accordance with a policy of constitutional defence, implying the maintenance

[1] *D'Ewes*, Coates, p. 213.   [2] Clarendon, *History*, I, p. 444.
[3] *Life*, II, p. 79.

of law and order in Church and State. Moreover, father and son were both high in the counsels of the King at this time. It appears that it now became Hyde's object to exploit the intimacy of his connexion with Digby. The Lords were 'containing' the Commons, and so long as they did so, a settlement, if less likely than before the passing and the subsequent printing of the Remonstrance, was not hopeless.

We may suppose that Hyde's statement in the original draft of the *History* that the Remonstrance was 'the first visible ground and foundation of that rage and madness in the people of which they could never since be cured',[1] is not purely the product of retrospective analysis, but reflects also in this instance his original feeling for the situation both as it was in itself and as it was built up into the policy he himself pursued. But we must not read too much into his retrospective estimate of its significance. The Remonstrance implied the defeat of his parliamentary policy and that policy was the most reasonable hope of settlement. With its defeat there was a great deterioration in the situation. The Remonstrance was a turning-point in events largely because it was a turning-point for Hyde himself. But though all this is true, the setback to the cause of peace was less decisive than the setback to himself. Because that was so, there might still be something he could do. He could do little now in the Commons; the Lords were not his concern; but through his free access to Digby and Digby's free access to the King something might be achieved. As Professor Coates has pointed out,[2] the continued success of the Remonstrants was dependent upon the continued mistakes of the King. Between the passing and the printing of the Remonstrance there were more of these mistakes. Without them 'the party would no doubt have rapidly dwindled'.[2] Pym was dependent upon a system of reactions to provocation—a system which as a result of his efforts now worked almost automatically. Hyde had failed to persuade

[1] Clarendon, *History*, I, p. 429.   [2] *Journal of Modern History*, IV, p. 16.

the Commons not to play. Now, the only hope was to persuade the King not to do so. The answer to the Remonstrance was a step in this direction. It must be considered in conjunction with a further and more important step, a step to which reference has already been made in connexion with Hyde's discussion of the King's conciliar policy in the final *History*.

At the beginning of the new year, Falkland was made Secretary of State and Culpepper Chancellor[1] of the Exchequer. In the manuscript of the *Life* occur the words: 'Mr Hyde wished the Lord Digby to advise the King to call the Lord Falkland and Sir John Culpepper who was Knight of the Shire for Kent to his Council.' The first eight words are erased.[2] We cannot be sure that the idea of taking this action was Hyde's. But it is probably safe to say that its execution was the offspring of Hyde's consultations with Digby and the latter's influence with the King. It was a bold stroke, and, within the limits of what was possible at that time, a hopeful one. It countered with the public the chief contention of Pym, now broadcast in the Remonstrance, that the King was still governed by evil counsellors. For no one could pretend that Falkland and Culpepper were that. They had no contact with the Court and had been prominent in the prosecution of the parliamentary cause. Even now, though clearly party men in a now party-ridden House, neither of them had suffered the parliamentary eclipse which Hyde had suffered. Culpepper's position, especially, seems to have remained strong. Pym's insistence was that the King should remove evil counsellors and appoint such as Parliament could confide in. There was as yet, it should be remembered, no positive demand on the part of the House of Commons that Parliament should appoint the Council. Though in the existing state of parties Falkland and Culpepper would hardly have

[1] Charles appears to have offered the office first to Pym. Gardiner, *History*, x, p. 127.　　　　　[2] Clarendon, *History*, I, p. 457.

satisfied Pym, in the eyes of the outside world they must have seemed such as ought to have satisfied the House of Commons. Hyde agreed with Pym about evil counsellors, especially in the Remonstrance sense that some of them were hostile to the Parliament to the extent of suggesting force. But he could not control the King in this respect and he knew that the Commons' harping on evil counsel only provoked him. The most that could be hoped was that the King would listen to, and act upon, the advice of the new *good* counsellors. It was possible to hope that they would 'have opportunity to give the King a truer information of his own condition and the state of the Kingdom than it might be presumed had been given to him, and to prevent any counsels and practices which might more alienate the affection of the people from the government'.[1] By far the most critical aspect of policy was the King's relationship with the Commons, and the new connexion afforded reasonable promise that this would be handled wisely.

As far as Hyde himself was concerned, he had no official position, and indeed now refused that of Solicitor-General on the grounds that that office was already occupied by St John.[2] In the *Life*[3] he explained that St John would do more mischief if removed than if he were allowed to keep it. But St John's present office, it will be remembered, was the consequence of an earlier instalment of just such a policy as Hyde was seeking to promote. To have acquiesced in St John's dismissal in order that a position might be found for himself would have been to defeat his whole purpose. In the circumstances it was enough that he was now established in a point of vantage from which he might hope to have some influence over the course of events.

It is a mistake to interpret this as an attempt, blessed by Hyde, to enhance the power of one group against another in a situation where both sides were prepared to take up arms

---

[1] Ibid. p. 459.
[2] There was no such bar in the other cases. Falkland got the post taken from Vane in November and Culpepper one that Cottington was ready to lose. *Vide* supra, p. 5.   [3] *Life*, II, p. 82.

rather than yield. Things had not moved as far as that. As long as the Lords held to their present course, there could be no war. Nor was war contemplated. It is true that the new appointments and what might be expected from them were the best possible guarantee that the Lords would stand firm, and it was necessary that they should, in order to contain the Commons, now under extremist control. But Hyde's object would not appear to have been merely to reinforce the Lords' stand and to bind the King closer to them in a purely passive defence of the *status quo*. Such a purely negative attitude would have contributed only to increase the tension. What were needed were measures to suggest to men's minds that the situation, as a whole, was not out of control, and that there was an alternative to deadlock. Only so was it possible to check the accumulation of partisanship.

The significance of Hyde's answer to the Remonstrance is that it was to serve, in conjunction with the new appointments, as the initiation of a line of action[1] that at least would not aggravate the situation, and by that very fact would ameliorate it. As we have seen, Hyde insisted that it be published as 'the King's answer with the advice of his Council', and so it was. His object seems to have been not only to oppose the contentions of the Commons about evil counsellors, and to associate the new conciliar appointments with the giving of counsel that all could see was good, but, perhaps, also to associate the body of the Council with the policy outlined in the Declaration. For he says that with such a superscription 'it could not be refused by them' (the Council). This may seem naïve, but his point was that the fact of the King issuing a counter-Remonstrance would annoy Pym, and the special title would 'engage them' (the Council) 'in some displeasure with the House of Commons'.[2] What Hyde wanted to do was to associate the Council with the Declaration and bind it together (even if only in a common

---

[1] Clarendon, *History*, i, p. 493.   [2] *Life*, i, p. 81.

unpopularity with the extremists) by means of the promulgation of this document.

What weighed at the time with Hyde as with all the Commons was the King's lack of good advice: in other words, his evil counsel. In such a situation as had developed good counsel necessarily tended to mean advice tendered by Parliament, and, in particular, by the House of Commons. The King, early in 1641, had, as we have seen (on the advice, Hyde says,[1] of the Marquis of Hamilton), made Privy Councillors of certain personages popular with the Parliament and the Scots but not with the Court. It was argued that this was politic as indicative of an accommodating temper; also that it might rescue the dignity of the Council as an institution menaced as it was by the reforming fury in respect of its recent excesses. But the result of this and of subsequent expedients of a similar character had been to enhance the tendency which always existed for the body of the Council to become merely nominal, and for the King to rely upon an inner group of confidants. Further, since these new advisers remained partisans of the Parliament against the Court, or were terrorized by the propaganda about evil counsellors into uselessness, the King naturally turned to people whose main qualification was partisanship on his personal behalf. Foremost among such people was the Queen. The tendency was for the Council to count less and less and for the Court to count more and more, with the consequent exacerbation of the conflict. That was what the process looked like to Hyde when he reflected upon these matters in after years. At the time he was probably thinking predominantly in terms of membership of the Council for the new men and of a project such as had been proposed in the Bedford plan earlier in the year. But it looks as though he may also have begun to think at this time of what the Council should be as an institution. Certainly he had much to say about the con-

---

[1] Clarendon, *History*, I, pp. 258–9

stitutional function of the Council in after years,[1] and it may
be that the roots of such views are to be found in the events
under discussion. In any case, a cohesive body of councillors
capable of pursuing a responsible line of policy was to Hyde
at the end of 1641 an indispensable prerequisite of any turn
for the better. Nicholas had been made Secretary of State at
the end of November.[2] Nicholas, Falkland, Culpepper, Digby
and Bristol (with Hyde in the background) might provide the
nucleus for the creation of an effective Council.

As for the Declaration itself,[3] the manifesto of good counsel,
there was no attempt in it to rebut the Remonstrants' bulky
story of the ills and misgovernment from which the kingdom
had suffered and which had now been reformed. In regard,
however, to the reformation lately effected, it was declared
that even if there had been no bills brought up to him from
Parliament, the King, for his part, had been determined to
relieve the people 'from those pressures which were grievous
to them'. To give this some plausibility, attention was drawn
to an aspect of the reign that was at least complementary to
the one emphasized in the Grand Remonstrance, namely, the
peace and plenty of the last sixteen years 'not only compara-
tively in respect of...neighbours, but even of those times
which were justly accounted fortunate'. If this had been not
entirely despite the Government, but reflected at least in part
a tradition of good intentions, it might be possible to graft on
to it a doctrine of the King's convinced adherence to, and free
personal interest in the recent institutional spring-cleaning.
But it was still necessary to deal with care and in detail with
'the fears and jealousies' which, however played upon by
Pym, undoubtedly existed. These, so ran the Declaration, were
of two sorts: for religion, and for liberty and civil interests.

[1] E. Carlyle, *E[nglish] H[istorical] R[eview]*, xxvii, p. 251.
[2] The secretaryship which had been Windebank's, not Vane's. Gardiner,
History, x, p. 94.
[3] *An Impartial Collection of the Great Affairs of State*, J. Nalson, 1683, ii, p. 746.
Clarendon, *History*, i, pp. 493–6.

The first, religion, was itself divisible under two heads: popery and the internal condition of the English Church. Under the former, there was a declaration of the King's convinced adherence to the Church, and of his determination to defend it against the Pope. Under the latter, the question was raised of the use of ceremonies at which certain tender consciences were scandalized. The conception of the difference between essentials and 'things indifferent in their own nature' was introduced at this point. Certain of these things indifferent were objected to by some as unlawful. The implication was that the controversy was taking place in the realm of inessentials, and that one side, the defenders, admitted that what they defended were inessential. The King, it was declared, would willingly comply with a parliamentary initiative for a law for the exemption of tender consciences in such cases. Now this was a significant proposal. Certainly, it did not suggest a wholesale capitulation on the Church question by the King. The main fabric of the Church and its government was left untouched by it. The Grand Remonstrance had requested a national synod, an expedient that would place the whole establishment in the melting pot, and the King, in his reply to the Petition which accompanied the Remonstrance, issued on 23 December,[1] expressed himself not unwilling to consider it. But it was an uncertain expedient, and safe, perhaps, for that reason, for the King to accept. The question of what clergy were to attend the synod was left unanswered. Moreover, the arrangements would take time. By contrast, the proposal in Hyde's document was clear and definite and, above all, immediate. Conservative as it was, and indeed had need to be, since it had been preceded by reiterated declarations of the King and of the Lords that they would defend and execute the law of the Church, it was considerably more liberal and constructive than the royal policy

---

[1] [S. R.] Gardiner, [Constitutional] Documents [of the Puritan Revolution, 1906], p. 233.

as announced up to date. The King, from the time Nicholas
had circulated the apostil amongst the peers, had created the
impression that his main personal interest and the hub of his
policy was to defend through thick and thin the whole existing
order in the Church. The point came out in his speech on his
return to London on 25 November,[1] and coloured his proclamation on 10 December,[2] and his answer to the Remonstrants' petition on 23 December. Both these last had referred
vaguely to measures to remove just scruples being under consideration, but the effect was marred, at least in the latter, by
a strong expression of regret that anybody could see corruptions in the present order, and by a statement that the Church
would be defended not only against Papists but against
'separatists and schismatics'. The latter was also the Lords'
point, culminating in their amendment to the Commons'
declaration against toleration.[3] The Commons had meant no
toleration for Papists. The Lords added that there should
be none for Protestant nonconformists either. This doctrine
was making some headway, since apparently the Commons
accepted the amendment. By contrast, Hyde's declaration
avoided partisanship in the ecclesiastical dispute: there was
no expression of pained surprise that anyone should wish to
modify the law, but rather a candid admission that the law
was changeable and that since some wished to change it,
measures should be undertaken at once to do so. Further,
there was no repetition of the statement that the ecclesiastical
law must be enforced, even in the meantime, and no hostile
reference to separatists and schismatics. There was merely
a passage deploring the licence in pamphleteering and
'preaching and printing of sermons' including an admission
of the government's remissness in not having enforced the law
against such things before, and a promise to do so in the
future on the ground that this 'virulent demeanour' was

[1] Gardiner, *Documents*, p. 201.   [2] Ibid. p. 232.
[3] Gardiner, *History*, x, p. 100.

'a fit prologue to nothing but confusion' which, if permitted to continue, would be a blemish 'to that wholesome accommodation we intend'. Having regard to the position taken up by King, Lords and Commons, respectively, up to date, it is difficult to see how Hyde's handling of this most difficult and dangerous matter could have been improved upon. It asked little of the King and of the Lords, and yet both in what it proposed and in the way it proposed it, conciliated their opponents. It ignored the Commons' discomfiture in accepting the Lords' amendment on toleration. Instead, it applied itself constructively to their real mind on the subject. For instance, it went some way to meet the Ministers' petition to the Commons occasioned by the King's Proclamation of 10 December. 'It seems most equal', they said, 'that the consciences of men should not be forced upon that which a Parliament itself holds needful to consider the reformation of, and give order in, till the same be accordingly done.'[1] Moreover, the Grand Remonstrance had protested, no doubt rightly, that 'the malignants' laid the spread of sectarianism at the door of the House of Commons. No doubt the malignants, too, were right. But it was true that the Commons did not wish to destroy the national establishment in religion. It was a highly delicate matter and the best thing to do was to omit all reference to separatists and schismatics, and that was what Hyde did.

In order to see the significance of the declaration in its ecclesiastical aspect, it is necessary to revert to the early days of the second session of Parliament: to the King's nomination of five new bishops. There was more in this than might be gathered from the way in which it was received in the House of Commons. Nicholas had suggested[2] to the King that it was important that the new bishops should not be Laudians and he had even gone so far as to suggest names which included two who seem to have been Puritans. He also urged that the King declare his readiness to reform the Prayer Book. The

---

[1] Ibid. p. 101.   [2] Nicholas to the King, 19 September, Evelyn, p. 88.

4-2

King complied only to the extent of nominating divines not notably Laudian.[1] In all other respects he maintained a position of great rigidity, with the result that the filling up of the five bishoprics made matters worse between him and the Commons. But there should be no doubt about the course Nicholas was recommending. In July he had seen the ecclesiastical dispute as the main issue between the King and the House of Commons,[2] and he was now in favour of the pursuit by the King of a positive policy of compromise. We have denied that there is ground for supposing any junction between Nicholas and Hyde before the opening of the second session, but it is very unlikely that by the time the latter had embarked upon the second phase of this activity he should not have established a connexion with Nicholas. The declaration of December represents a reassertion of the policy suggested to the King by Nicholas in September, and of the policy embodied in Bedford's scheme in the spring. What Hyde did was to seize upon the fact that the anglicanism for which Falkland had contended in the House of Commons was of a liberal and accommodating nature, and attempt to make of it a bridge between the King and the Commons. The loss of the two previous opportunities had greatly narrowed the chances of success. But to make a third attempt was still the only possible course.

In moving forward to treat of 'civil liberties and interest' the declaration stressed again the King's assent to the reforming Bills and reminded the public that the reformation was guaranteed by triennial parliaments. Nor did the King

[1] It is to be noted that Hyde, in the *History* (i, pp. 401–2), comments upon the moderate and non-Laudian character of the divines chosen by the King.

[2] Shaw, i, p. 75. Compare Shaw, i, p. 46, where reference is made to the 'remarkable paper preserved in *State Papers Domestic*, CCCCLXXVII', containing proposals for an ecclesiastical compromise. Shaw writes: 'It seems almost incredible that Nicholas could have put such propositions to paper, and I doubt exceedingly his authorship of the paper and the date of it'. (He assigns it to March 1641.) It will seem the less incredible if compared with the letter of September.

imply that there was nothing more that could be done. He would refuse nothing presented to him for the 'completing and establishing that security'. However, so ran the argument, it should be clear in this connexion that since the King had done so much for the rights of the people he could not doubt that they would do the same for him, for upon the preservation of his rights their own security depended. This was the formula that had come naturally to hand in the circumstances of the Remonstrance debate—that it was the interest as well as the duty of both King and people to maintain one another's rights and liberties. This was not a platitude either at the time of the Remonstrance debate or now. The parliamentary cause had been threatened by the breach with the King at that time, and the threat was the greater now. For the Remonstrance adopted had not been Hyde's, but Pym's. It had been a manifesto not of conciliation but of provocation. But if the Remonstrance had been Pym's, its answer was Hyde's. A break was made with a purely negative and provocative policy—the continual harping by the King and the conservatives on the royal prerogative in the appointment of ministers. There was no specific reference to this point. In this respect the declaration trod as delicately as it had trodden round that equally explosive point, the Church. True, the Commons' demand was not conceded—it could not be. But nothing was gained by saying so, and something might be gained by the stressing of a formula of reciprocity, the validity of which it was impossible for anyone to deny. Moreover, the King now had counsellors to whom it was difficult to deny confidence, especially if, as Hyde hoped, the King would listen to them. Even the Commons' majority could not style them evil counsellors.

Finally, the declaration made a general appeal for obedience to the laws and for an abatement of dissension in face of the danger to Ireland. There were two senses in which the reformation of 1641 was theoretical. First, it was not certain whether or in what sense the King accepted it, or whether, indeed, even Pym and his party regarded what had been achieved as sufficient. Secondly, the destruction of the regime of the prerogative had not uncovered a rule of law. It had left a vacuum. These two things were connected. The circumstances of mutual suspicion prevented the working of the new order; the breakdown of government precipitated the taking of sides. Moreover, threats to enforce the law amounted, if they stood alone, to partisan and inflammatory action, as, for instance, in regard to the Church and to the London mob. It was impossible to restore law and government unless a measure of confidence were first achieved, or unless one of the contending parties defeated the other by force. Hyde still hoped, or at least still worked, for confidence as a prelude to reconciliation, and he did not suppose that without it the administration of the law was possible, still less that the administration of the law could be a means to achieving confidence. The earlier part of the declaration makes this clear. The statements in the declaration about law and its enforcement should be taken as the attempt to emphasize and to consolidate the doctrine of the King's positive acceptance of the Common Law Revolution. Further, they drew attention to the fact that order of any kind, let alone order based upon the law, was disappearing. This was the most fundamental and the most obvious aspect of the situation as it would appear to a detached observer and also to each man as he was touched in his private concerns. That it should have been necessary or possible to make such a point as this is a fair indication how bad the situation had become.

That the situation was to get much worse was proved even while Hyde was launching this second bid for its improvement. Even before Falkland's and Culpepper's appointments were announced, the breakwater provided by the attitude of the Lords had been shaken to the foundations by the Bishops' Protest. The bishops announced that since they were prevented by hostile crowds from attending the House, proceedings in their absence ought to be deemed void. The King was a party to this, and so, in Gardiner's judgement, was Digby.[1] On 28 December Digby had striven without avail to make the Lords formally declare they were no longer free by reason of the tumults. Two days later they were invited in effect by the bishops to agree that the decision against Digby had been a mistaken step. This spectacular and clumsy stroke played into the hands of Pym. Hyde leaves us in no doubt what he thought of it.[2] The bishops' claim was false, for though they constituted, Hyde held, the third estate of the realm, they did not constitute a third House of Parliament with a consequent negative voice. It is true that their molestation was in principle an infringement of the freedom of Parliament, but that was a matter to be decided by the whole House. The House had declined so to decide, unfairly, perhaps, to the bishops. But the reaction of the latter was unparliamentary in a much more obvious sense. They were carrying the principle of protestation to an unheard-of length. And whereas the Lords' action was politic, theirs was impolitic in the extreme, since thereby they added the Lords to their enemies and lost the Lords for the King. Hyde blamed Archbishop Williams, but his account does not exclude—it rather suggests—Gardiner's view.[3] His hopes of a new Council following a continuous and responsible policy were frustrated since the conditions necessary for its working were destroyed before it could begin, destroyed, moreover, by that very agency by which he had tried to bring his plans to fruition. A few days after Holles[4] had clamoured against Digby for his action

[1] Gardiner, *History*, x, p. 123.
[2] Clarendon, *History*, I, p. 476.
[3] Ibid. p. 463. 'And from this unhappy composition in the one and the other [the King and Digby] a very unhappy counsel was entered upon, and resolution taken, without the least communication with either of the three which had been so lately admitted to an entire trust.' These words are immediately followed by Hyde's account of the Bishops' Protest.
[4] *D'Ewes*, Coates, p. 361.

in the Lords on the 28th, he was revealed to Hyde also as an evil counsellor. Digby did not deliberately deceive him. He was, Hyde wrote, 'equal to a very good part in the greatest affair, but the unfittest man alive to conduct it, having an ambition and vanity superior to all his other parts, and a confidence peculiar to himself, which sometimes intoxicated and transported and exposed him'.[1]

But the Bishops' Protest was only a beginning. Charles, with Digby deeply implicated, proceeded to impeach and then personally to attempt to seize the Five Members—and that without informing the new Council. This was the culmination of a succession of impolitic and foolish actions,[2] the effect of which was to submerge[3] Hyde's attempted new departure in pacification in an access of confusion and mistrust unparalleled up to that moment. 'This last accusation of divers members of the House has occasioned a greater distance between the King and the parliament than before', wrote an observer; 'all things are now in so great distraction...that there is no thinking of doing anything, but everybody are providing for their own safety, as if everything were inclinable to ruin.'[4]

The words 'royalist' and 'parliamentarian' are commonly and justifiably used as opposite and mutually exclusive terms and the fact is that royalist policy in this sense emerged and came to a head at this time. The Court resorted openly to measures to overthrow men whom it regarded as its enemies.

[1] Clarendon, *History*, I, pp. 461–3.
[2] 1. The King's passing through to Hampton Court on his return from Scotland instead of remaining at Whitehall (Clarendon, *History*, I, p. 433). 2. The handling of the question of the lieutenancy of the Tower (ibid. pp. 447–9). 3. The entertainment at Whitehall (whither the King returned at the prayer of the City) of 'many officers of the late disbanded army' (ibid. p. 456).
[3] It submerged Hyde's project so completely that Gardiner omits altogether to consider it. He makes no reference to Hyde's declaration in the *History*, mentioning it only in a footnote to p. 104 of the [*History of the Great*] *Civil War*, [1886,] vol. I.
[4] Carteret to Pennington, Jan. 6, *Cal[endar of] S[tate] P[apers] Dom[estic]*, 1641–43, p. 241.

This was in line with at least two of the three aims of a royalist party that showed itself, as Gardiner has pointed out,[1] amidst the excitement of the King's return to London from Scotland at the end of November. Those aims were: to put down the non-conforming Puritans and sectaries, to overthrow the power of Pym, and to check the Papists. The rumours that the King considered resorting to force against the Commons leaders, or at least to legal measures which assumed that they were traitors, were never entirely baseless, and as the year drew to its close, they were, as was now apparent to all, far from being so. The policy now acted upon assumed that the parliamentary movement had become a rebellion.

It should be unnecessary to state that Hyde had not now become a Royalist. The Royalists had now emerged, and in doing so had wrecked his schemes. He was still a Parliamentarian, even though after the Remonstrance he was detached from the prevailing party and policy in the House of Commons. Hyde and also D'Ewes commonly use the epithet 'violent' to describe the party and the policy which from the passing of the Remonstrance came to prevail there. Such terminology suggests both the convenience and the accuracy of employing the expression 'non-violent' to describe Hyde's parliamentarism and the policy for which he stood not only up to the passing of the Remonstrance but at this latest juncture. The words 'conservative' and 'moderate' are both misleading for they suggest if employed in his case a defection from the ideals of the Long Parliament, the one in the realm of doctrine, the other in that of practice. In neither of these senses had such a defection taken place. There is no call to quarrel with the use of the words 'royalist' and 'parliamentarian' as opposite and mutually exclusive terms. It tallies with events as they shaped themselves in the end. The parliamentarism of the Parliamentarians known to history,

[1] Gardiner, *History*, x, p. 85.

however, was from Hyde's point of view the parliamentarism of the party of violence, and if we seek a definition of the 'non-violent' attitude, we have but to understand that both in the time of his parliamentary leadership and in the subsequent period of his concern with the membership of the Council, Hyde had worked precisely to prevent the emergence of any such disastrous distinction as came to be established in the end between Parliamentarian and Royalist.

If Hyde, furthermore, was detached from Parliament in that since the passing of the Remonstrance he had deplored the policy of the House of Commons, he had certainly not now become attached to the King in the sense that Digby was attached to him. Digby had been at the outset an adherent of the reformers, and as such, it may be presumed, had grown intimate with Hyde. But he had clearly changed sides in a sense which it is quite incorrect to apply to Hyde. It was as a disgruntled courtier that Digby had joined the cause of reform. When 'he made private and secret offers of his service to the King',[1] he deserted that cause and became a courtier in a way that cannot be made to fit Hyde. It is not merely that the *History* is critical of actions which when studied in retrospect turned out to be politically mistaken. The detached historian's style and the intervening years of royal service conceal the fact that those actions must have been precisely those against which he himself had worked at the time. He had known them to be disastrous because, this time not from the side of the Commons as in the Remonstrance, but from that of the King, they were actions which seemed to destroy all prospect of a settlement.

[1] Clarendon, *History*, I, pp. 461–2.

§ 2. *From the Attempt on the Five Members to the Arrival of the King at York*

WHEN THEY have described the attempt on the Five Members, historians often suppose that they have gone far enough in explaining the outbreak of the Civil War. The King's action impelled Parliament to make its claim to control the militia, and the remaining months of peace appear in retrospect to have been a time of manœuvring preparatory to what was now the inevitable war. It is not quite in conformity with such a judgement that Gardiner declares the policy recommended by Hyde at the beginning of 1642 to have been of no historical importance.[1] For he appears to agree with Ranke[2] in placing in March rather than in January the date at which a resort to arms can be said to have become inevitable.[3] But he can make this statement about Hyde's policy only because he believed him to have been one of the leaders of the Royalist party since the previous autumn. If, as I have argued, such a notion is misconceived, not only must it be asked what became after 4 January of the ideas and policy traced out for Hyde up to that date, but the assumption that they have necessarily become of no historical importance must also be examined. In so far as his reaction to the changed circumstances can be reconstructed, there is ground for believing that, so far from his views being of no historical import, a correct appraisal of them may illuminate the paradoxical process by which the country was led into civil war.

---

[1] Gardiner, *History*, x, p. 128.
[2] [L. von] Ranke, [*A*] *History* [*of England principally in the 17th century*, 1875], II, p. 345.
[3] Gardiner, *History*, p. 172, though compare p. 146: 'Compromise was hardly possible now' (i.e. after the attempt on the five members), and p. 157: 'Up to that morning [14 January] hopes of an accommodation may possibly still have been entertained.'

Hyde shows in the *History* that the new councillors were of necessity deeply compromised by the attempt on the Five Members. Falkland, Culpepper, and also Hyde, could not avoid being looked upon as sharing in responsibility for what had happened. As councillors and as the friends of Digby they were marked men.[1] But the fact that they now appeared Royalists in the eyes of the parliamentary leaders tells us nothing about their own views, and does not justify a historian in agreeing without more ado with what would have been Pym's verdict in the matter. Little can be inferred from the profoundly unsympathetic terms in which Hyde refers in the *History* to the conduct of the parliamentary leaders after the attempted coup. He spoke in the same way of their conduct in connexion with much earlier events when we know that he was acting in concert with them. In retrospect, certainly, he declared that their proceedings justified the charge of treason, and he was prepared to distinguish between the manner and the matter both of the charge and of the attempted arrest. Moreover, we know[2] that in debate on 12 January he dared to affirm that 'he thought there was no privilege of parliament in cases of treason, felony and breach of the peace'. It is of far greater significance that even as a historian Hyde could find no terms strong enough to convey the disapprobation and dismay with which he and the other two reacted not only to the manner but also to the matter of the King's action.[3] The new councillors were, Hyde says, tempted to give up the line of policy begun when Falkland and Culpepper took office, not only because of the difficulty, henceforward, of their position in the House, but also out of grief and anger over counsels to which they were 'absolute strangers', and which they 'perfectly detested'.[4] Their own purpose had been the reconciliation of the King and the two Houses of Parlia-

---

[1] Clarendon, *History*, I, p. 487. *Life*, II, p. 84.

[2] D'Ewes' Journal, Harleian MSS. 162, fo. 319 *b*. I owe this and subsequent references to D'Ewes' Manuscript to the kindness of Professor Coates.

[3] Clarendon, *History*, I, pp. 487, 505, 525.   [4] Ibid. p. 487.

ment by means of an initiative on the King's part which should make clear that he accepted the achievements of Parliament and sympathized with its anxieties. The latest events made that assumption untenable. The turn of the year saw the culmination of the evil counsel which Hyde, as much as Pym, had always deplored. If he had rejected the political system which Pym had reared upon his suspicions on the ground that it could only incite the King to resort to evil counsel, those suspicions had now received confirmation in the attempt on the Five Members, and they were to be confirmed yet again in transactions which immediately followed. If such a thing had not been precluded by his own past action, and, now, by the action of the King, one might have expected that the divergence between Hyde and Pym over the Grand Remonstrance would have been forgotten. Indeed, it may be noted in this connexion that on 3 January, the day before the King had appeared in person in the House, Falkland and Culpepper were both made members of the committee which was immediately appointed, upon the King's request to the Speaker to deliver the Five Members. The committee was to wait upon him and tell him in reply that his message concerned the privilege of parliament 'and therein the privilege of all the Commons of England'.[1]

After the collapse of his position in Westminster and in London, through his alienation both of the Upper House and of the City, the King, on 10 January, retired to Hampton Court. The following day, which was the day on which the threatened members made their triumphal return to Westminster, Charles, egged on by his wife, appointed the Earl of Newcastle Governor of Hull, and dispatched an officer to take possession of the town. This was part of a design involving the seizure not only of Hull, but also of the Tower of

---

[1] C[ommons] J[ournal], II, p. 367. Lady Theresa Lewis, *Lives [of the Friends and Contemporaries of Lord Chancellor Clarendon*, 1852], I, p. 93. I should state that the thesis in her study of Falkland is the nearest I have been able to discover to the thesis of the present work.

London, and of Portsmouth. Digby and Lunsford, the Royalist whom Charles had made lieutenant of the Tower in December 1641, and then removed from that position in favour of Sir John Byron under pressure from the Commons and the City a few days later, were to seize the Surrey magazine at Kingston-upon-Thames, and from there the King would be able to strike south to Portsmouth. On 13 January the King and Queen moved to Windsor. The obvious purpose of these proceedings was to reassert the royal authority in consequence of the initial failure to arrest the parliamentary leaders, by the seizure of arms and strong places, two of which, lying on the coast, would give access to such help as the King might be able to procure from abroad. It is probable that the whole of this phase of policy, beginning with the impeachment of the Five Members, was touched off in the King's mind by his fears on behalf of the Queen. For he had reason to believe that the leaders of the Commons contemplated her impeachment. An object in seizing Portsmouth was that she should leave the country, not only to seek for aid, but also to assure her own safety.

In face of this resort to force, Pym's counter-measures were immediate. He was always well informed of what the Court was planning. Sir John Hotham was immediately dispatched to Hull by the authority of both Houses with instructions not to deliver it up till he was ordered to do so by 'the King's authority signified unto him by the Lords and Commons, now assembled in Parliament'.[1] Both Houses accepted a guard appointed under their own authority in preference to the guard proposed for them by the King. The train-bands were called out in Surrey and in the neighbouring counties to forestall Digby's attempt on Kingston, and Skippon was ordered to invest the Tower. On the same day Byron was summoned before the Lords to explain the attempt which had

[1] [The] Parl[iamentary or Constitutional] Hist[ory of England from the earliest times to the restoration of Charles II, 1751–62], x, p. 198.

been made to strengthen the Tower garrison. On 13 January it was the Lords who moved that the measures taken to meet the emergency at Kingston should 'be made general for all England',[2] and this called forth from the House of Commons a declaration which, explaining to the whole country the gravity of the situation, called upon it to put itself into a posture of defence.[2] In this attempted *coup d'état* on Charles's part and in the measures taken for its frustration, there was a situation which amounted to a momentary outbreak of civil war. But it was not the Civil War which was to come later, for though there was great and widespread fear of confusion and bloodshed, a fear which was inflated by the wilder and more fantastic apprehensions which had prevailed for many months past, the parliamentary leaders assumed that, provided they acted with vigour, they could master the situation, and that the Court had only a small faction to rely upon. The Buckinghamshire petition, presented on 11 January, in which Hampden's constituents offered to live and die with the Parliament, was of importance in this respect. It was clear before long that the parliamentary assumption was a sound one. Hotham reached Hull before the officer dispatched by Charles, Kingston was saved and Byron safely blockaded in the Tower.[3] Parliament soon had things under control, and, moreover, perceived that it had enhanced its strength beyond all computation.

Hyde in the *History* lays the greatest possible stress upon the collapse of the King's position, and the vast enhancement of that of Parliament, and he attributes it, rightly, to the attempt on the Five Members. He has little enough to say about the designs of Charles which immediately followed the failure of that attempt. But if he reprobated the latter, it is safe to say that he reprobated the former also, and that he included the

[1] L[ords] J[ournal], II, p. 510. Gardiner terms this 'the first proposal of a new militia bill'.
[2] *Parl. Hist.* x, p. 206.
[3] Byron obeyed the Lords' summons on 13 January.

later phases of the projected coup under the condemnation addressed to the drastic departure from his own policy which the King had made at the beginning of January. Can it also be assumed that he and his colleagues were as ignorant of these later plans as they were of the attempt on the Five Members, and that the King continued to keep his new councillors in the dark? Hyde says[1] that before he left Whitehall, the King renewed his commands to Falkland, Culpepper and himself 'to consult upon his affairs' in Parliament, and that after his departure they remained in correspondence with him. But such information is not evidence on which can be based a negative answer to the question, though Ranke implies that the parliamentary councillors dissuaded the King from the attempt on Hull.[2] This opinion is based on a passage in one of the Queen's letters which may well refer to a later stage in the story.[3] On the whole it seems more likely that Hyde was in ignorance of these plans and heard of them only as they became known in Parliament. It was a situation in which, as Hyde explains,[4] he and his colleagues carried on the work of advising Charles in his dealings with Parliament, begun at the end of the previous year, but with reluctance and embarrassment, and only out of duty and conscience and out of consideration of the present ill condition of the King. In this sudden polarization of events into an actual confrontation of armed forces, Hyde and his friends had, it seems, no part or lot on either hand, though it is, as we have seen, hard not to suppose that, in the circumstances, they accepted the measures of Parliament as inevitable. This is the more likely in that the House of Lords, whose attitude up to the beginning of the new year had been a factor which not only made possible but encouraged Hyde's

[1] *Life*, II, p. 83.
[2] Ranke, *History*, II, p. 340.
[3] *Letters of Queen Henrietta Maria* [*including her private correspondance with Charles the First*, M. A. Everett Green, 1857], p. 117. *Vide infra* p. 104.
[4] Clarendon, *History*, I, pp. 487–8.

policy, since it had remained standing on the ground which he had tried in vain to make the Commons adopt,[1] now agreed with the Lower House, and even took the lead in proposing measures of security.

Such measures, however, were successful, and in that the designs of the turn of the year had from the King's point of view proved so disastrously abortive, there was now no alternative open to him but to adopt some such course of action as Hyde had recommended before those designs had been embarked upon. It now became clear to the King that it was necessary to go some way towards conciliating Parliament. On 20 January he sent a message to the two Houses. He animadverted upon the distracted condition of affairs, which could not, he said, admit of the delays of ordinary proceedings in Parliament, and though normally proposals should come from Parliament to the King rather than from the King to Parliament, he asked them with all speed to 'fall into a serious consideration of all those particulars which they shall hold necessary, as well for the upholding and maintaining of His Majesty's just and regal authority, and for the settling of his revenue as for the present and future establishment of their privileges; the free and quiet enjoying of their estates and fortunes; the liberties of their persons; the security of the true religion now professed in the Church of England, and the settling of ceremonies in such a manner, as may take away all just offence; which when they shall have digested and composed one entire body, that so His Majesty and themselves may be able to make the more clear judgement of them',[2] he undertook to do everything in his power to make such concessions as should conduce to a settlement.

Hyde does not claim that it was he who was behind the message of 20 January and there is no conclusive evidence

---

[1] The House of Peers, he wrote, 'was well disposed, and might have been managed with a little patience, to have blasted all the extravagances of the Commons'. Ibid. p. 524.

[2] *Parl. Hist.* x, p. 226.

that it sprang from an initiative on his part.[1] It cannot, therefore, be affirmed that it had the same kind of background as
the declaration in answer to the Remonstrance. Though, as
has been mentioned, Hyde seems to imply that there was
contact between himself and the King at this time,[2] the indications are that he was much in the background, even when
compared with Falkland and Culpepper.[3] It will, however,
be clear enough that the message represents a continuation
of the idea of Hyde's answer to the Grand Remonstrance, the
idea of staging a pacificatory gesture from the King's side.
It actually recalls the terms of that document in respect of its
liberal ecclesiastical policy, and in regard to the settlement of
the civil state there is the same indication that the King has
by no means come to the end of all the things which he will
do for his subjects. There is also a repetition of the formula of
reciprocity which Hyde had imported into the debate on the
Remonstrance (since the King will do something for Parliament, they must do something for him), but in the circumstances of the now much wider breach which was, moreover,
one which divided the King from both Houses of Parliament
and not from the Commons alone as before, the formula has
been promoted into something resembling the framework for
a treaty between the King and the estates of the realm. If,
then, it is impossible to say that the message of 20 January
was directly suggested by Hyde, it must certainly be maintained that it was a step with which he would have been in
sympathy, and it will be possible to argue that he endorsed
it approvingly at least at a later stage in the course of events.

The House of Lords was delighted with the King's message.
Though they had been united with the Commons in the
security measures recently adopted, they had not concurred
on all points. They had refused to join the Commons in

[1] Lister asserts that it was framed with Hyde's assistance (1, p. 154). This is
presumably an inference from the fact that Hyde and Falkland were still giving
Charles advice on his dealings with Parliament.
[2] *Life*, 11, p. 83.   [3] Ibid. p. 90.

54

petitioning the King to remove Sir John Byron from the command of the Tower and appoint Sir John Conyers instead,[1] and they had objected to the preamble of the Commons' declaration announcing the state of emergency. The message of 20 January seemed about to reconstitute the difference between the two Houses as it had existed prior to the attempt on the Five Members. The Lords refused to allow the Commons to add to the answer of thanks to the King's message a petition for the dismissal of the lieutenant of the Tower and for the disposition of the forts and militia in the hands of such commanders as they could confide in, though they were willing to enclose the Commons' request that the King should clear the Five Members. The Commons' petition, therefore, went to the King merely on the Commons' account. But though he had asked for all proposals to be digested into one body before they were presented, the King now showed that he would not reject out of hand the amendment to his scheme thus put forward by the Lower House. On 28 January he sent an answer, in which, though in an imprecise manner and with reservations about his own rights, it was implied that he might consider nominations from Parliament for the control of the forts. As for the militia, he said that he would entertain a Bill for the ordering of it. He could not allow their request in respect of the Tower, unless grave objection could be made to the lieutenant, but he urged them to go forward with the scheme of 20 January.

This answer did not satisfy the Commons, and they proceeded to press the Lords to join them in demanding the guarantees. In a few days, the Lords gave way, 'through', as Ranke says, 'various concurrent circumstances'.[2] But the problem of the change of front on the part of the House of Lords is not a difficult one. Firth declares[3] that Hyde is in

---

[1] The Commons first asked them to do so on 11 January.
[2] Ranke, *History*, II, p. 327.
[3] C. H. Firth, *The House of Lords during the Civil War*, 1910, p. 111.

error in attributing it to riots since these did not occur at this stage. But the pressure through mass petitions cannot be ignored. Pym on 25 January at a conference between the Houses made a long speech in which he aimed to shake the Lords by reading such petitions, and by asserting that men now leading the Irish rebellion had landed in Ireland with royal passports. Nor, in the same connexion, is it possible to ignore, as an instance of the type of intimidation to which the more conservative peers might expect to be subjected, the treatment of the Duke of Richmond, who in a debate following Pym's speech was understood to have moved an adjournment of six months. For this action he was censured and threatened with worse. But it is more important to recall that the Lords had acted in unison with the Commons earlier in the month and it is not surprising that they should ultimately have agreed with the Commons in asking for guarantees for the future. It is to be noted in this connexion that on the very day in which the Lords received the King's message (20 January) the Commons had received news from Hull that the municipal authorities, perplexed by contradictory orders from King and Parliament, were standing out against the execution of Sir John Hotham's instructions to strengthen the place. Until such matters could be cleared up the Commons could not feel that they were sitting in safety, and the same considerations could not but work upon the Lords. In the Upper House it was always a middle party which had mattered,[1] and, after what had happened, that middle party was not to be won over once more without concrete concessions.

To the joint petition of Lords and Commons of 2 February requesting, as a necessary preliminary to adopting the course proposed by him on 20 January, that the Tower of London, the forts and the militia be placed in the hands of men recommended to him by Parliament, Charles replied on 6 February.

[1] Both Gardiner (*History*, x, p. 163 n.) and Firth (*The House of Lords during the Civil War*, p. 111) make this point.

This time he clearly stated that he would accept parliamentary nominees for the control of the forts and the militia, if they would tell him the extent of the power they were to exercise and the length of the time they were to exercise it. In reply to the simultaneous petition that he would clear the Five Members, he declared that he would drop his charge against them altogether and grant a general pardon. This was a big step. Two previous messages which had shown signs of a weakening on his part in this matter had done no more than suggest a reconsideration of procedure and a willingness to safeguard parliamentary privilege.[1] On 11 February he gave way even in the matter of the Tower, agreeing to substitute Conyers for Byron. On the following day Parliament presented to him its list of nominees for the forts and the militia.

It indeed looked as if affairs had taken a turn for the better from Hyde's point of view. There were now hopes of quietness, wrote a correspondent, through the King accepting the militia petition and abandoning the accusation of the members, and the dismissal of cavaliers attending the Court now that the King had left town, had rid the latter of its fears.[2] Even Gardiner admits that at last a basis for settlement had been laid. But he hastens to point out[3] that the King's motives were highly questionable. His actions now, he says, were probably inspired by the same motive as those which had precipitated his resort to force a few weeks earlier, namely his fear for the safety of the Queen. It had been decided that Henrietta Maria should leave the country. It should be understood, however, that in consequence of his present weakness and isolation the King's motives could no longer have the importance which they had previously possessed, and if we are inclined to discount the royal concessions, it must be

[1] One on 13 January, *Parl. Hist.* x, p. 203, and the other on 14 January, ibid. p. 209.
[2] Slingsby to Pennington, 10 February. *Cal. S.P. Dom.* 1641–43, p. 282.
[3] Gardiner, *History*, x, p. 164.

57

recognized that the parliamentary leaders were probably threatening the Queen for the precise purpose of extracting them. The Queen, as Hyde viewed matters, would be a good riddance. Indeed, he would hardly have dissented from the thesis put forward later by the Grocers' Hall Committee that the influence which she exerted over the King was a root cause of all the troubles.[1] The equally disastrous Digby had already fled. It looked like the clearing of the field for Hyde and the new councillors. It did not, of course, follow that, because the Queen was to leave England, she would do no more harm, especially as it was believed that she was to carry with her the crown jewels. There were plenty of suspicions on the part of Parliament. But these, though he doubtless shared them, and most probably on a similar basis of ignorance, would weigh the less with Hyde if it could be assumed that the King would stay near London, or, at least, that he would return to its neighbourhood after he had escorted the Queen to her ship, and that the negotiation on the militia, and, thereafter, on all outstanding points would go forward.

The course of events, as Hyde would now see it, was as follows. On 5 February, the Saturday before the Monday on which the King's second message on the militia had been received, the House of Lords had at last passed the Bill to deprive the bishops of their places in Parliament. The King, everybody knew, was greatly disinclined to pass this, and much discussion, as a matter of fact, took place in his circle, as Hyde was later able to relate, on the course which he should now pursue. In the meantime, he put Parliament off with a temporizing answer which was read in the Lords and in the Commons on 8 February and on the following day left Windsor for the south coast. On 14 February Parliament received a further and a most notable instalment of concessions from the King. Greatly to everyone's surprise, he passed the Bishops' Exclusion Bill. He also passed the Impressment

[1] Ranke, *History*, ii, p. 327, and *vide infra*, p. 110.

Bill for Ireland, and put the reform of the Church into the hands of Parliament, requesting only, in accord with the terms of the message of 20 January, that its proposals be digested into a body before presentation. The King also suggested that Parliament should take steps to meet the decline of trade, and promised, for his own part, to enforce the laws against the Papists. Both Houses formally expressed their gratitude. On the same day, however, Pym produced an intercepted letter from Digby, who was now abroad, and also the order which had been given to Lord Newcastle in the middle of the previous month, to take over the governorship of Hull. Digby's letter to the Queen clearly seemed to envisage that the King should 'betake himself to a safe place where he may avow and protect his servants from rage and violence'. It also disparaged the attempts which were being made at accommodation. These disclosures, against the background of the anxieties induced by the King's absence, made the Commons, and then the Lords, pass the arrangements for the militia which had so far been made in concert with the King, but in the form of an ordinance to be presented for his acceptance. In these circumstances it was certainly no less necessary than before to obtain such guarantees. Without them the other concessions would be worthless. But in reply on 19 February the King would only say that the matter required time for his consideration, and that he would attend to it when he returned, which he intended to do as soon as the Queen had left the country. Parliament's united view was that in the anxieties of the situation such a message must be counted a denial, and on 21 February they decided to send again to press the King to accept the militia ordinance. All they could elicit from him was yet another temporizing statement, reported on 25 February. In the meantime, the Commons had heard that the Prince of Wales had been summoned from Richmond to attend his father. This circumstance naturally seemed a very sinister one. Parliament had already expressed anxiety in

59

regard to the movements of the Prince.[1] Was he now to be
sent out of the country too? Could the King himself be counted
on to return to the neighbourhood of the capital? In such
doubts and fears regarding the King's intentions, both Houses
sent off a deputation post haste begging him not to allow the
Prince to be moved. Of this deputation Hyde was made
a member.[2]

These events, or some of them, are discussed by Hyde in
the *Life*. But not only was that document written at a great
distance of time from the events described, with attitudes and
ideas which he later adopted under the impact of succeeding
events read back as having been firmly held at even these
early junctures in his career, but the *Life* is inspired, also, by
the aim of showing with how much devotion and, in view of
what transpired, with how much perspicacity its author had
always served the King's interests. Hyde asserts that in the
matter of the two Bills, the Bishops' Exclusion Bill and that
of the militia,[3] though he explains that he was not consulted,
he and the King were independently of the same judgement,
namely that both should be rejected. He implies that his own
view was 'that nothing was so necessary as the most obstinate
resolution'[4] and that the King could do more good for himself by standing firm than by yielding. In the matter of the
bishops' exclusion, the inference, as at earlier points in the
story, is that he was impelled by his concern for the Church
and for the Constitution, in regard to both of which his view
tallied with the view of the King.[5] He explains that Culpepper
pressed for the acceptance by the King of the Bishops' Exclusion Bill on the ground that the opposition would thereby
be appeased not only in regard to the Church but also in
regard to the militia, and that when not at first successful he
was able to win his point by playing upon the Queen's fears

[1] See *Parl. Hist.* x, p. 208.   [2] *Life*, ii, p. 98.
[3] It should be noted that it was a question at the time not of two Bills, but of
a Bill and an ordinance.
[4] *Life*, ii, p. 93.   [5] Ibid. p. 94.

that she would be prevented from embarking if the Bill were refused. Hyde proceeds to point to the vindication of his own judgement, which he identified with the better judgement of the King, in the immediate falsification of Culpepper's arguments by events in Parliament, the pressure of which for an agreement on the milita was increased rather than relaxed by the concession on the bishops, and also in the harm which was done to the King's interest by his surrender in a matter in which it was common knowledge that his deepest feelings were implicated. Men concluded, said Hyde, that there was nothing to which the King would not agree if pressed hard enough to do so, and, therefore, stood aside or allowed themselves to be swept along by Pym's brilliantly manipulated torrent.

Now if, at this time, Hyde had already taken sides in a conflict which, however lamentable, he now thought inevitable, it is possible to maintain that he would, if consulted, have recommended rigidity on the King's part in Church matters and in all others as both the right and the politic course to pursue, and even, since the evidence does not allow us to be positive that they had been made on his advice, that he believed the concessions made since 20 January to have been misconceived. The fact is, however, that it is his own account of these matters which makes it difficult to accept such an estimate of the way Hyde viewed events at this juncture. For the crux of his story in the *Life*, as he originally told it,[1] lies in the account of the difference which emerged at this point between Hyde and Falkland on the one hand, and Culpepper on the other, and in the importance which Hyde attaches to it. Culpepper, unknown to the other two, now recommended, Hyde shows, that the King, after seeing the Queen safely on board ship, should repair to the north with the object of making a second attempt to secure the magazine at Hull, while he and Falkland desired, as did Parliament as a whole,

[1] Ibid. p. 91.

that he would return to the capital and assumed, moreover, that he would do so.

Culpepper, as Hyde makes clear, was now converted to the Queen's doctrine which was analogous to that of Pym; namely, that even if there were to be a treaty, it must depend on mutual respect for strength, and, moreover, that confidence had become so hard to establish that it was a prime duty to prepare for the worst. Following the failure of the designs at the beginning of January, Henrietta Maria had not abandoned her policy. She had merely postponed its application. And Culpepper was now converted to her way of viewing the situation, converted, in short, to that royalism in the usual sense of the word, of which the attempt on the Five Members had so far been the most spectacular manifestation. To men of such a mind it was impossible to give way on the militia. Even compromise on that point was unthinkable. There is no reason to doubt that Hyde and Falkland, on the other hand, despite the deplorably changed circumstances flowing from the attempted arrest of the Five Members, remained rooted in the line they had inaugurated at the end of the previous year, a line in which they would have been confirmed by the reversion to their policy which was on the face of it involved in the King's message of 20 January. If Hyde counted on the King returning to London, as his own account makes it apparent that he did, it is difficult to believe that he can have envisaged a completely unbending attitude on the King's part once he was back there. Hyde may indeed have preferred intransigence in the matter of the bishops. He had certainly himself opposed the Exclusion Bills in 1641. The King's acceptance now would accelerate the fall in the number of the Lords attending Parliament, and so smooth the path for Pym, and he may have foreseen such a thing. Moreover, he must have assumed that nothing would induce the King to accept the Bill. But how could the King's return to the capital have been conceived save as involving that the negotiation pro-

posed on 20 January was conducted in good faith, above all
that for the settlement of the militia? And how could there
have been such negotiations without concessions? In fact even
in his own account he admits the necessity of 'moderate con-
descensions' had the King returned to London.[1]

Retrospectively, Hyde stressed the question of the bishops'
exclusion for the reason that from the later point of view
which glorified intransigence the King had acted wrongly in
this matter. He desired to reveal to the King his mistakes.
It was intransigence, especially in the matter of the Church,
which was decisive as it turned out in building up the strength
of the King. But that was in the future. At the time his
attitude to the situation was most probably not unlike that of
the majority of the House of Lords, as it had been in the
month of January, that is, before its numbers began to thin
out. The Lords in passing the Bill to exclude the bishops had
gone further than it could be supposed that the King would
follow them. But it was also not impossible to suppose that
a refusal of the Bill by the King need not necessarily have
wrecked an accommodation on the militia. Culpepper's
argument, indeed, was based on an exaggerated estimate of
the importance at this time of the ecclesiastical issue. This
issue had now been put in the shade by the King's actions
early in January, and far more effectively than by either
Hyde or Pym in the parliamentary tactics of an earlier phase.
It was the question of the militia which was now the central
one in the view of Parliament and probably also in the view
of Hyde. It was the necessary outcome of the attempt on the
Five Members and a compromise on the question, together
with the withdrawal of the King's charge against the members,
was the obvious recipe for the inauguration of settlement.
Moreover, the question of the militia actually required constitutional clarification. A compromise embodied in a legislative enactment would have seemed necessary and, in addition,

[1] *Life*, ii, p. 103.

not impossible, provided too great a strain was not put upon
confidence. Up to the King's departure with the Queen the
compromise settlement in this matter seemed to be going
forward.

The indications of Hyde's close relations with the Earl of
Essex are suggestive in the present connexion. For it is known
that Essex, together with Holland, had begged the King not
to leave Whitehall in January.[1] Now Whitelocke writes,
'this was another and great wonder to many prudent men,
that the King should leave this city . . . and by his leaving the
town bring great disadvantages upon himself and his affairs:
this was thought not to have been done advisedly'.[2] It would
appear that Hyde, together with Essex and Holland, must
be included amongst Whitelocke's prudent men. In the *Life*
there is a section in which Hyde explains that Essex was
desirous of an accommodation at this period, 'and did hope
nothing more than to make himself the instrument to reconcile the Parliament to the King, by some moderate and
plausible expedient'.[3] It is possible (we can, of course, say
no more) that the position of such a statement at the point in
his text at which it occurs can be accounted for in terms of
a policy in which Hyde himself, in common with Essex, had
been concerned. Moreover, in the original *History* there is
a similar passage about Essex which is immediately preceded
by the following. 'And I have heard many of the fiercest
concurrers, and who have ever since kept them company, at
that time profess that if any expedient might be found to reconcile the present difference about the militia, they would
no more adventure upon demands of a like nature.'[4]

It cannot be denied that in the *Life* Hyde would have it
believed that not only the King but also he himself was opposed to any significant concession in the matter of the militia.

---

[1] Gardiner, *History*, x, pp. 149, 150.
[2] Whitelocke, *Memorials*, 1853, 1, p. 156.
[3] *Life*, II, p. 103.   [4] Clarendon, *History*, II, p. 13.

In the *History*,[1] too, he describes even the answers of 28 January and 6 February as having been denials. But it must be remembered that Parliament always treated the King's answers on this matter as in effect denials, that the King in his own mind may have meant them to have been such, that his subsequent action certainly encouraged a retrospective interpretation in that sense by Hyde, and that, in any event, the King did not and never would have accepted what Parliament actually proposed in the militia ordinance, and that Hyde could not have recommended that he should have done so. The fact remains, nevertheless, that in later declarations inspired and penned by Hyde the King's answers are emphatically declared to have been denials not in substance but only in details, and Hyde's account of Culpepper's change of policy and his admission that Falkland and he were unaware that it had taken place is a clear indication that he cannot at the time have viewed the question of the militia in the way in which he viewed it in retrospect. The search for just such an expedient to reconcile the difference about the militia as was desired by men like Essex[2] is the most reasonable explanation of Hyde's conduct at this time.

Hyde, as we have seen, had been put on the deputation sent by Parliament to request the King that the Prince should not be moved. This brought him to the fore again, and gave him an opportunity of renewed contact with Charles with whom he had discussions at Canterbury, after the King's return from Dover, and again at Greenwich. In the *Life*, he tells how he persuaded the King to substitute a paper drafted by himself for the reply it had been intended at first to give about the Prince's movements. This reply, Hyde told Charles, 'had much sharpness in it, which at that time could only

[1] Ibid. pp. 537, 557.
[2] Hyde did not necessarily work, of course, in concert with Essex. Indeed, there was embarrassment when the latter came upon Hyde and the King in conversation in the privy gallery at Greenwich. *Life*, II, p. 102.

POLITICS

provoke them '.[1] He says nothing about having also discussed
with Charles the answer to the militia ordinance, but since
that answer was dated the same day as the reply about the
Prince (28 February), and since Hyde declares that the upshot of this latest contact was the agreement that he should
draft the King's papers, we may accept the view of both
Ranke[2] and Gardiner[3] that the answer to the militia ordinance was drafted by him. No reference is made in this document to the King's decision to go to the north. Hyde implies[4]
that he knew by this time that the suspicions of parliament
to the effect that Charles did not intend to return to London
were well founded. But we cannot be certain that his memory
was trustworthy upon that point. Nicholas, writing to Sir
Thomas Roe from Dover on 19 February,[5] still apparently
assumed that the Court would shortly return to Whitehall,
and, even on 4 March,[6] still seemed to be in ignorance that
it had been decided to go to the north. But at least it would
seem possible to say that these interviews between Hyde and
the King were an attempt on Hyde's part to salvage what he
could from the wreckage of confidence resulting from the
suspicious character of the King's movements.

What then was Hyde able to secure from the King? Charles
had made up his mind, says Hyde, to make no more concessions until he could be satisfied regarding the full extent of
what Parliament had it in mind to demand.[7] Such a decision
was congruent with the offer of 20 January, and even if the
mood of the King was now unmistakably more defiant than
it was when he had first made it, such a decision conformed
more closely with the letter of that offer than the concession
made when the King had left Windsor with the Queen had
done, namely, his acceptance of the Bishops' Exclusion Bill.
Hyde, of course, knew that Parliament would not entertain

[1] *Life*, II, p. 99. [2] Ranke, *History*, VI, p. 7.
[3] Gardiner, *History*, X, p. 171. [4] *Life*, II, p. 101.
[5] *Cal. S.P. Dom.* 1641–43, p. 287. [6] Ibid. p. 293.
[7] Clarendon, *History*, I, pp. 554, 556.

66

the proposal of 20 January without satisfaction in the matter of the militia. It is necessary, therefore, to look at the King's reply (28 February) to the militia ordinance.[1] In this reply the King refused to accept an ordinance, and, moreover, objected to its preamble which harped on the attempt on the Five Members and was obnoxious in that he had agreed to drop all charges against them and had offered to pass any Bill Parliament liked to offer for the safeguarding of its privileges. Furthermore, he stipulated that the rights of town corporations should not be infringed by what was proposed. But he would accept Parliament's nominees, and would grant them the same powers as had been granted during the present Parliament, and with its advice, to certain Lords Lieutenant. If those powers were not enough, 'but that more shall be thought fit to be granted to these persons named, than by the law is in the crown itself', he invited new legislation to meet the case. As for the length of time during which the nominees were to have power, the King could not agree that they should have it for an indefinite period. Parliament, it was implied, must make a proposal on that point. It was hoped that these offers would dispel Parliament's fears and jealousies, and enable the members to proceed in accordance with his message of 20 January. The King, it was pointed out, had now granted all that was asked of him in the original petition. Although this is undeniably a rejection of the militia ordinance, it was a rejection only because an ordinance was objectionable in form, and because the time during which the nominees were to act was left unspecified and left to parliamentary discretion. The acceptance of Parliament's nominations, subject to clarification on this latter point, was a great concession, and if, as seems clear, the drift of this reply was an invitation to prepare a Bill in any case, there was no reason why Parliament should not accept it.

It cannot be known what passed between the King and

[1] Ibid. p. 577.

67

Hyde. All he says in the *Life* (and what he says has reference only to the answer to the petition about the Prince), is that he disapproved of the provocation and sharpness of the King's attitude, and prevailed with him to make a more restrained reply. It looks as if Charles was so relieved by his wife's safe departure from the country and by his son's safe arrival at Greenwich, that he was prepared to let Hyde send Parliament what answer he pleased[1] both in regard to the Prince and in regard to the militia, and to suggest, or to agree to Hyde's suggestion, that he should draw up all his answers to Parliament in future. Apart from such an attitude in the King it is difficult to account for this extraordinary arrangement. The practicability of such a scheme derived from the terms of the offer of 20 January, and from the immediate reaction to it. For Hyde would proceed upon the assumption that, from the King's side, there would be a negative answer to every isolated new request, and that, from Parliament's side, an agreement on the militia was the indispensable preliminary to digesting all other proposals into the outline of a settlement. But did not the inception of this plan which for Hyde meant the all important continuation of discussions on the militia depend upon the fact, as Gardiner asserts, that negotiations with Parliament had at this time become a secondary object with the King?[2] We shall be disposed to comment that the very factors which made the new arrangement possible should have made it obvious to Hyde that no improvement of the situation could be expected to spring from it. We shall be tempted to endorse the disparaging tone in which Gardiner refers to Hyde's efforts at this time. But the situation had to be accepted for what it was, even if Hyde had known, as he must at least have suspected, the nature of what the Queen was advising. The fact that the prospects were bad only heightened the necessity of seeking an improvement, whatever the expectation of success.

[1] *Life*, II, p. 101.   [2] Gardiner, *History*, X, p. 171.

It must be recalled that, as a member still attending the House of Commons, he would still have been working from Parliament's assumptions regarding the King's weakness and in agreement with its view that, if he would not freely come to terms, he would not, as an alternative, be able to resist its demands. In fact, he admits in the *Life*[1] that he shared these assumptions. Such considerations would be even more potent now than they had been before the message of 20 January. The King's absence from London merely invited Parliament to increase its hold over the country and to do so with success. Nothing the Queen could devise could alter this. Indeed, anyone placed as Hyde was, must have believed that her devices would only further it. The King had brought the present situation on himself, and his own interest, as much as the prospects of settlement depended, it could be pointed out, on a cessation of actions which aroused suspicion. Hyde may still have been in ignorance that Charles intended to try once more to seize Hull. And the King would have been able to stress that aspect of his undertaking with the Queen which implied a treaty. If Hyde shared Parliament's suspicions and mistrust, as he most probably did, by the same token he would not have envisaged civil war, but rather alternatives which were, on the one hand, a freely negotiated settlement, or, on the other, an abject capitulation by the King.

In considering this point, it is important to recognize that from the Queen's correspondence with Charles, it is clear that, in her view at least, he had not been guiltless of deviations into Hyde's policy. What is more, she would hardly have filled her letters with reproaches and threats to retire into a convent every time there was a rumour that the King was seeking terms with Parliament, if she had felt she could trust him in the present and in the future. In the *Life*, Hyde states that so great were the Queen's doubts about the reliability of her husband's policy, that had she not been so much

[1] *Life*, II, p. 90.

afraid of what would happen if she remained, she would never have left the country at all.[1] The Queen's letters confirm this. She writes as if she knew there was too much reason to fear that rumours which reached her ears were not baseless. The fact that she was as critical of the King's divergences from her policy into the policy of Hyde as Hyde was of the King's divergences from his into hers, indicates that Hyde and the Queen had been struggling to win the King's mind. She did not yet regard that struggle as having ended in her favour. The Queen was confident[2] on receiving a letter dispatched from Greenwich at the time of the safe arrival of the Prince, but before long she was 'troubled almost to death'[3] over rumours that the King was returning to London. The tone and content of her letters with their continual insistence that he be firm to the resolutions made at the time of her departure can only mean that it was not a foregone conclusion, even now, that the King would listen to her in preference to the parliamentary councillors, and this is confirmed by a correspondent of Digby writing from York with a point of view similar to that of Digby himself. All would be well, he wrote, if the King did not listen to an accommodation. But he was too much inclined to do this.[4]

Whatever Hyde's part may have been in conceiving the original offer on 20 January, that offer had become the basis now for yet another effort at pacification on his part. The same principle was involved as before—to think so far as possible of the future in preference to the past, with the condition and the sanction that for the future the King's action must be impeccable. Such a project was not, apparently, an absurd one: 'a long debate', says D'Ewes, ensued upon the reception by the House of Commons of the King's message of 28 February, 'whether this were a denial by his Majesty of

[1] *Life*, III, p. 158.   [2] *Letters of Queen Henrietta Maria*, p. 52.
[3] Ibid. p. 56.
[4] Thomas Elliot to Digby. D. Townshend, *George Digby, 2nd Earl of Bristol*, 1924, p. 31.

our desires or not'.[1] But the reasons behind the failure of Hyde's previous efforts to apply his principle must operate with even greater force now. The wall of mutual distrust was now of a formidable height. If it was possible at least to hope that Parliament might now think itself strong enough as a result of the King's failure over the Five Members to accept his present offers of a settlement and so demonstrate to Charles the force of Hyde's arguments (and the 'long debate' shows that such an attitude was not an unreasonable one), it has to be understood that the very strength of Parliament and the weakness of the King worked to abate the consideration with the former that its pursuit of the less accommodating alternative might result in war. 'After long agitation it was at last Resolved upon the Question that this Answer of his Majesty is a denial to the desires of both Houses concerning the settling of the militia.'[2] The line Pym had taken since he had beaten Hyde in the previous November, which he was still taking, and was to continue to take, applying ever increasing pressure, was that of a settlement through the complete capitulation of the King to his demands. Even if the King's past actions had not been enough to settle the matter, his refusal to return to London was decisive for the maintenance of a policy based on mistrust, and the misgivings of such men as Essex had no chance of asserting themselves, especially as the desertion of the House of Lords by the more conservative peers, and the removal of the bishops, made it a much smaller body in February than it had been in January.

But there was a difference between this effort of Hyde's and his previous ones. Whereas, before, his failure had been due

---

[1] Harleian MSS. 163, fo. 10b.

[2] Ibid. D'Ewes gives no details of the debate. We cannot therefore tell whether Hyde spoke in it. He recounts that earlier in the day Hyde reported the mission to Canterbury and Greenwich. D'Ewes' account of Hyde's speech adds nothing to our knowledge though it confirms what Hyde relates in the *Life* that the King substituted a second answer about the Prince for the one he had originally intended. The report includes no explanation of this.

6-2

to the actions of the side from which he was trying to act (Parliament had refused to endorse his views on the Grand Remonstrance, and the King would not act in terms of his answer to it), now the refusal came from the side ranged over against the one which he was advising. However great the past faults of the King, and Hyde would have been no more likely to minimize them than any other parliamentarian, the fact remains that it was Parliament which refused to make any response, and that at a time when what the King wanted and what Hyde wanted, or, at least, in the matter of the King's absence Hyde had to accept, were for a time running parallel in the realm of means. In telling the story, Hyde speaks[1] of the 'resolution' of the King's present policy, a quality which his present counsellors had infused into him. Transposed back into the circumstances of 1642, it may be inferred that Hyde now thought that the King would act on his advice, and that he had abandoned the policy which he had pursued from the attempt on the Five Members to the departure of the Queen. And it is a fact that, whereas at the end of 1641 royalism and the purposes of Hyde were mutually exclusive, now, though unknown to Hyde, and also to the Queen (each hoped that the King's 'resolution' excluded the other's definition of it), the King, bombarded from both sides, was effecting something like a fusion of the two, a fusion which had perhaps been facilitated by the defection of Culpepper to the Queen's views.

From this novelty in the pattern—the fact that it was less from the side from which he was trying to act than from that to which the initiative towards a better understanding was addressed that the check was to come, there stemmed the most important consequences. Because, at this point, it was Parliament and not the King which the more obviously would not respond to Hyde's urgent pleas for an accommodation, and because of what this was to mean for Hyde's personal

---

[1] *Life*, II, pp. 107, 110. *History*, II, p. 7.

safety, Hyde, in the literal and local sense of the word, was to abandon Parliament for the King. Because of the part he was privately to play as public spokesman for the King, the circumstances of that abandonment are a large part of the explanation of the fact that the King acquired a party and an army. Because of that, there was a civil war, and out of the Civil War, beginning in the way which Hyde judged that it did begin, namely in the uncompromising aggressiveness of the leaders of Parliament, there sprang the interpretation of events which forms the fundamental framework of the *History of the Rebellion.*

Having resolved that the King's answer of 28 February amounted to a denial of the militia, both Houses of Parliament proceeded to resolve also that the men who had advised that answer were enemies of the State and declared their intention of finding out who they were. They resolved that it was necessary to act forthwith for the defence of the realm, and that those who had already begun so to act be deemed to have done no wrong in the sight of the law. It was resolved, also, that the King's removal northwards hazarded the peace, and that he be asked to return to his Parliament. The Prince was also to be brought back.[1] These resolutions were embodied in a message to the King to be sent to him at Theobalds. It was presented there on 1 March. The King replied that he had his own jealousies and fears and that he dare not come back to his Parliament. He declared that on the questions of the militia and the Prince he had nothing to add to what he had said before.

On 2 March, both Houses, being informed of this reply, again threatened to take action on their own for the defence of the realm; in other words, they threatened to put the militia ordinance into execution. They also determined to draw up a declaration[2] which should expound 'the just causes

[1] *Parl. Hist.* x, pp. 325, 326.   [2] Ibid. pp. 329, 330.

of the fears and jealousies' which had inspired the militia ordinance, and also clear them of the imputation cast on them by the King when he said that he dare not return to Parliament. By 5 March both Houses had passed the militia ordinance in a new form. Previously, it had read: 'It is ordained by the King, Lords and Commons, now in Parliament assembled, that etc.' The King's name was now omitted. The same day the Commons' draft of the declaration of fears and jealousies was read in the Lords. It was a long paper outlining all the past actions of the Court of which there had been reason to complain. It was declared that the King was still guided by evil counsel in that he had left his Parliament. Reference was also made to the intercepted letter from Digby. On such grounds, so it was argued, the militia ordinance was imperatively necessary. It was stated that the King had no cause for fear, and that his fears were implanted by evil counsellors. Let him, it was urged, divest himself of them, and return, with the Prince, to London.

It was on the ground of the King's absence from the capital that the Parliament declined to negotiate further on the militia, and insisted on the ordinance which now stood in an extremely offensive form. The King's declaration of 28 February and his absence were taken together and assumed to be the product of a single piece of evil counsel. Such a hypothesis would have been bitter for Hyde, who had himself assumed precisely that successful negotiations depended on the King's continued presence near the Parliament. That assumption was now vindicated. His absence now became the crux of the situation. The significance of the King's answer at Theobalds lay in the fact that he gave, or implied, a reason for this absence. The doctrine of Parliament's rejoinder—the doctrine of the declaration of fears and jealousies which was presented at Newmarket on 9 March—was that whereas the Parliament had always had good grounds for mistrusting the King, at no time had he any reason for mistrusting the Parliament.

74

Such a turn of events was infinitely regrettable when compared with the idea of a Bill for the militia to be followed up with action as proposed on 20 January. Nothing was less desirable than that King and Parliament should embark upon a course of self-justification and mutual recrimination. But Hyde could have sympathized with the complaints made by the King, if not with his having used them as a pretext for deserting Parliament. He himself had opposed the tumults and the licence in pamphleteering and preaching the year before. Some attention to these matters would have had to be included in the settlement as proposed on 20 January, and it was evident that actions of mutual assurance must now be undertaken if the proposals of that date were to be taken up. It was therefore of the utmost importance that whatever the provocation the King's reply to the declaration of fears and jealousies should be something other than merely a reply in kind, and that in tone and content it should not close the door to the measures that were appropriate.

Hyde says [1] that when 'the persons designed for the message withdrew to prepare themselves for their journey, the message being read and agreed upon, Mr Hyde went likewise out of the House; and that the King might not be surprised with the sight of the message before he heard of it, he sent instantly to the Lord Grandison (in whom he had entire confidence) to

---

[1] *Life*, II, pp. 104, 105. Hyde says that the action here described was in connexion with the Theobalds incident. But it obviously relates to the Newmarket one. Whereas Hyde refers to 'the length of it', the parliamentary message to Theobalds had been a very short one. Secondly, Hyde refers to his own detailed answer to it, but there was no answer of this kind to the Theobalds message though there was to the one delivered at Newmarket. Thirdly, though the answer put by the *Life* into the mouth of the King might at a stretch be taken as a description of either, and is, indeed, almost a conflation of both, the emphasis in Hyde's description upon the King's 'quick and sharp treatment' of the envoys, and upon its effects, would seem to make that account tally with the Newmarket interview rather than with the one which took place at Theobalds. Lastly, Lord Pembroke was not a member of the deputation to Theobalds, as is stated in Hyde's account, though he was a member of the one sent to Newmarket.

speak with him; and desired him...that he might with all possible expedition carry a letter to the King....He writ to the King, that such persons would be presently with him, and the substance of the message they would bring to him; which in respect of the length of it, and of many particulars in it, would require some time to answer, which he should receive soon enough; and for the present, he might upon the delivery make some short resentment of the houses' proceeding with him; and conclude, that he would send an answer to their message in due time.' Hyde was anxious that the form of the parliamentary message to Newmarket, with the total refusal to admit any royal grounds for complaint, and the mere self-justification in respect of the refusal to negotiate further on the militia, should not take the King by surprise and provoke from him a rejoinder that would make things worse. Hyde recommended a simple acknowledgement by the King with the promise of a detailed answer to follow.

The formal preliminary answer[1] which the King made, was restrained enough. He said that he could not give an immediate and complete reply to a document of so strange and unexpected a character, and reproached Parliament for preferring this method to the one propounded on 20 January. He undertook to allay their fears and jealousies, and also briefly indicated his own, making particular reference to Pym's speech of 25 January in which he had implied the complicity of the King in the Irish rebellion. On this head, though he had sought it, he could, he said, obtain no satisfaction. He reminded them of all the concessions he had made and of his offer of amnesty and pardon. In the informal exchanges, however, which accompanied this transaction, it may well be that the King's 'quick and sharp treatment' of the envoys was contrary to what Hyde had thought desirable when he had forewarned him. While the Earl of Holland was

[1] In Hyde's own account in the *Life* he fails to distinguish between this and the longer answer which was to follow.

reading the declaration, the King interjected comments, asking, for instance, what he had denied the Parliament. The Earl replied that he had denied the militia. To this the King retorted that there had been no Bill. 'It was a necessary request at this time', said the Earl: to which the King's retort was that 'he had not denied it'. He referred, presumably, to the necessity. The next day these informal exchanges took a more serious turn. The King again asserted that the two Houses were mistaken in treating his answer in respect of the militia on 28 February as a denial. Whereupon the Earl of Pembroke asked whether the King would not grant the militia, as was desired, for a time. But the King burst out with the words, 'By God not for an hour; you have asked that of me in this, which was never asked of a King, and with which I will not trust my wife and children.' Did this mean that the King would now refuse even a compromise solution, thus vindicating the attitude of Parliament?

Hyde's detailed reply, however, to the message which thus provoked the King was so conciliatory that he thought it necessary in the *History* to justify it in the eyes of those who might think it unprincely and consider that a more indignant and resolute tone would have been preferable. He argues that the King had lost so much ground by the attempted *coup d'état* against Pym's leadership that he had to descend 'to all possible arts'[1] to win supporters. But to define in this way the objective of his paper is a result of that alteration in perspective which, while intelligible enough, falsified his own part in events. The declaration, in the original perspective, was addressed to Parliament and was part of a still-continued attempt to make a settlement between that body and the King. The fact that it was published did not mean that it was primarily an appeal to the country for support, but was rather a consequence of the fact that Parliament had published theirs, a circumstance which Hyde seems to have deplored.

[1] Clarendon, *History*, II, p. 7.

In this declaration[1] Hyde justified the King's answer at Theobalds. He denied, as he would have held himself well qualified to do, that the King was taking evil counsel, and protested the King's good intentions both in Church and State. In respect of religion he made reference to the answer to the Grand Remonstrance. To the Parliamentary catalogue of the Court's misdeeds, he proceeded to reply in detail. There had been no design of altering religion. The war with the Scots which Parliament said was part of that design was, it was answered, buried now by a solemn act of oblivion. If, as was charged, the Irish troubles had been fomented by English malignants, then every effort ought to be made to discover them. In regard to the army plots of 1641 and the 'dangerous petition delivered to Captain Legg by His Majesty's own hand', Hyde declared it was not dangerous and suggested that it should be published. The question of Jermyn's[2] escape in the face of a parliamentary charge, an escape which the King was accused of facilitating, was dispatched by a reference to dates. As for the Five Members, the King had withdrawn the charge against them and made all possible amends. He could do no more. In regard to the entertainment of army officers at Whitehall, they were asked to remember the tumults which had threatened the safety of the King's person and that of his family. Digby's departure from the country in January with the King's permission in the face, as it was averred, of a parliamentary accusation was, like that of Jermyn, disproved by reference to dates. 'What their advisements were' from abroad 'or from what persons such informations came, or how the credit and reputation of such persons had been sifted and examined', he knew not, but was confident no sober honest man could believe the King was so desperate or so senseless as to entertain designs of resorting to foreign arms against his own subjects. When con-

[1] Clarendon, *History*, II, p. 1.
[2] Sir Henry Jermyn, royalist, promoter of Army Plots.

sideration had been given to these explanations, it was hoped that Parliament would agree that no ground existed for continued misunderstanding, or any grounds that would necessitate on their part 'the use of any other power than what the law had given them'.

In regard to the King's own fears which prevented him from returning to London, he had not meant to accuse them of the responsibility, but he asked that something should be done about the tumults. 'If they had not yet been informed of the seditious words used in, and the circumstances of, those tumults, and would appoint some way for the examination of them, he would require some of his learned counsel to attend with such evidence as might satisfy them.' He then listed all the concessions made by him since the meeting of Parliament, above all the Act by which the dissolution of Parliament was rendered impossible without its own consent. To round it all off he was willing to offer a free and general pardon 'as ample as themselves should think fit'. He sincerely desired, it was declared, to return to the neighbourhood of his Parliament. If something could be done about the state of the capital, he promised to do so. In the meantime, neither Ireland nor anything else should suffer by his absence.

Unless Hyde knew in detail of the Queen's projects for getting foreign help[1] and believed that the King had committed himself to them in the same spirit as the Queen, or unless, which is unthinkable, he both knew and approved of such projects, in which latter case alone this declaration is a mere dishonest playing for time, we can only take it at its face value, and, at that, it is the clearest of pleas for a reasonable accommodation.

This declaration did not reach Parliament until after the King had arrived at York on 19 March. It is dated 21 March,

[1] It should be noted that years afterwards Hyde made an unsolicited admission that he had never known about the business of the crown jewels, and that Culpepper had kept him in the dark about it. S[tate] P[apers collected by Edward, Earl of] Clar[endon], III, [1786] p. 8.

and was received on 24 March. In the meantime, Hyde had written[1] to the King in a way which shows that in his judgement the sharp interchanges at Newmarket had indeed been, to say the least, unfortunate, and which confirms that he was still thinking in terms of negotiation with Parliament. The letter is an extremely tactful one, but the following points in it seem clear. Though the royal message, that of 9 March, was, Hyde said, unobjectionable, the quick and sharp remarks made to the deputation at Newmarket have 'begot notable doubts' of the Royal intentions. He enclosed a declaration to be dispatched from Huntingdon for the purpose, first, of making reference to Ireland 'which Your Majesty knows to be the envious argument, in which you must never appear less jealous'; secondly, of giving public notice of the journey to York, which, so far, the King had not given: thirdly, 'of satisfying your Majesty's end of a proclamation, which will be very hard at this time, if not impossible, to pass, and may hereafter, if there should be necessity (as I hope there will not) be set forth with more advantage to your Majesty than now'. 'Proclamation' presumably means a proclamation prohibiting obedience to the militia ordinance. For the present, it was sufficient that the point be covered in the context of an incitement to mutual respect of privileges as between King and Parliament and the joint maintenance of the law, and that the prohibition be enveloped in a conciliatory message to Parliament. The letter proceeds:

Men's discourses here are full of your Majesty's designs of immediate force, of a retreat into Scotland, of the divisions there, to none of which your servants give the least credit; assuring themselves that, however your affairs and conveniences have invited you to York, you intend to sit as quietly there as if you were at Whitehall. For your Majesty well knows that your greatest strength is in the hearts and affections of those persons who have been the severest assertors of

[1] *S.P. Clar.* II, [1773] p. 138.

the public liberties, and so besides their duty and loyalty to your person, are in love with your inclinations to peace and justice, and value their own interests upon the preservation of your rights. These your Majesty will not lose by any act which may beget just fears in them; neither can there be so cunning a way found out to assist those who wish not well to your Majesty, (if any such there be) as by giving the least hint to your people that you rely upon anything but the strength of your laws, and their obedience.

The above is a familiar passage, but its significance has not been fully recognized. It is unnecessary to suppose that 'the severest assertors of the public liberties' refers exclusively to the so-called 'Constitutional Royalists' conceived as sharply distinguished from the men who followed Pym. For though the phrase about 'valuing interests' is no doubt a reference to the fear on the part of members of Parliament in face of the disorderly manifestations in London and elsewhere, a fear which had played a great part in the inspiration of such op-position as Pym had had to face, it would be rash indeed to assume that the fear of social upheaval was not shared by those whom Pym was contriving to sway. Hyde, with the most penetrating acuteness, was later to explain in the *History* the process which he himself had experienced and watched, the process by which, with Pym's help, both Lords and Com-mons had persuaded themselves that there was no alternative to pursuing the course which they actually pursued. From these men, Hyde himself had differed in no important respect. It should be noted that in the letter he makes no distinction between parties—the King, he implied, had no ill-wishers. He expressed his parliamentary sympathies even when he came to write the *History*, though not, of course, sympathy for the leadership. But even in regard to the latter, it is apparent that it was, in his opinion, the fears of the leaders for their personal safety which drove them on. Nor, as Hyde's whole account makes clear, could they have succeeded in leading as they did but for the depth and widespread character of the mistrust for the King. Apart from the King's mistakes, things could never have gone the way they did. Hyde in the letter under discussion is pointing out to Charles even at this late hour that he still had it in his power to arrest the course of events which was plunging the country into anarchy in Church and State and precipitating unnecessary and unwanted extremities. It was his implication that the King's going to York gave handle to the extremist leaders. Hence the form of the declaration from Huntingdon which balanced the announcement of the journey to York with yet another emphatic recommendation that the course proposed on 20 January be embarked upon. Irish affairs, also, always played into Pym's hands. Hence the necessity of a reference to Ireland in the declaration.

Hyde and Pym had, in truth, all along been saying the same thing. They had been saying that it was the King and the King alone who was responsible for the line of policy pursued by Parliament. Both men were bent on persuading him of the fact, the difference between the two being that Pym was using the method of threats, while Hyde used the method of reason. This letter drives it home that Hyde's advice to the King was still rooted, as it had been throughout, in unshakable assumptions regarding the personalities and consequent possibilities in Parliament. He was conveying to Charles the nature and the logic of parliamentary thought. The letter brings out at the time what we can also see in the *History*; namely, Hyde's conviction that great as was the mistrust inspired by the King, there was at the same time nothing the King could do which could alter the fact that Parliament as a whole included him in its picture of the future. In other words, the talk about evil counsellors was sincere: it was a change of policy by the King, not a change of the constitution which was sought. That is what Hyde meant when he spoke, as he frequently did in his historical work, of the 'ambition' of the leaders.[1] It was peace with security which they wanted, not a programme of constitutional innovations. This conviction of his, based on his judgement of the political situation, was the foundation of his desire for a settlement, and the reason why he was able to return to the charge again and again. Even now he was trying to convince the King that Parliament was not composed of men sworn to overthrow the monarchy. There was, therefore, still all the difference in the world between Hyde and the Royalists proper, despite the fact that the plea and the warning in the letter are couched by him in terms of an appeal to the King's own prospects. Hyde is still working to prevent a situation in which Royalist and Parliamentarian confront one another. If he is a Royalist in the eyes of Parliament as then led, he was not a Royalist in his own eyes or in those of the Royalists such as there were at this time. Employing the terms sanctioned by historical usage, it is correct to describe him as remaining as much a Parliamentarian as ever.

§ 3. *From the Arrival of the King at York to the Nineteen Propositions.*

IF THE message from Huntingdon and the long answer to Parliament's address to the King at Newmarket are compared with Hyde's next paper, the message of 26 March, the difference is clear. The latter, and all succeeding papers, are harsher and harder and far less restrained in tone than all that went before. Hyde himself, in the *History*, having apologized for the mildness of the long answer to the Newmarket address, is soon speaking of the bitterness of the papers which were exchanged and of the part they played in preparing the outbreak of hostilities. But if it be supposed that a point has been reached at which it is necessary at last to describe and account for a conversion to royalism, we must hasten to point out that

[1] E.g. Clarendon, *History*, II, p. 14.

it is impossible to discover any modification of Hyde's desire
for peace or any cessation of activity on his part to obtain the
settlement which he continued to think both desirable and
possible. Still less can one discover any change in his fundamental political beliefs. What did begin to change at this
point was the situation in which he found himself. It was not
that Hyde changed sides, but that the sides which were to
contest the war, and on to one of which Hyde was to be precipitated, now and only now began to appear. The party
which opposed the Parliamentarians in the Civil War was
a different thing from the Royalist party of which, up to now,
there has been occasion to speak. The King's party in the war
was naturally to include the early Royalists, the Queen,
Digby, Jermyn, Lunsford, Newcastle and the rest, but their
outlook, which remained throughout the war what it had
been before, was not the same as that of the bulk of the King's
adherents, and they never converted or for long adequately
represented the latter. The later royalism was the spawn of
Parliament. Just as the King by his royalist actions in late
1641 and early 1642 had provided the material out of which
the later parliamentarism, that of the men who were to contest him in the war, had been moulded, so the proceedings of
this later parliamentarism created the material of the later
royalism. If Pym could have done nothing of what he did
against the King apart from what the King himself had done,
so the King would never have been able to contest the field
with Pym without the involuntary assistance afforded by the
latter. Given nuances of political opinion and political judgement, and given a variety of personal connexion and situation
and the differences of conviction in matters of the Church,
the mere operation of what was becoming a parliamentary
terror, gave Charles, in that he was now established at York,
a party in the sense in which he had not had one before. We
must instance the important case of the Kentish petition
(25 March) and the harsh treatment of the petitioners by

Parliament. On 3 April a band of gentlemen rode out of London, making for York.[1] On 8 April Benyon, a wealthy citizen of London, was sentenced in connexion with a petition in which it was urged that the militia ordinance infringed the privileges of the city, and there were other cases.[2] There was also coercive treatment of dissident members of Parliament.[3] So long as the King was free in the north, the very attempts of Parliament to strengthen its hold by intimidation and force were bound to create opposition for itself, especially when the King, to maintain his freedom after the second failure to secure Hull at the end of April, took an armed guard. He could now protect anybody who felt in need of protection.

In the *History* and especially in the *Life* Hyde stresses the part played by his State papers in gaining men to the King's service. So far as can be judged, that claim is by no means a baseless one, but it misleads if it is allowed to imply an explanation of what Hyde thought he was doing between the end of March and the end of May, when he went to York. It would be a mistake to regard him now as a royal servant who strove to strengthen the King's position for war. In reality, Hyde was much more the creature than the creator of the process which with the remorseless sweep of tragedy now embraced the country in its operation. In reality, there was no change in his attitude or his purpose save such as was caused by, and is entirely explicable in terms of the circumstances, though the change in the circumstances was momentous enough, and though that change meant for Hyde the departure into partisanship, a realm he had so far stood outside. As a Parliamentarian who had sought to eliminate the friction between the King and the Parliament which had been incidental to the first year's legislative achievement, the essence of his position had been that it was not partisan. But

[1] Gardiner, *History*, x, p. 184.
[2] E.g. those of Edward Sandeford, and Sir William Wilmer.
[3] E.g. The Duke of Richmond, Sir Ralph Hopton, Sir Edward Dering.

7   WC

in what now rapidly became the starkest of breaches between the parliamentary leaders and the King, he adhered to the King.

On 15, 16 and 17 March, there were momentous steps taken by both Houses of Parliament. On the 15th, the House of Commons resolved that there was an urgent necessity of putting the kingdom into a posture of defence: that in respect of the extreme danger and of the King's refusal to accept the militia ordinance, obedience to the latter was required in law, and that the Lords be moved to concur. The Lords did so.[1] It was on this day, also, that the Lord Admiral, Northumberland, was requested to appoint Warwick to take command of the fleet. Parliament was clutching at the navy. Next day, which was the day on which was received the King's Huntingdon message, that is, the last of the series of conciliatory papers, Holles reported to the Commons that in respect of that message the Lords insisted on adhering to their former votes on the militia, and that, in connexion with the King's statement that the ordinance was contrary to law, they recorded the observation that 'when the Lords and Commons in parliament which is the supreme court of judicature in the kingdom shall declare what the law of the land is, to have this not only questioned and controverted, but contradicted; and a command, that it should not be obeyed, is a high breach of the privilege of parliament'.[2] Holles also reported that the Lords were in favour of appointing a committee to inquire where the King's message had been framed, 'for by comparing this with the votes that passed both Houses yesterday, it is, as it were, a contradiction of those votes: they do either think there was some prophetical spirit in it, that this should be so express an answer to those votes, or that it was framed nearer hand'.[2] On the 17th, the Commons reported their own votes on this matter. These were an endorsement of what the Lords had

_____
[1] _Parl. Hist._ x, p. 361.   [2] Ibid. p. 368.

communicated to them the previous day with additional resolutions to the effect that the King's absence from Parliament
was destructive to the affairs of Ireland, that those who had
advised him so to absent himself and those who had advised
the recent message were to be condemned, the latter as
enemies to the welfare of England, the former as enemies to
the welfare of both kingdoms.[1]

The resolutions of 15, 16 and 17 March do not represent
any notable departure from the attitude which Parliament
had previously been maintaining. They do, however, constitute the decisive indication that Parliament would reject
all further discussion on the militia and the decisive indication
that it accepted as irreversible the breach of relations with the
King. They possess this significance in that they threatened
Hyde's safety. Hyde now saw himself in peril for no other
reason than that he had sought to maintain negotiations
between King and Parliament. It is at this point that Hyde
himself is confronted with the fact that it was impossible to
deflect Parliament, the Lords now, as much as the Commons,
from the course it was bent on pursuing. 'And from this last
resolution, by which the law of the land, and consequently the
liberty of the subject, was resolved into a vote of the two
Houses. . . all sober men discerned the fatal period of both,
and saw a foundation laid for all the anarchy and confusion
that hath followed'.[2] These events of the middle of March are
not a turning-point in the same way that the night of 22 November, when Pym had defeated Hyde on the Grand Remonstrance, had been a turning-point. But because Hyde had
been the chief, the only active exponent of a negotiated settlement of the type proposed on 20 January, and because of the
change which his policy now underwent, the point at which
Parliament condemns and projects the discovery and punishment of the author of the King's conciliatory messages must
be regarded not only as having had significance for Hyde,

[1] Ibid. p. 370.   [2] Clarendon, *History*, I, p. 594.

it has significance also as a turning-point for the historian of the events of 1642.

In the *Life*[1] Hyde asserts that he had been suspected of penning the King's messages from the answer to the Grand Remonstrance onwards, but it was from the beginning of March that the threat to his personal safety had begun to materialize. Both Houses, as we have seen, after declaring the King's answer to the militia ordinance given on 28 February to be a denial, had resolved that whoever gave the King this evil counsel was a public enemy, and declared their intention of finding out who had done so.[2] 'Your Majesty will pardon me that, in these public dangers [so concluded the letter which he had written to the King at Newmarket], I can have so particular a care of myself, as to remember your Majesty to burn these papers, and to vouchsafe me to transcribe anything with your own royal hand out of them that you think fit for your service, without communicating it to any other eye.'[3] The message from Huntingdon brought the matter to a head, and though Falkland pointed out[4] that the Lords were in error in supposing that the Huntingdon message must have been based on a knowledge of the votes of 15 March, since similar ones had been passed some days previously, a parliamentary investigation into the drafting of the King's replies now looked like being taken up in earnest. It is Hyde's story that it had been planned to seize Falkland, Culpepper and himself, simultaneously, when all three were in the House of Commons together, and that they therefore decided that only one of them should be there at a time, and that they should refrain from speaking. Be that as it may, the infrequency of Hyde's attendance in the last part of March certainly attracted notice. Ironically enough it so happened that at this time proceedings were broached which should, in the ordinary course of Parliament, have involved Hyde's

[1] *Life*, II, p. 110.
[2] *Parl. Hist.* x, pp. 325, 326.
[3] *S.P. Clar.* II, p. 138.
[4] *Life*, II, pp. 110, 111.

presence. On 23 March the House of Lords sent a message to the Commons requesting the speeding up of the proceedings against Archbishop Laud 'and other delinquents'. The Commons agreed, requesting in their turn that the Lords would take up the case of the delinquent judges,[1] a matter which had been postponed at the request of the Lower House at the end of the previous October.[2] 'Upon Sir Arthur Hasilrigg's motion it was ordered that Mr Hyde, a member of the House, should attend the House tomorrow, he having the managing of the charge given in against Mr Justice Berkeley.'[3] Not only had Hyde been chairman of the committee which had drawn up the charges against the judges, but he was also one of the witnesses whom Berkeley himself desired to call.[4] On 29 March the Lords were asked to postpone Berkeley's trial pending the summoning of the witnesses, and Hyde was again ordered to attend the House, 'all excuses laid aside'.[5]

The charge against Berkeley, the most notorious of the ship-money judges, was that of 'endeavouring to subvert the fundamental laws, and introduce an arbitrary and tyrannical government against law'. Hyde was expected to take up again the work of asserting the Common Law constitution by the punishment of the royal servants who in the eyes of the men of 1640 had flouted it, at the very moment when he himself was faced with imminent subjection to proceedings at the hands of Parliament which would have seemed to him as arbitrary and, indeed, as unparliamentary as the proceedings of the ship-money judges had been. It is not difficult to account for the spirited character of the papers drafted by Hyde from this time forward.

In the declaration of 22 March, which Parliament sent to

---

[1] D'Ewes's Journal, Harleian MSS. 163, fo. 43 b.
[2] D'Ewes, Coates, p. 49.
[3] D'Ewes's Journal. Harleian MSS. 163, fo. 43 b. C.J. II, p. 493. See also Falkland's letter to Hyde about this order; he told Hyde that he had explained the latter's absence as due to ill-health. S.P. Clar. II, p. 141.
[4] D'Ewes, Coates, p. 33 n.   [5] C.J. II, p. 504.

the King in reply to the interim answer he had given at New-market, without waiting for the long and detailed document which on Hyde's advice he had promised, they defended their departure from the procedure suggested on 20 January as 'more proper for the removing the distraction of the Kingdom', but claimed that they were going some way towards complying. They instanced the Book of Rates they were drawing up, and the digestion of certain 'material heads' which it was intended to present 'for the good and contentment of his Majesty and his people'. They pointed out, however, that it was the King's own denial of the militia which held up procedure along the lines he had suggested. They referred perfunctorily to seditious pamphlets and sermons and to tumults, defending the concourse of people at Westminster on the ground that while the King had refused them a guard to their liking, he had taken one for himself which frightened both Parliament and people. The King had asked when he had violated the laws. They answered by reminding him of the regime which had preceded the calling of Parliament and of the attempt on the Five Members which they chose to regard as the culminating point of its arbitrary and illegal acts. If he had passed Bills for reformation, concurrent with them there had, they said, always been designs calculated to frustrate their effects. They denied that they had done nothing for him, recalling the two armies they had paid off in the previous year, and the expenditure in connexion with Ireland. They dismissed the offer of a free and general pardon as irrelevant since their fears 'arose not from any guilt of their own actions, but from the evil designs and attempts of others'. In this connexion, they had received further information from abroad which, when added to the expressions in Lord Digby's intercepted letter and 'his majesty's succeeding course of withdrawing himself northward from his Parliament', gave very just cause for anxiety. They concluded with a request that he should return to his Parliament.

To this, in the declaration of 26 March,[1] Hyde replied in terms which up till that moment it had been precisely his object to prevent the King from using. Bitterly and angrily, he proceeded to assail Parliament for its impatience. Had they waited for the full answer promised at Newmarket, they could have saved themselves the trouble of saying much that had been said in their paper of 22 March:

...we must tell you, that if you may ask any thing of us by message or petition, and in what language (how unusual soever) you think fit, and we must neither deny the thing you ask, nor give a reason why we cannot grant it, without being taxed of breaking your privileges, or being counselled by those who are enemies to the peace of the kingdom and favourers of the Irish Rebellion, (for we have seen your printed votes upon our message from Huntingdon,) you will reduce all our answers hereafter into a very little room.

Was this the way to compose all misunderstandings? The scheme of 20 January was a better way, and the King could not see why his refusal to consent to the militia ordinance was a reason why that scheme should be rejected. For the refusal of the ordinance was not a denial of the militia 'which we always thought necessary to be settled'. He had never denied the thing, only the way proposed by them, namely, an ordinance with an obnoxious preface and the exclusion of the King from a joint control with Parliament and for a time unlimited. 'We tell you, we would have the thing done', but by a Bill, which was the right way, and the time spent in arguing disproved their contention that the necessity and danger were so acute that there was no time for such a thing. They might reject his offer of a Bill, which was still open, but he would never accept the ordinance, or permit his subjects to obey it, or allow the two Houses to make law apart from him, for

[1] Clarendon, *History*, II, p. 10.

'what is this but to introduce an arbitrary way of government'?

The proferred explanation of Pym's speech of 25 January was rejected, and the declaration went on to speak bitterly of the seditious literature which abounded on all hands. In regard to the tumults in the capital it was insinuated that the parliamentary leaders had arranged them, thereby nullifying the freedom of Parliament. The King was made to express angry surprise that they should, in affirming the view that he had violated the law, have brought up again the irregularities which had preceded the Long Parliament, when it was the King's 'resolution, upon observation of the mischief which then grew by arbitrary power, (though made plausible to us by the suggestions of necessity and imminent danger; and take you heed, you fall not into the same error upon the same suggestions,) hereafter to keep the rule ourself, and to our power require the same from all others. But above all, we must be most sensible of what you cast upon us for requital of those good bills you cannot deny'. He defied the devil himself to prove the existence of the designs which they declared had been aimed at nullifying them, and demanded full reparation for the charge. Let them reject the offer of pardon if they wished. If they did not like it, they need not have it. He took it extremely ill that they should continue to credit on such slight evidence the rumours that he sought foreign aid against his own subjects. For that also, he must demand reparation, not only to clear his own honour, but to quiet the public, 'whose fears and jealousies would soon vanish were they not fed and maintained by such false and malicious rumours as these'. As for his return to London, from which, as he now declared, he had been driven, they need not expect it unless they could give satisfaction in the matter of the pamphlets and sermons and tumults, or before they had made reparation for 'those insupportable and insolent scandals that are raised upon us'. If they could not enforce order in the capital, let Parliament be adjourned elsewhere. In conclusion, though he would neglect no just or honourable means of re-establishing understanding, 'we are resolved that no straits or necessities to which we may be driven shall ever compel us to do that which the reason and understanding that God hath given us, and our honour and interest with which God hath intrusted us for the good of our posterity and kingdoms, shall render unpleasant and grievous to us'.

Succeeding papers hardly surpassed this one in vehemence of tone and bitterness of language, and succeeding events served only to develop themes explicit or implicit in it. The business of Hull, which after the King had on 23 April appeared before the town, and been refused admittance by Hotham, was the main one, in particular served to clarify the argument that it was Parliament now which was the aggressor against law and property, and that the rights of the subject now stood or fell with the maintenance of the rights of the King. Much space is taken up by the vindication of the sincerity and the reasonableness of the King's attempt to reach a settlement, and by the exposition of parliamentary intransigence, in particular, over the militia.

If Hyde had been the man chiefly concerned in this attempt at settlement, we should expect a vein of self-justification in his papers, and the expectation is not disappointed. In the answers to the two parliamentary papers of 19 and 26 May (the former of which was a reply to the King's papers of 21 and 26 March), which Hyde seems to have penned after he had left Westminster for good, this strain is very much in evidence. The first[1] of these parliamentary papers complained that in the King's papers of 21 and 26 March the malignant party had 'with much art and industry, advised his majesty to suffer divers unjust scandals and imputations upon the Parliament to be published in his name', and that it had succeeded in withdrawing His Majesty from his Parliament. The very man

[1] Clarendon, *History*, II, p. 135.

who had, in a parliamentary spirit, been working upon the King's mind in opposition to the policy of the Royalists, who had objected to the removal from London, and striven to moderate the King's replies to the parliamentary papers, was now classed as the chief of malignants, and the difference between the declaration of 26 March and the preceding ones ignored. Even that minimal recognition in the resolutions of 17 March that Hyde and Falkland differed from Digby and the Queen which was implied in the fact that the advisers of the Huntingdon message, unlike the advisers of the King's withdrawal from Parliament, were not styled favourers of the Irish rebellion was now apparently withdrawn.[1] It is not to be wondered at if Hyde now retorts that the true malignants were those who had contrived and countenanced the tumults which had encouraged the King to abandon the neighbourhood of London, and whose subsequent violent courses had made a reasonable 'settlement and composure of public affairs' impossible. No one, he argued, could seriously desire a settlement who put forward as obstacles those past irregularities of prerogative government which it had been the precise purpose and effect of the King's acceptance of the legislation of the Long Parliament to end once and for all. Hyde had always believed that settlement depended upon an ability to bury the past. In the Remonstrance debate he had opposed the looking too far back and that requirement had continued to be axiomatic in his subsequent efforts. The refusal on the part of the leaders of Parliament to relinquish the past and their evident determination to emphasize it was exasperating proof of their disinclination to contemplate what was for him the prerequisite of any settlement.

Safe from the clutches of the parliamentary leaders, he now dared them to name the evil counsellors of whom they complained. It was, he declared, a new device they had found out, 'instead of answering' the King's 'reasons or satisfying

[1] *Parl. Hist.* x, p. 370.

94

his just demands, to blast his declarations and answers as if
they were not his own'. There was no assertion of what was
not true, and what no one could have been expected to believe,
namely, that the King had composed the papers himself. But
Hyde was in a position to state his belief that every answer
and declaration published by his Majesty 'was much more
his own, than any of those bold, threatening, and reproachful
petitions and remonstrances were the acts of either or both
Houses'. The King had not, in fact, acted by any means on
the lines which Hyde could approve since going to York, but
he found it easier to identify his own papers with the mind of
the King than to imagine that the Parliament, the mentality
of whose members he understood and sympathized with so
thoroughly, could have been brought to support declarations
of this sort without trickery and intimidation. He spoke now
of 'a now major part of both Houses of Parliament (infected
by a few malignant spirits)'. He was weary now of the militia
business: 'God and the law [the existing law] must determine
that business.' As for the resolutions of mid-March, those of
the 15th, 16th and 17th, they were 'the greatest violations of
his majesty's privilege, the law of the land, the liberty of the
subject, and the right of Parliament, that could be imagined'.
He explained how they had first declared a fact—that 'the
kingdom was in imminent danger (it was now above three
months since they discerned it)', and then declared a law for
dealing with it. 'Who could not see the confusion that must
follow upon such a power of declaring? If they should now
vote that his majesty did not write this Declaration, but that
such a one did it, which was still matter of fact; and then
declare, that, for so doing, he was an enemy to the commonwealth; what was become of the law that man was born to?'
He inveighed, as he well might, against the imputation that
the King still preferred and countenanced those who had
exercised power between 1629 and 1640. For this imputation
covered not only the bridge-appointments which had failed

of their object, but also those of Falkland and Culpepper. 'He would know one person that contributed to the ills of those times...whom he did or lately had countenanced or preferred; nay, he was confident...as they had been always most eminent assertors of the public liberties, so, if they found his majesty inclined to anything not agreeable to honour and justice they would leave him tomorrow.' He countered with the suggestion that it was the men who at present controlled Parliament who were falling, 'under the specious shows of necessity and danger, to the exercise of such an arbitrary power they before complained of'.

The personal note is even stronger in the first part of the next paper,[1] the answer to the parliamentary paper of 26 May, and the break between Hyde and the parliamentary leaders emerges more widely. The latter are now 'a faction of malignant, schismatical, and ambitious persons; whose design was, and always had been, to alter the whole frame of government both of Church and State, and to subject both King and people to their own lawless, arbitrary power and government'. These men he looks upon now as not so much the leaders of Parliament as the destroyers of its procedures and true purposes as an institution, and as the perverters of the real intentions of its present membership. Those, on the other hand, whom this conspiracy of wicked men called 'malignants' were so far from deserving the name that they were the true parliamentarians as distinguished from, and in opposition to themselves:

...nothing was more evident by their whole proceedings than that by the malignant party they intended all the members of both Houses who agreed not with them in their opinion... So that if, in truth, they would be ingenuous, and name the persons they intended, who would be the men...but they who had stood stoutly and immutably for the religion, the liberties, the laws, for all public interests, (so long as there

[1] Clarendon, *History*, ii, p. 149.

was any to be stood for;) they who had always been, and still were, as zealous professors, and some of them as able and earnest defenders, of the Protestant doctrine against the Church of Rome, as any were; who had often and earnestly besought his majesty to consent that no indifferent and unnecessary ceremony might be pressed upon weak and tender consciences, and that he would agree to a bill for that purpose?

Such men had behind them the better, if not now the more numerous, part of Parliament. He went on to specify the actions which Parliament described as resulting from evil counsel. First, the withdrawal to York 'where his majesty, and all such as would put themselves under his protection, might live...very securely'. Secondly, his majesty's 'not submitting himself absolutely' to their votes and resolutions. Thirdly, his refusal to be content that his subjects' lives and fortunes should be disposed of by their votes.

This was the evil counsel given and taken: and would not all men believe there needed much power and skill of the malignant party to infuse that counsel into him? And then, to apply the argument the contrivers of that Declaration made for themselves, was it probable, or possible, that such men whom his majesty had mentioned, (who must have so great a share in the misery,) should take such pains in the procuring thereof, and spend so much time, and run so many hazards, to make themselves slaves, and to ruin the freedom of this nation?

This was Hyde's apology. In the act of joining the King at York, an action which, though free, was imperatively dictated by his immediate circumstances, he made these vehement protestations of the parliamentary convictions which he had cherished. He had not now abandoned them. Nor, indeed, was there any reversal of the original purposes or a radically changed conception on Hyde's part of the course of action which he thought the King should pursue. It was simply that, whereas up to and including the declaration of 21 March, Hyde's papers had been directed primarily to the Parliament in an attempted compromise on the militia, a compromise which was to be the prelude to a comprehensive agreement as suggested on 20 January, thereafter, when it was clear that the parliamentary leaders would not consider such a thing, they were addressed primarily to the public with the object of disabusing its mind of the interpretation put upon events by the parliamentary leaders, and of counteracting the poison which they were infusing into it. It would be foolish, in the light of Hyde's past attitude, and of the evident weakness of the King's position, a weakness which could escape nobody, least of all Hyde, and a weakness upon which the whole of the strategy of Parliament was based, to conclude that his object now was to enable the King to make armed resistance. That was the effect, not the cause, of his continued activity. It was only when the policy had definitely failed which he had for six months devoted his energy to pursuing, and when the situation seemed really hopeless, that he began to achieve any success. It was to be more profitable to work with the grain of divisiveness than against it as he had worked hitherto. And, as we have seen, divisiveness now took the form of a process which was creating two parties and two systems of military strength. Moreover, the declarations themselves from that of 26 March onwards become more impressive as documents than the earlier ones had been. Hyde was not only in danger, and personally insulted and misrepresented by the extension of the parliamentary definition of malignancy to cover himself in addition to Digby, he could now write with a clear conscience, having striven so much for settlement. In such circumstances it was good, as well as easy, to be able to expose the arbitrary and unconstitutional nature of Parliament's actions: better and easier than trying to defend or explain away the King's past failings and mistakes, a task which he had had to undertake in the long answer to the Newmarket address for the purpose of sustaining the negotiations with Parliament. Such a defence had still to be maintained, but it was an aspect of his work which was put into the shade by the new circumstances in which he could not but blame the parliamentary leaders for the breakdown of relations and in which, better still, Pym's own definitions of law and liberty could be used against him. He would appeal to reason and ask the people to judge 'without resigning their reason and understanding' either to the King's prerogative or to 'the infallibility of a now major part of both Houses of Parliament'. Hyde rose to the occasion with a brilliant device, itself suggested by Parliament's own insistence that the King even now had in reality made no break with the eleven years 'tyranny'. He expounds Pym's present aims and methods as being identical with those of the hated regime which Parliament had confounded. This return of the old monster in a new form, the King as an inseparable component of Parliament with the support, open or tacit, of all true parliamentary spirits, would now struggle to resist. He was able to end by declaring, without any surrender of convictions or contravention of the facts, that the people had been better off under the previous form of arbitrary government than they were under the present form of it.

Civil war lay ahead, and Hyde did not regret either in 1642 or when he wrote the *History* the part his papers played in gaining men to fight for the King. But that was because at both periods, placed as he was, while very far from absolving the King from responsibility, he could not but put most blame upon the reckless and relentless conduct of the leaders of Parliament. But it must be understood that it is unlikely that the purpose of these later declarations was anything more than what, in fact, even in the *History* Hyde indicated that it was—namely, to disabuse the public, and, by lessening Parliament's hold and making its position more difficult, to force it to adopt a more accommodating type of policy. With respect to those who controlled Parliament, it clearly mattered little how the King now proceeded to act. They had proved

99

beyond possibility of doubt that, in their eyes, nothing he did could be right or other than a reason for driving even harder along the line they had adopted than before. But with respect to the parliamentary rank and file, and with respect to the country at large, what the King did was still of as great importance, from the viewpoint of peace, as it had been in the days when Hyde had thought that Pym could somehow be contained and a change be brought about by the joint action of the King and the House of Lords.

It is in the light of that fact that Hyde's activity in the last weeks before he went to York can be understood. Up to the middle of March, he had been a member of Parliament in touch with the King, representing to him the parliamentary point of view, and trying, from that standpoint, and in the interests of accommodation, to influence the royal counsels. Thereafter, circumstances were to make of him a royal servant whose task it was to maintain touch with Parliament (though he went in fear of his safety there) in order that no time might be lost in answering the Parliament's papers. But since it still mattered what the King did, if the public was to be disabused and if the future was to be affected to the good, it will be found that Hyde continued to advise and to act much as he had done before.

One of the earliest things the King did on arrival at York was to set himself to deprive the Earl of Essex and the Earl of Holland of their positions at Court. This had been part of the plan arranged with the Queen,[1] and the method was to send them a summons to attend upon the King at York. Now it is clear that Hyde and Falkland had been connected with the Earls in acquaintance. Hyde says as much.[2] They may even have been connected in policy above all in the matter of

---

[1] *Letters of Queen Henrietta Maria*, p. 53. Clarendon, *History*, II, p. 14 (from the *Life*).
[2] *Life*, I, p. 57.

a compromise over the militia. When the King sent to ask for advice in the matter of depriving the Earls, Hyde and his colleagues 'did all they could to dissuade the pursuing it'.[1] They knew 'that they did not desire to drive things to the utmost extremities',[1] and we may well believe that the reason given in the original *History* for Falkland's disinclination to do the King's work after the Lord Keeper had refused to do it—the reason, namely, that it would 'inflame the present distemper'[2] was the true one. The objection made to the King against the dismissal of Essex and Holland was the same as that given in the case of St John, that he would do more harm out of the office than in it.[3] Hyde had been in favour of these bridge-appointments. After the attempt on the Five Members there could be little hope of further expedients of this nature on the King's part unless a negotiated settlement could be substituted for the determination of the parliamentary leaders to fulfil their 'ambition' by forcing themselves upon the King. Hyde nevertheless was opposed to undoing what had been done in this respect, especially when the intended victims had been advocating a less violent course, and had begun precisely to fulfil the purpose for which such appointments had been made. We should disregard the point which is based on the knowledge of the part played by the Earls against the King in the war: if Essex had been allowed to keep his place, Hyde wrote, he would never have commanded an army against the King.[4] This found its way into the narrative through the play of a later perspective, and at a time when Hyde was magnifying the contribution he made (or, in this instance, could have made had his advice been taken) to the King's prospects. Of much more significance in the present connexion is the distinction drawn in the original *History* between, on the one hand, those who opposed the dismissal

[1] Clarendon, *History*, ii, p. 16 (from the *Life*).
[2] Ibid. p. 60.   [3] Ibid. p. 16 (from the *Life*). *Life*, ii, p. 82.
[4] Clarendon, *History*, ii, p. 16 (from the *Life*).

of the Earls, and, on the other, those 'who only looked upon the bold scandals that were every day raised and countenanced, and the disservice that was every day done to his Majesty',[1] and who, in consequence, only wondered that they had not been dismissed before. Hyde was very willing in the declarations to exploit the injured dignity of the King for the purpose of mobilizing sentiment and detracting from the prestige of the parliamentary leadership. But this episode and the comment he makes upon it, indicate how far he still was from the position of the true Royalists. The true royalist view had long been that those who were not with the King were against him and should be treated accordingly. But Hyde was still sharply removed from sympathy with the measures contemplated or taken by the Royalists at this time with the object of strengthening the King in the material sense. It was the implication of their position that moral factors, and so even the possibility of a treaty, could supervene only as a consequence of the possession by the King of arms and strong places. The Queen, in pressing the King to seize Hull, urged that it was precisely the King's moderation and apparent desire for a treaty which made Parliament's demands so excessive.[2] They would be more reasonable, she said, if the King took a stronger line. Hyde's position was the reverse of this. The attempt of the King to strengthen himself materially would only weaken him still further, and strengthen the present leadership of Parliament both morally and materially. That had been the result of his trying to do so in the past. It would be different if as a result of a shift in the moral balance potential material strength accrued to the King. That is what Hyde sought to further, and thereby, even yet, the achievement of settlement by negotiation.

It is probable that the same point was involved in the affair of the Earl of Northumberland, the Lord Admiral. Parliament, in the course of the measures for securing the fleet,

---

[1] Clarendon, *History*, ii, p. 61.   [2] *Letters of Queen Henrietta Maria*, p. 60.

had requested Northumberland to appoint the Earl of Warwick to command it, and the proposal had been made the
matter of a petition to the King. The King refused, but
Northumberland, early in April, nevertheless granted his
commission to Warwick. Men wondered, Hyde says, that
the King 'upon so apparent a breach of trust and act of un-
dutifulness' did not at once dismiss the offender. But he goes
on to point out that the revoking of the Lord Admiral's commission was at that time uncounsellable since it was hard to
see who could take his place, and that his dismissal might
have prevented the fleet from going to sea, and thereby work
to confirm with the people the violent party's doctrine that
the King was seeking to arrange a foreign invasion.[1]

After an initial period at York in which the King, apart
from the affair of the Earls of Essex and Holland, seemed to
be following the course which Hyde approved, he proceeded
once more to deviate into actions which in Hyde's judgement
only played into the hands of Parliament and weakened the
effect of his appeal to the country. In answer to a petition of
the Yorkshire gentry that he should come to terms with his
Parliament, he replied that all would be well if Parliament
would proceed according to the offer of 20 January and settle
the militia by a Bill. But on 8 April he informed Parliament
that he proposed to go to Ireland, and submitted to them
a Bill for settling the militia. Thus the King now adopted,
and in a spectacular form, Hyde's suggestion that he should
express solicitude for Ireland, and moreover, took up again
the project of the militia compromise upon which Hyde had
previously staked so much. But he did so only because the
suggestion and the project could now be fitted, as he thought,
organically into the concert with the Queen, which was to
secure arms and a seaport. The Irish expedition was to be
armed from Hull. This was very different from 'sitting as
quietly at York as if he were at Whitehall'. Hyde implies[2]

---

[1] Clarendon, *History*, II, p. 21.   [2] Ibid. pp. 41, 42.

that the Irish project came as a surprise, and that he disapproved of it. Not only did such a design confirm the plausibility of parliamentary propaganda, but, what in the present phase was worse, the King's absence in Ireland, together with his offer that, while away, the militia should be under parliamentary control would expose everybody who was menaced by Parliament, and so disposed to turn to the King for protection, to the unrestricted fury of parliamentary dictatorship. In the event, the King changed his mind about going to Ireland, and his Militia Bill came to nothing, since Parliament made substantial changes in it to the King's disadvantage, and he refused to pass it. As for Hull, it has already been mentioned that a direct but unsuccessful attempt to secure it was made by Charles on 23 April. This was not 'sitting as quietly at York as if he were at Whitehall' either. There is no proof, but the Queen's statement to which Ranke refers about the King having been hindered from taking Hull by those advisers who sought an accommodation with the Parliament may throw light on Hyde's attitude to the King's action at this point in the story.[1] At any rate such an attempt as he had now made could not but vindicate the parliamentary case in the eyes of the country at large.

The King's Militia Bill is illuminating in more than one respect. If Hyde disapproved of it, the Queen objected to it no less. The King with his fusion of the two policies contrived equally to alienate the exponents of each of them in its pure form. The Queen was horrified when she heard of his offer. 'You are beginning again your old game of yielding everything.'[2] She continued with an argument the gist of which is nothing less than an admission that Hyde's policy could have succeeded supposing that it had been the right one to

---

[1] *Letters of Queen Henrietta Maria*, p. 117. 9/19 September 1642. Gardiner (*History*, x, p. 179), says that at the beginning of April 'Charles thought it expedient to abandon for a time his projects upon Hull'.

[2] Ibid. p. 68.

adopt, which in her view it had not been, and supposing that the King had adopted it without reserve, which he had not done. 'If you had been willing to cede the militia when I was in England, I could have satisfied The Parliament, as I said; but you have done in this, I am afraid, as you did in the affair of the Bishops; for at one time, you could have entered into an accommodation about that, and you were obstinate that you would not, and after all, you yielded it.'[1] The King, as the Queen rightly pointed out, had pursued neither policy but had vacillated between them. The best he could do was to try and pursue both at once, making a synthesis of the two. Thereby he made the worst of both worlds. It is hard to see that there could have been civil war if the King had from the beginning of 1642 pursued either Hyde's policy or that of the Queen in its entirety. Instead, there would have been either an accommodation had he listened to Hyde or a total collapse and surrender to the wishes of Parliament had he listened wholeheartedly to his wife. As it was, he pursued enough of the Queen's policy to prevent the one and enough of Hyde's to forestall the other. The Queen, in fact, from her own point of view, had reason to be grateful for the extent to which Charles had deviated from her policy into that of Hyde. For realistic as were her arguments, and they were the same arguments as those employed by Pym, they ignored the peculiar circumstances in England. Those peculiar circumstances consisted of the fact that, as a result of the moral supremacy of Parliament, threatened, perhaps, towards the end of 1641, but overwhelmingly re-established by the attempt on the Five Members, it was Pym and Pym alone who at such a time could use the Queen's arguments to advantage. Hyde recognized this, and precisely because he himself was a Parliamentarian.

By the end of April the King had almost done enough to set the stage for the third and least likely possibility, civil war.

[1] Ibid. p. 68.

The King's Militia Bill brings out sharply the extent to which circumstances had changed since the end of February and the beginning of March. In January and February, though he would have regretted, it may be supposed, a design of going to Ireland as destructive of confidence, Hyde would have rejoiced at, and worked for such a Bill as was now proposed. Now he could only deplore it. The breakdown of relations between the King and the parliamentary leaders which had now taken place was accelerating the process which set up two armed camps. Whereas before he would have worked for such a Bill to prevent this, he now opposed such a Bill. He was now in favour of maintaining a situation in which men could disengage themselves from Pym's system with hope of personal safety if they did so, and he adopted such an argument for urgent public reasons and for still more urgent private ones. He now concurred with the Queen, at least to the extent that he held that all was lost if the King continued in a state of isolation. He disagreed with her regarding the means whereby it could, and therefore should be ended.

Furthermore, the King's Bill helps to explain Hyde's reticence in the *History* and the *Life* in regard to the whole original project of a compromise on the militia. It was not only that events brought it to nothing in circumstances which endorsed and made intelligible the line of policy taken by Culpepper as opposed to his own. Events brought it to nothing in a peculiarly embarrassing way. In 1642, Hyde had a reason for objecting to 'the King's treaty and overture of a bill', over and above the fact that it would, if successful, have exposed Pym's opponents to destruction. He had a reason which derived from its failure. The King's offer was to the effect that the militia should be placed in the hands of the original nominees of February under the joint control of the King and the two Houses for one year. The King, in other words, now came forward with that proposal specifying the duration for which the compromise was to run which

Parliament, in spite of the King's request, had never been willing to make. But Parliament now amended the Bill by excluding the King and making it run for a maximum of two years.[1] This the King rejected. But despite the very careful paper[2] published on 28 April which explained why he was doing so (careful, because Hyde had used the fact that so far the King had accepted every Bill Parliament had presented to him as an argument that he would accept a Bill for the militia), Parliament was able to make it appear that it was his own Bill which he had rejected. In their paper on the militia, ordered to be printed on 5 May and issued concurrently with the instruments putting the militia ordinance into execution, this supposed repudiation by the King of his own offer was made the climax of the whole story of the negotiation on the militia which they now publicly recounted. In this way they were able to turn all that Hyde had tried to transact in that matter against the King, and to suggest that the foundation of what was to have been a comprehensive settlement of all outstanding points as suggested on 20 January, had never been laid in good faith. Such was the end of the militia negotiations. Hyde at the time had not relished the King's Bill for the reason already given. Very soon, he was compelled to contemplate the whole affair in terms of the great tactical triumph which the parliamentary leaders were able to achieve.

The affair of the Lord Keeper Littleton illustrates even more vividly than that of the projected Irish visit on the King's part what was happening to the country, and makes it clear that it is the movement of the situation as a whole rather than any supposed change of allegiance or reversal of conviction on Hyde's part which explains his actions at this time.

The affair of the Keeper of the Great Seal was a later and a larger affair than that of the Earls of Essex and Holland. It is difficult to trust the details of Hyde's account of it because

---

[1] Gardiner, *History*, x, p. 191.   [2] Clarendon, *History*, II, p. 42.

the acquisition by the King of the Great Seal proved to be so great a prize that those unreliable qualities which play in the *Life*, knowledge of the event and meritorious service of the King, have the fullest play: Hyde makes Littleton speak of inevitable war and of the need the King would have for the Seal.[1] He may have done so. There is no telling. But it should be noted that an object of Hyde's story as told in the original *History* and even in the *Life*, was to vindicate Littleton from royalist calumny. It looks as though, at the outset, Hyde regarded this case in the same way as he had regarded the case of the Earls. Littleton's had not been a bridge-appointment, but he had gone along with the prevailing party in Parliament even to the extent of approving the militia ordinance, and Whitelocke implies that it was his attitude in this matter which was decisive in swinging the Lords over unreservedly to the policy of the Commons.[2] But Littleton, too, had been, and remained, despite his approval of the ordinance, a friend of Hyde's;[3] and him, too, the King was now determined to relieve of his function. In this case, as in that of the Earls, Hyde disapproved of such action, believing that he was not as black as he was painted by royalist partisans, or even as black as he had contrived by his actions to paint himself. The difference between the case of the Earls and the case of the Lord Keeper lay in the fact that the King was this time persuaded to change his mind and to invite the Lord Keeper to York, and in the fact, also, that he accepted the invitation and left Westminster at the end of May. What the King wanted, of course, was not the Lord Keeper but the Great Seal, and he was persuaded by his London counsellors that the only way to get it was to give Littleton the benefit of the doubt. It had been objected by Hyde and Falkland to the deprivation of the Earls that they were not as bad as they seemed, and that their dismissal

---

[1] Clarendon, *History*, II, p. 112 (from the *Life*).
[2] Whitelocke, *Memorials*, I, p. 165.   [3] Clarendon, *History*, II, p. 111.

would inflame the present distemper. There were the same
grounds for opposing the deprivation of the Lord Keeper. On
the other hand, to secure that he took the Seal to York would
inflame the distemper even more. But Hyde was no longer
in a position to judge and to act by such a simple criterion.
It would appear from the letter to Newmarket that he had
tried to postpone the issue by the King of a proclamation for-
bidding obedience to the militia ordinance, on the ground,
apparently, that Littleton could not be relied upon and in
the hope that the prohibition would not be necessary. The
King, however, would now delay no longer and was determined to have the Seal. But so, it seemed, was Parliament.
If Littleton were not summoned to York, or if he did not obey
the summons, the King would not get it and Parliament
would, and if Hyde did not work to get Littleton to the King
his inaction would give it to Parliament. Events had now
made the question of the location of the Great Seal, in London
or in York, one of the utmost consequence, and this fact,
together with Hyde's existing relationship with the King, had
made of an episode which was at first comparable with that
of the Earls, something that was an outstanding service to the
King from a true royalist point of view. We should not fail to
note, however, that the *History* suggests that even this 'service'
was related in Hyde's judgement with the purpose of shaking
the Parliament into a more accommodating frame of mind.

From the beginning of April, the parliamentary leaders,
indeed, had shown signs that they were aware that a reaction
against them was taking place. On 5 April the Lords agreed
to the Commons' proposal for a joint committee to examine
such information on seditious literature and tumults as the
King's law officers should submit. On 8 April there was
issued a declaration of the parliamentary objectives in the
matter of the Church which was couched in moderate and
reassuring terms. All that was contemplated, it was stated,
was 'a due and necessary reformation', and nothing was to

be taken away but what was 'evil and justly offensive, or at least unnecessary and burdensome'. To help in the task Parliament proposed 'speedily to have consultation with godly and learned divines'.[1] Moreover, as has been seen, Parliament entertained, though with fatal alterations, the King's Militia Bill and, while entertaining it, forbore to execute the militia ordinance. But, in reality, there was no lessening of the terror and no relaxation of the pressure upon the King. Nor indeed had he done anything which might have encouraged such a relaxation. On the contrary, he had suggested or attempted actions which Parliament regarded as hostile and, what was worse from his point of view, having suggested or attempted them, he was unable to carry them out. The Grocers' Hall Remonstrance which appears in the journals under 19 February was taken up in April. This was a document which emanated from the committee appointed just after the attempt on the Five Members, and it at least contained positive proposals for a settlement with the King. Whether or not it had originally been intended as a response to his invitation of 20 January, it had enabled Parliament to affirm in the declaration of 22 March that they were engaged upon the preparation of 'material heads', and Pym thought it necessary, in presenting the Remonstrance to the Lords on 1 April, to explain why its form differed from that asked for by the King. The King had asked for separate Bills, but Pym said there was not time for these; moreover, 'it will be a great comfort to the Kingdom to have the King's assent beforehand, and it will much conduce to the settling the minds of men'.[2] The proposals, however, were of such a nature that acceptance of them by the King would amount to total capitulation on his part, and the matter dictated the form. The form was that of an ultimatum.

Hyde's account of the last weeks he spent in the south is misleading, since he states that he stayed on there long after

---

[1] *Parl. Hist.* x, p. 425.   [2] Ibid. p. 417.

he had received a summons to York. The reader imagines he
has to do with a final scene of dare-devil courage and may
even speculate whether Hyde was not still acting in the
detached and mediatorial manner of earlier months. But in
reality Hyde was summoned to attend the King not as he states
'about the end of April'[1] but on 21 May.[2] In the relationship
with the King in which first his own attempts at settlement
and now a new and more sinister pattern of events had involved him, he could neither have left without the King's
permission nor have stayed after having been called away,
and though he appears to have delayed a little (though only
about a week) after hearing from the King, in order to see the
Lord Keeper safely on the way northwards, and to carry with
him the parliamentary declaration of 19 May, he was probably glad enough not to have to stay any longer. He can
have seen nothing in public affairs to justify any change of
mind, and he probably owed his own freedom during April
and May only to Parliament's superficial reaction to the
growth of opposition. Its failure to act on the suspicions
aroused about him at the end of March was most probably
yet one more instance of that tactical moderation which has
been noticed above.

The parliamentary declarations of 19 and 26 May, followed
as they were in a few days by the Nineteen Propositions, were
merely the culminating expression for Hyde of the impenitence
of those in control of Parliament, and we have already discussed the tone of acute exasperation which was expressed in
the King's answers. When he wrote the answer to the declaration of 19 May he already had knowledge of that of 26 May,
and when he wrote the answer to the latter he was already
aware of the Nineteen Propositions, if, as is improbable, he
did not know even before that date that they were to be
expected. And since an answer to these drafted at Westminster

[1] Clarendon, *Life*, II, p. 113.
[2] Clar[endon] MSS. 21, 62, endorsed 'received at Ditchiy'.

after Hyde's departure by Falkland and Culpepper was
doctrinally, it will be recalled, of such a character that he
could not at first recommend its publication, he at first
suggested that the answer to the parliamentary declaration
of 26 May was a sufficient, and indeed the only response
which a king could be expected to give to a document of such
an outrageous nature. These Propositions were nothing less
than that ultimatum, now in final form and at last presented to
the accompaniment of mobilization, which the Grocers' Hall
Committee had prepared. In effect, the King was asked to
surrender all the powers of government both civil and military
and the entire reformation of the Church into the hands of
the two Houses of Parliament. It should be recognized that
Hyde himself would not have denied the ills which were complained of, and that he had desired a settlement which would
not only have amounted to what was now demanded, but
would actually have included much of what was now desired.
For instance, it was demanded that the militia be settled by
a Bill, and that Lord Kimbolton and the Five Members be
cleared by an Act of Parliament. 'Bridge-appointments', or
the giving of offices both civil and military to parliamentary
leaders, and legislation to liberalize the Church would at one
time, Hyde believed, both have satisfied those leaders and
guaranteed the achievement of the Revolution, and also
satisfied the King. Moreover, the King himself had offered
a parliamentary reformation of the Church in February and
had agreed to put the anti-Romanist legislation into execution. But in another sense, and in a sense which was now the
sense that mattered, the Nineteen Propositions were the
exact antithesis of what he had worked for, and the precise
reverse of a settlement. For they were completely one-sided.
They admitted none of the grievances on the King's part
which had accumulated since the Grand Remonstrance and,
moreover, were intended to leave him no choice but acceptance. Hyde knew at least this about the King; that however

weak his position he would never rest quiet under terms which he had not freely accepted in negotiation. But it was precisely the same knowledge, and because they believed that he would never freely accept the terms they sought, since it included their own elevation to power with him, which made the parliamentary leaders determined to reduce him to impotence, both actual and legal.

The Grocers' Hall Remonstrance was a continuation of the method, and a repetition of the form of the Grand Remonstrance: it was an appeal to the people by means of a description of the situation which magnified every grievance and aggravated every danger. But this time the leaders gauged the success of their appeal by the response to the militia ordinance. Hyde had watched them delay their application to the King for the remedies to the ills which they had for so long and so heavily stressed until they were sure of their military resources, and then, cutting out the catalogue of ills from the Remonstrance, present its demands as if they were the response to the King's request of 20 January. It was the crowning piece of cunning thus to exploit the popular approval of the fact that the King had for long been asking for propositions,[1] by making it appear that what was in reality an ultimatum was but a modest compliance with his request. With this object they made a few perfunctory and, from the King's point of view, unconvincing suggestions regarding what they would do for him if he complied with them. The King had either to make a complete surrender or else allow it to appear that it was he and not the Parliament that now rejected a settlement and thus permit the parliamentary leaders to repeat the trick which they had played over his Militia Bill.

[1] Clarendon, *History*, II, p. 166.

§ 4. *From the Nineteen Propositions to the End of the First Civil War*

THE POINT in the story has now been reached at which it becomes easier to tell. That is because the factor which has so far worked to distort the evidence for it which Hyde himself provides is henceforth diminished in its operation. The movement of events has opened a new kind of division between the parliamentary leaders and Hyde, and he has become a partisan and a servant of the King in a way he was not before. The gap, therefore, between what he was aiming to do at the time and his retrospective interpretation of it narrows. It is still necessary to guard against distortions due to knowledge of the event, but, apart from that, it is possible now to rely to a greater extent upon Hyde's own narrative.

It must, however, be pointed out that although Hyde's own accounts are clear enough regarding his own attitude to the Civil War, and the policy he favoured, the significance of his remarks on those heads has not been correctly appreciated. That has been due to the misconception of the aim he cherished, and the policy he pursued between the autumn of 1641 and the spring of 1642. Lister was as much on the right track when he implied that Hyde belonged to the peace party in the Royalist camp after the outbreak of hostilities, as he was when he rejected the ecclesiastical explanation of Hyde's activity from 1641 onwards. But because he also rejected the notion that Hyde could have been trying to mediate from the latter part of 1641, and assumed, instead, a change of sides and a conversion to royalism, his story of him as a peace party man in the war is not as convincing as it might be. Gardiner's picture, on the other hand, achieves a rotund coherence, which is superficially more convincing. Having disposed of Hyde as a fanatical Churchman and rigid constitutionalist before the war, he allows it to be inferred that he was not amongst those who desired a negotiated peace after it had broken out. The picture is achieved at the price of ignoring the significance of statements made by Hyde which Lister rightly allowed to tell their own story of his attitude to the war. For having explained that Hyde, like Falkland, became a Royalist out of his concern for the Church, at a later stage Gardiner implies[1] that those who had become Royalists for high religious reasons were always those most eager for a peace of compromise. Since Hyde is not placed by Gardiner in the peace party, we are left to assume that Hyde both before and after the outbreak of the war was motivated by an irreligious ecclesiasticism, and by an outlook and a programme which was not only unattractive but futile. Hyde's idea of the constitution, says Gardiner in speaking of the part he played in the early part of 1642, 'was the idea of an essentially mediocre statesman. It was based on negations, and provided so elaborately that nothing obnoxious should be done, that there was no room left for doing anything at all.'[2] In speaking of the outbreak of war Gardiner classes Hyde and Charles together as men who were unable to perceive that 'the use of force only renders the object aimed at more difficult of attainment'.[3]

But if the *History* and the *Life* are allowed to tell their own story of Hyde in the Civil War, that story, which is one of a desire, and of a striving for a peace other than that of complete victory, will be found to be the natural outcome and continuation of the aims and efforts so far described, aims and efforts which had nothing of ecclesiasticism about them and nothing of constitutional orthodoxy as an end in itself. From the passing of the Grand Remonstrance to the end of March 1642 Hyde spent his time trying to persuade the King

---

[1] What he actually asserts is that it was the Royalists who were least under the influence of religion who clamoured loudest for war, whereas amongst the Parliamentarians the reverse was the case. Gardiner, *Civil War*, I, pp. 1, 13.

[2] Gardiner, *History*, x, p. 169.

[3] Gardiner, *Civil War*, I, p. 31.

to adopt the policy which was precisely the one which Gardiner himself judged that the King ought to have pursued. During that period, Hyde's attitude was exactly the one which it was Gardiner's lament that nobody was capable of achieving, namely that each party to the dispute, the King and the parliamentary leadership, should, especially in the matter of the Church, go some way to meeting the other. Even the great campaign for the law of the land which Hyde conducted in the series of declarations following the rupture of relations over the militia, was not conducted for the sake of the law in itself, was not inspired merely by a spirit of legalism, but, instead, with the object of stirring the people out of the bemusement induced in them by Pym, and by so doing, to force him to slacken his pace and change his direction into that of accommodation. It is probable, as we have seen, that this consideration was in Hyde's mind when he assisted in the removal of Littleton and the Great Seal to York. It is probable that the same consideration was not absent when he, amongst others, deserted Parliament. In this latter connexion, allowance must be made for Hyde's conscience as a Parliamentarian prompting him to justify at great length in the *History* the exodus of so many members of both Houses. But he certainly made use of the fact of the exodus in his attempt to bring about a public discrimination between the institution of Parliament and its present leadership and actions, and Thomas May vouches for the considerable and disturbing effect which that exodus had.[1]

This last phase of attitude and activity, that which dates from the end of March, was that in the midst of which Hyde entered the war, and the actual outbreak of hostilities should not be regarded as making any difference to it. In the manuscript of the *Life* there is to be found the following summing up of his view of the origin of the Civil War: 'on the Parliament side the opinion that the King could never raise an

[1] May, *History*, p. 176.

army was the true reason that they did raise one, and so the cause of the war, together with the general opinion that the Parliament would never raise a rebellion.'[1] The fact that this was written so long afterwards does not detract from its value as indicating Hyde's attitude in 1642. For the outstandingly obvious political fact in the middle of 1642 was the strength of the parliamentary leaders and the weakness of the King. The parliamentary leaders mobilized because the King was weak and in order to make him weaker, both in the sense of preventing any attempt on his part to clutch the sword, but more especially for the purpose of isolating and overawing him. So weak was he, that they were under no necessity of believing that they would ever have to fight him. 'But the kingdom', writes May, 'was not much affrighted with any forces which the King could so raise.'[2] Moreover, it was only because the moral prestige of Parliament was so great and because men were incapable of entertaining the notion that the two Houses could ever actually draw the sword against the King, that the leaders were able to acquire sufficient support both in Parliament and in the country to raise military forces. The King was in a position to make neither peace nor war. Peace could be had only on the terms of capitulation on all the public issues and the proscription of all who had sought his protection. On the other hand, he had neither money nor armament, and the attempt to acquire, and, still more, the attempt to apply such things, could have little effect beyond confirming the interpretations proclaimed far and wide by Parliament. In a situation where both courses appeared equally hopeless, but in which, also, it was imperative to adopt one of them, the King opted for resistance and raised his standard at Nottingham on 22 August. Only thus could he make a virtue out of the necessities he had

[1] Clarendon, *History*, II, p. 341.
[2] May, *History*, p. 175. Cf. D'Ewes, commenting on the lamentable state of the King's prospects in September 1642. Gardiner, *Civil War*, p. 25 n.

brought upon himself, and the virtue was indeed virtuous enough to attract some and bind together others, the Digbys on the one hand and the Hydes on the other, who save for such a bond, had little in common.

Since, however, the forces Charles could raise proved vastly inferior in number to those already serving under the Earl of Essex, it was not long before he was compelled, though with great reluctance, and only, according to Hyde, because the advocates of peace used the argument that an overture would be rejected, to give way to those who preferred the alternative course, and to sue for terms. Hyde had no place in the Council and it was his part merely to draw up the message. His judgement on the matter, according to his own accounts, was that Parliament would probably refuse, but in the expectation 'that an entire submission would shortly attend it',[1] and that the King by making the offer might be given a breathing space in which to muster more strength: but that, by the same token, the overture was untimely since a prospect of capitulation with all that that might mean for the King's adherents, was hardly likely to encourage such armed support as he was, in fact, gradually acquiring. As we have seen, the King had been winning adherents since his establishment at York, and it must be assumed that at some point in the summer Hyde had come to the conclusion that such adherents would be, and, in consequence, should be, armed, despite the vindication thereby afforded to the parliamentary contentions. But in this respect, Parliament's rejection of the King's offer made up for the harm done in making it, and Hyde emphasizes that the episode resulted in a marked increase in the King's moral and material strength. Not only did Hyde see that there was nothing now to be gained by any course that further weakened the position of the King, but he himself, especially after the episode of the peace offer, worked by the raising of money to strengthen it.[2]

[1] Clarendon, *History*, II, p. 302 (from the *Life*).

It is important, however, to recognize that if he judged the origin of the war to lie in Parliament's opinion of the King's weakness, and in its own reputation for impeccability, he went on to explain that the principal cause of the war's continuance was the confidence on the King's side that a single battle could be decisive, and the consequent direction of all energies to the one end of fighting.[1] Behind this observation there lay much experience and conviction which from the start of hostilities seems to have cut him off from the Royalist leaders. Again and again in the *History* he declared that military influence was too prevalent both in the conception and in the conduct of the war. It is impossible, therefore, not to believe that while at the outset the interest of peace as Hyde envisaged it required that it be proved to the world that the King was stronger than was expected and the parliamentary leaders more wicked than was supposed, once those facts had been demonstrated by the outbreak of fighting, Hyde regarded the King's power as the means to a negotiated peace. Hyde, in other words, had come to accept the Queen's thesis, the thesis to which Culpepper had been secretly converted at the beginning of the year, that a settlement would be impossible so long as the King disposed of so little power. But Hyde did not accept it until the precise moment at which that thesis was expanded by the royalist leadership into the doctrine that a settlement could be founded only upon the total destruction of the military forces of the Parliament, and it is true to say that not only was the difference and the distance between Hyde and the Queen as great in the military phase as it had been before, but it has exactly the same significance. Then and now, the Queen's policy meant the crushing of a revolt to which the Revolution had been incidental. Then and now, Hyde's policy meant the healing of a breach that had been incidental to the Revolution.

If 'the King had only stood upon the defensive in all places

[1] Ibid. p. 341.

where he had power, and declined all occasions of fighting as much as had been possible, and so ordered all contributions and supplies of money to the equal support of the army, it would probably have succeeded better'.[1] Hyde seems to have been amongst those who doubted whether the King could ever expect to have the strength to do more than this. In addition, he objected that the aggressive military policy caused it to be thought that the King was implacable. The meaning of these views is clear. Hyde was still a Parliamentarian in his unquestioning conviction that the moral prestige behind the parliamentary leaders was such as would always prevent the King from acquiring enough merely material strength to destroy it. And it was as a Parliamentarian that he was able to appreciate the axiomatic monarchism of the vast bulk of those who fought for the Parliament. There was an intense desire for peace with the King which came out into the open in Parliament as soon as it was apparent that the King would fight, as soon, in other words, as it was clear that the parliamentary resort to arms was leading not, as was supposed, to peace, but to war.[2] The only thing in Hyde's view which could prevent this desire from prevailing was fear: fear for personal safety at the hands of a totally victorious Royalist army, and fear, also, for the fruits of the Revolution.

Hyde's difference, then, from Southampton and Falkland at the beginning of the war was not one of principle. It is impossible to make that difference imply that he was not of the peace party. He was with the war party only in the sense that the armed strength of the King was a requirement as indispensable to the making of peace as to the making of war.[3]

[1] Clarendon, *History*, II, p. 341.

[2] Ibid. p. 340 (from the *Life*), and p. 378 (from the original *History*).

[3] Both Ranke (*History*, VI, p. 7) and Lewis (*Lives*, p. 123) imply that Hyde was of the peace party to the extent of backing the overtures of August and September, but the evidence does not seem to me conclusive on this point, and I prefer the interpretation given above.

The phraseology of the message of 25 August drafted by him may be taken, save in one particular, as fully representing his idea. Observing that the method of bringing peace pursued up to date, through 'messages, petitions, and answers, betwixt us and our two Houses of Parliament' had failed, it was now necessary, he declared, to find some other method of treaty 'wherein the matters in difference may be more clearly understood and more freely transacted'. Representatives of the contending parties must be chosen to engage, under safe conduct, in a free discussion. What 'opinion soever', he went on, 'other men may have of our power, we assure you nothing but our Christian and pious care to prevent the effusion of blood hath begot this motion; our provision of men, arms, and money, being such as may secure us from further violence, till it please God to open the eyes of our people'.[1] Hyde's complaint was that because the last part of the sentence quoted was untrue, and known to be so, nobody could be expected to believe the first part.

It soon, however, began to come true, and in so far as the King's power increased the issue between Hyde and the military leaders was clarified. After the battle of Edgehill it was possible either to sit still at Oxford and await overtures from Parliament, or to set out with the object of reducing the capital.[2] Military counsels prevailed, and the latter course was adopted. To Colnbrook Parliament sent a message desiring the King to advance no further and to await negotiators, to which he replied in a way which they took to be in the affirmative. But 'all things were in a hurry, and the horse still engaged the King to follow, so that he advanced with the whole army to Brentford...all thoughts of a treaty were dashed; they who most desired it did not desire to be in the King's mercy, and they now believed, by his majesty's making so much haste towards them after their offer of

---

[1] Clarendon, *History*, II, pp. 304–5.
[2] Ibid. p. 388 (from the *Life*).

a treaty, that he meant to have surprised and taken vengeance of them without distinction'.[1] Besides, it was seen by his opponents that the King's strength had been overestimated.

The harm done was not, however, irreparable, and nothing could deter the movement in Parliament for the opening of negotiations from coming to a head. At the beginning of 1643 commissioners from the Parliament arrived at Oxford. It is unnecessary to recount in detail the story of the abortive Treaty of Oxford. It is enough to point out that in his personal memoirs and to a lesser degree in the *History*, Hyde, while of course blaming the Parliamentarians, was concerned to emphasize the royal and the royalist share of responsibility for its failure. He was critical of the extent to which military considerations were kept in view, and of the legalistic rigour upon which the King insisted while negotiating. Above all, he deplored the cloud cast over the proceedings by the Queen's return to England and by the King's inclination to defer decisions until her arrival at Oxford.

That this is something more than retrospective criticism, and indicates how greatly Hyde was concerned for the success of the negotiations at the time they were being conducted, becomes plain when the circumstances of the treaty are scrutinized more closely in connexion with Hyde's statements regarding his own part in it. It will be recalled that the so-called Constitutional Royalists, and pre-eminently their leader, Hyde, had been, before they were driven into the King's camp by the trend of events, the original exponents of the policy now being pursued by the peace party in Parliament. By far the most hopeful aspect of the prospect of a treaty was that, first, the leaders of these successive peace parties in Parliament achieved, by the very fact of that prospect, high peaks of influence in their now separated spheres of action. The Marquis of Hertford, a friend of Hyde's, came to Oxford from the west 'about the time when the treaty

[1] Clarendon, *History*, ii, p. 389 (from the *Life*).

began'.[1] Hyde, through the strong advocacy of Falkland, was sworn of the Privy Council[2] and made Chancellor of the Exchequer.[3] The Queen was still at a distance. The parliamentary commissioners could muster a majority of both Houses. In the second place, they now, in this treaty, effected a junction. What had happened was that the shock of hostilities had in effect vindicated Hyde's policy as against Pym's, and not only given it an ascendancy in the Houses, but, in the circumstances of the treaty, momentarily restored him to the bosom of his followers. This is the significance of the statement in the original *History* that 'at this time the number of those in both Houses who really desired the same peace the King did was (if they had not been overwitted by them) superior to the other'.[4] The fact that Hyde no longer sat at Westminster, and had indeed been excluded from pardon under the instructions given to the Earl of Essex in the previous September,[5] was more than counterbalanced by the influence he had attained on the other side, and by the fact that this position did not adversely affect his relationship with the parliamentary commissioners. A re-embodied non-violent parliamentarism was now in a position to address itself to the repair of the disaster which the action and the counter-action of violent Parliamentarians and Royalists, respectively, had brought upon the country.

The terms proposed by Parliament were considerably more moderate than the terms of the Nineteen Propositions for the extreme claims to control the executive were abandoned. The King was requested to accept the abolition of episcopacy and the settling of the militia by a bill. It was also desired that certain men should be given offices, and that others who had been deprived should be restored. After the first exchanges

[1] Ibid. p. 529 (from the *Life*).
[2] On 22 February.   [3] On 3 March.
[4] Clarendon, *History*, II, p. 495.
[5] Ibid. p. 327. He had been expelled from the House of Commons on 11 August 1642. *C.J.* II, p. 715.

the parliamentary commissioners were instructed to demand an armistice to be followed by a twenty days' discussion of the first proposition of Parliament, namely disbandment of the armies, and the first proposition of the King, namely restoration to him of the command of forts and ships. To Hyde's regret, Charles's attitude precluded success in getting the armistice, 'and therefore', says Hyde,[1] 'the articles for a cessation were the sooner declined, that they might proceed in the main business', discussion of the conditions of peace.

There is a passage in the *Life*[2] which describes the mind of the parliamentary commissioners, but which is true also of Hyde himself. 'The Commissioners, who had all good fortunes and estates, had all a great desire of peace, but knew well that there must be a receding mutually on both sides from what they demanded; for if the King insisted on justice, and on the satisfaction and reparation the law would give him, the lives and the fortunes of all who had opposed him would be at his mercy; and there were too many concerned to submit to that, and that guilt was in truth the foundation of their union. On the other side, if the parliament insisted on all that they had demanded, all the power of the crown and monarchy itself would be thrown off the hinges, which as they could never imagine the King would ever consent to, so they saw well enough their own concernment in it, and that themselves should be as much involved in the confusion as those they called their enemies.' The method devised, as might be expected, was none other than the one which dated back to 1641, the method of bridge-appointments. The parliamentary commissioners proposed, and Hyde concurred, that Northumberland who had been dismissed at last from his position as Lord Admiral at the end of June 1642 should be reinstated. No doubt it was contemplated that other appointments of this kind should follow.[3] But Northumberland was chief parliamentary Commissioner for the treaty and the

---

[1] *Life*, III, p. 150.   [2] Ibid. p. 151.   [3] Ibid. pp. 156–7.

head of the peace party at Westminster. In regard to the King's proposition about the forts and ships Parliament had replied with the suggestion that the King should nominate men in whom it could confide. In other words, it had reverted to the terms of the militia negotiation of precisely a year previously. The relevance to this proposal of the main expedient pressed by the joint commissioners, that of bridge-appointments, is obvious. Moreover, as we have seen, the parliamentary propositions included requests for offices for certain persons and requests that others, deprived, should be restored. The great advantage of the expedient offered was that it circumvented the clash of principle which must other-wise exist as between the King and the Houses, but at the same time met the fundamental requirements of the parliamentary leaders with whom the preservation of the principles of the Revolution had become identified with the safety of their own persons.

It should be noted that Hyde's attitude to church matters was the same as it had been up to and at the time of the passing of the Grand Remonstrance, and during the period of the attempted composition on the militia. That aspect received no emphasis. It was clear, now that the Houses had agreed to the abolition of episcopacy and had desired the King's assent to that measure, that to concentrate on this issue would destroy all chance of success. The parliamentary commissioners agreed with Hyde that it was hopeless to expect Charles to surrender here.[1] But they argued, as he would have done, that Parliament's consent to the abolition had been obtained from considerations of military and political security rather than of ecclesiastical conviction, and that if the point of security could be met in some other manner, the church issue might be expected to dispose of itself.[1] The commissioners had passed from this issue to that of the militia bill, and since the latter also resolved itself with

[1] Ibid. p. 152.

125

Charles into a point of principle, they had passed from that to suggesting bridge-appointments.

Hyde relates that he pressed the King as hard as he could to fall in with this suggestion, arguing that he could not expect the ill condition he was in to be improved by a continuance of the war, and that there was no possibility of getting out of it on easier conditions than what were now proposed.[1] The King, however, was not to be persuaded. He thought rigidly not only in terms of his rights but of his honour. Worse than that, he thought less ill of the military prospects than did the Chancellor of the Exchequer, and was encouraged by the return of the Queen with money and military supplies.[2] The truth is that the outbreak of war while on the one hand it restored non-violent parliamentarism to a position it had not held since the night of the passing of the Grand Remonstrance, on the other assured the ascendancy of military thought. Not only did each side have to consider what would happen if the treaty came to nothing, the stronger, at this moment that of the King, was invited by its very strength to prefer a peace based on victory to one based on negotiation. The King wrote to tell the Queen that the treaty was worth pursuing if only 'to undeceive the people'[3] and to prove that the Westminster Parliamentarians were the aggressive party. As he had done before, the King was following recommendations made by Hyde in a context to which Hyde himself considered them totally inapplicable. It was one thing to have taken such a line in the summer of 1642. It was quite another to do so in the spring of 1643, for the significance of the treaty was precisely that the people had been at last undeceived.

The Treaty of Oxford was in reality the culmination of the third and last phase of Hyde's activity on behalf of settlement and peace. The first had run to the passing of the Grand Remonstrance, and the second to the complete rupture of the

---

[1] *Life*, III, p. 154.   [2] The Queen landed on 22 February.
[3] Gardiner, *Civil War*, I, p. 110.

militia negotiations in March 1642. The third one was a phase
in which, unlike the previous two, it had been necessary that
the King and the two Houses should fall further apart before
they could come together again. That phase having begun in
the spring of 1642, it was nearly a year before the process had
worked itself through to the pattern which had been desired
by Hyde. In the Oxford negotiation the contending parties
had been brought as near together as the process could bring
them. But if the treaty was in this sense a culmination, its
failure did not mark another decisive break for Hyde, for the
pattern in the situation continued to subsist. Retrospectively,
Hyde dated both the internal decomposition of the Royalists
and also the internal decomposition of the violent party from
about the time of the failure of the Treaty of Oxford, and as
will be seen in the second part of this work, those were the
factors which, since their operation was ultimately to change
the entire landscape, introduced a new and most important
dimension into his mentality. But because the decomposition
of the King's opponents looked as yet merely like decomposition rather than the birth-pangs of a novel and more terrible
adversary, the failure at Oxford cannot be regarded as possessing a decisive significance for Hyde.

Even with regard to the failure of the Oxford treaty itself,
it is probable, for instance, that the discovery by Pym of
Waller's 'plot' at the end of May was a greater blow than the
departure of the parliamentary commissioners from Oxford.
In origin, the so-called plot of Edmund Waller seems not to
have been a plot at all, but merely a circumstance of that re-
emergence and reunion of non-violent parliamentarism of
which we have already spoken. Waller had left Westminster
in the summer of 1642, but had, with the King's approval,
returned thither, and had reappeared as one of the parliamentary commissioners at Oxford. After his second return to
Westminster, on the failure of the negotiations, he remained,
through his brother-in-law, Nathaniel Tompkins, in corres-

pondence with Falkland at Oxford, and also worked to maintain the solidarity and coherence of the peace party in London. It was hoped, by holding the group together, sooner or later to be able to secure the reopening of negotiations. It led, instead, to the collapse of non-violent parliamentarism. While Falkland and Waller maintained contact, the King had, unknown, Hyde says, to any of his ministers, issued a Commission of Array to be smuggled into and executed in London in order to effect an armed rising in the City. The two projects, Hyde maintained (and he declared he had as much reason to know the truth of the matter as anybody),[1] were distinct, and remained distinct, even at the London end. The most that was contemplated in the way of resistance by the Falkland-Tompkins-Waller combine was resistance to taxation. But Pym discovered both schemes, and wove them into one with the most disastrous results to the prospects of a negotiated peace. He was able to suggest not only that members of the peace party were implicated in a bloody conspiracy, but that the latter was what Oxford really had in view when it talked about peace. In this connexion, it was unfortunate that, a few days before the discovery, the King had sent a message to Parliament inviting the resumption of negotiations. With the parliamentary covenant of 6 June, the violent party re-established its ascendancy, and affirmed that there would be no peace until the King had been deprived of the ability to resist. The capture, it is true, of Bristol by the King's forces at the end of the following month momentarily shook the leadership of the violent party. The House of Lords drew up proposals for peace and, on 5 August, succeeded in evoking a favourable majority in the Commons. But two days later the House of Commons, after being subjected to pressure from the City, changed its mind.

This last flicker of the peace party in August 1643 was merely the result of the oncoming tide of the royalist military

---

[1] Clarendon, *History*, III, p. 38.

success, and it bore the same relation to the Treaty of Oxford as the King's last desperate peace moves following the erection of his standard in the previous August had borne to the offer of 20 January and the negotiation over the militia, and it may be pointed out that the reasons given by the Commons on 10 August 1643 for rejecting the Lords' proposals were to all intents and purposes identical with Hyde's reasons for objecting to the suggestions of the peace party in August 1642. 'We could not,' argued the Commons, 'in this time of imminent and pressing danger, divert our thoughts or our time from those necessary provisions as are to be made for the safety of the kingdoms to the framing of new propositions, we having so lately presented propositions to his Majesty, and by his answer received no satisfaction, that we cannot, at least with any hope, present others at this time, when we have cause to doubt his late success will make his royal assent more difficult.'[1] Within the space of a year the respective positions of the King and the parliamentary leaders had undergone a reversal so complete and so exact that the prospect of an amicable settlement was about as distant in the summer of 1643 as it had been in the summer of 1642, and there is no ground for doubting that Hyde's attitude to the King under the predominating influence as he then was of the Queen and the military leaders was a much less critical and exasperated one than had been his attitude to the parliamentary leadership when, a year before, it had believed it could get all it wanted by intimidation. If it be objected that there was now little love lost between Hyde and the violent party at Westminster and that he could therefore sympathize with the King's frame of mind, it is only necessary to remind the objector that in the previous year, also, he had been sufficiently critical of royalist thought and action to enable him at least to understand Pym's reactions to it.

In 1643, when at last the wheel had come full circle and it

[1] Gardiner, *Civil War*, I, p. 220.

was possible to think of peace, Hyde had to regret as obstacles
to its advancement a whole catalogue of intentions and actions
on the King's part. Following the lamentable spirit which
had been allowed to prevail during the Treaty of Oxford there
was the Commission of Array issued to Sir Nicholas Crispe
which had given Pym the opportunity to destroy at a blow
a movement which had been nothing less than the reversal
in Parliament of the whole trend that had prevailed since the
passing of the Grand Remonstrance. Next, there came a
development which seemed to menace non-violent parliamentarism even at Oxford, a development which, had it not
been scotched by Hyde, would have completed the parallel
between the King in 1643 and the Houses in 1642, presenting,
as it does, a constitutional analogy with the militia ordinance
and the declaration of 17 March. The King instructed Hyde
to draft a proclamation for the dissolution of Parliament despite the fact that he had given his assent to the Bill of 1641
whereby Parliament could not be dissolved without its own
consent. Against that Act, and in favour of his proposal to
dissolve Parliament, the King adduced, according to Hyde,
first, the doctrine of inseparable prerogative whereby such an
Act must be considered inherently invalid, and second, the
view that by reason of the treason and rebellion of the members, their right of sitting in Parliament was forfeit.[1] Hyde
saw at once that the whole revolutionary achievement would
be put in jeopardy if the King dissolved the Parliament. If
the 'Own Consent Act' could be put aside in virtue of inseparable prerogative, there was no telling whether much of
the rest of the legislation of the Long Parliament would not
be put aside on the same grounds. At least, Parliamentarians
on both sides could be pardoned for thinking so. As for the
second argument, it was manifestly unjust to the many members of both Houses against whom it was impossible to impute
either treason or rebellion. For over a year Hyde had laboured

[1] *Life*, III, p. 179.

to drive home a distinction between the criminality of the parliamentary leadership on the one hand, and both the constitutional status and the moral and political integrity of the bulk of its members on the other, and if, from a parliamentary point of view, such a distinction raised the same difficulties as did his attempt to assert a right of protestation for the members of the Lower House in 1641, at least it was a distinction which sprang from a depth of parliamentary conviction which Hyde was far from alone in cherishing. In the end, the King was persuaded to accept an alternative plan which, while meeting his requirements, was less detrimental to the principles with which Hyde was concerned. There was to be no dissolution of Parliament. Instead, the freedom of its actions and the validity of its proceedings were to be questioned in consequence of the pressure exerted upon it from outside. To concede even so much to royalism was dangerous enough; it had been part of Digby's policy at the end of 1641, part of a policy Hyde deplored so much at the time, and we may suspect that, despite the drift of argument in his declarations, he would not have recommended it even now save as the lesser evil, or apart from an idea, which had already been mooted, and which was now outlined in the proclamation of 20 June, the idea of summoning the members to Oxford.[1] The idea of an adjournment of Parliament to a quieter place than Westminster had, as a matter of fact, appeared in the Declaration of 26 March 1642, the declaration which had marked, on the King's side, the breach of the militia negotiations.

If the events at Westminster on 7 August substantiated the view of Parliament which Hyde had now accepted, they also gave rise to an opportunity, the missing of which was in Hyde's view (though he suppressed the passage in the original *History* from which we quote) 'one of the greatest if not the only omission on the King's part of any expedient during the whole distractions which might reasonably have been

[1] J. Rushworth, [*Historical Collections*,] 1692, pt. III, vol. II, p. 331.

depended on to promote or contribute towards a fair accommodation'.[1] When the violent party succeeded in defeating the Lords' motion for peace at the beginning of August, a number of the peers left Westminster and made their way to the King. Hyde seems to have exerted the greatest efforts to secure a favourable reception for them at Oxford, but in vain. To have received them back, and to have buried the past would have been to cut clean across the spirit of royalism which now informed the policy of the King. But the result, in Hyde's judgement, was deplorable. Those at Westminster —and it was reasonable to believe there were still many there who desired a negotiated peace—could only conclude that the King was implacable and that the breach was unbridgeable, and that if as now seemed to be the case, settlement was unattainable without a military victory, it was unsafe to allow the victorious side to be that of the King. Hyde put the greatest of emphasis on this point, and he might well do so.[2] For this was indeed the application of the *coup de grâce* to the peace party. The King had now rounded off a course of policy the effect of which was to seal off at each end two apparently irreconcilable blocs, and had brought about within each of them the submergence of non-violent parliamentarism.

That he blamed the King did not, of course, mean that he thought no ill of Pym and the violent party at Westminster. He had thought ill enough of them since the Grand Remonstrance and as ill as possible of them since the rupture over the militia negotiations in March 1642. The abolition of episcopacy prior to the Oxford treaty, and, following its failure, the calling of the Westminster Assembly of Divines, the instrument for an exclusively Presbyterian and partisan reformation of the Church, was a violent aggravation of the breach. Moreover, in calling in the Scots, with which action the two aforementioned were connected as preparatory measures, Pym and the violent party were to provide him with a reason

---

[1] Clarendon, *History*, III, p. 148.   [2] Ibid. pp. 196, 199 (from the *Life*).

for regarding their guilt as of an order of enormity quite incompatible with that of the King. The point, rather, is that up to that final stage of the present story, the stage in which the Scots appeared irremediably upon the scene, instead of contenting himself, as a Royalist would have done, with reflecting on the virulence of a rebellion which required so long to crush, Hyde considered that it was precisely because Royalists, and the King under their influence, viewed the situation in that way that peace had not been restored.

If, however, the foregoing interpretation is correct, and had no further circumstances to be considered, Hyde could hardly with consistency have blamed the London Parliamentarians for calling in the Scots as vehemently as he did. He held that it was on grounds of self-preservation that they did so, and strongly implied that the King had made that argument a more than plausible one. It should be recognized, however, that the final condemnation of the parliamentary leadership was made in virtue not of the fact that they called in the Scots to protect themselves from the fury of the Royalists, but rather of the response they made to what was the last expedient adopted by Hyde in the cause of peace which could be thought to afford any prospect of success, namely the Oxford Parliament. It was the upshot of this episode which finally shifted for him the moral balance against the men of Westminster.

As has been seen, by August 1643 the non-violent Parliamentarians had suffered eclipse both at Oxford and at Westminster, an eclipse upon which the death of Falkland at the Battle of Newbury in September of the same year was a melancholy and for Hyde personally an acutely painful comment. The King offered Hyde the vacant secretaryship. But the Queen preferred the candidature of Digby, and Hyde could not agree to associate himself at the close quarters which would be involved with the lamentable policies which now prevailed. He declined to compete with Digby for the

office.[1] To summon, however, members of Parliament to
Oxford would be to re-embody what was left of the non-
violent party and even to some extent to reunite it, in so far
as it might be hoped that some members, at least, could be
enticed from Westminster.[2] If such a thing were too much to
hope at this time of day, the introduction of parliamentary
institutions at Oxford would alter the situation there and
potently qualify, if not put an end to, the dominance of
Royalist counsels, both civilian and military.

Hyde states[3] that he suggested the summons of the members to Oxford as an expedient in prospect of a Scottish
invasion, and in the proclamation of 22 December,[4] the
reason given for the summons was that the world might see
that the major part of Parliament abhorred the action of the
men at Westminster in promoting the invasion. But in view
of what had been happening, and in view of his opinions and
aims, and in view of the passages in the proclamation of
20 June which expressly referred to the project, it is impossible
to credit that Hyde desired such a thing, still less that he
thought of such a thing, only in connexion with a Scottish
attack. Moreover, the argument about the Scots is in itself
unconvincing. He implies that since the country continued
to accept whatever the Parliament at Westminster did, however outrageous, as infallible, it was time in face of this latest
and greatest outrage, namely the calling in of the Scots, to
demonstrate that it was no longer the Parliament. At the
same time, however, he is contending that the summons of
the Scots was unpopular not only in the country at large, but
in the Parliament at Westminster, and if that was so (as there
is no reason to doubt that it was), there was a less and not

[1] *Life*, III, p. 177.
[2] The proclamation of 22 December, which summoned the members, offered
a general pardon, without exception, to those who would leave Westminster and
come to Oxford. *Parl. Hist.* XIII, p. 4.
[3] Clarendon, *History*, III, p. 256 (from the *Life*).
[4] *Parl. Hist.* XIII, p. 4.

a greater necessity of disabusing the people at such a time. On the other hand, if he already desired on other grounds to effect the convention of the members to Oxford, the unpopularity of what the violent party at Westminster had now brought upon the country would work to the advantage of a new assembly at Oxford. It was a good moment to summon such a body, assuming that it was wanted, and Hyde did want it. The project would not forcibly suggest itself, so long as there was a chance of the peace party predominating at Westminster: for the pattern which subsisted up to the exposure by Pym of Waller's 'plot' was a happy enough one. But it is known that the King was reluctant to accept the idea even as an expedient in face of the Scots.[1] It is not, therefore, unreasonable to suppose that it was in the circumstances of the entry of the Scots upon the scene that Hyde was finally able to achieve a purpose which was in his mind from the time that he had warded off the King's intention to dissolve Parliament in June. We can only suppose that the argument of the proclamation and the argument of the text of the *History* is the one which he used to convince the King, who did not want to summon Parliament at all. In the text, he stressed that aspect of the matter which was involved in his relations with the King. The argument was one which at least followed on easily from the first expedient proposed by Hyde, namely, a letter from the English peers to the Scots which should demonstrate that there were more peers with the King than there were at Westminster.

The reason why Hyde wanted Parliament at Oxford is usually assumed to be a concern for the weakness there of the civilian element, and also, and more particularly, his wish that constitutional courses should be followed, especially in the matter of the financing of the war. That, and especially the latter, is probably a part of the truth, for Hyde was Chancellor of the Exchequer. But this is a view which

[1] Clarendon, *History*, III, p. 260 (from the *Life*).

derives from the assumption that Hyde was a Royalist and, in consequence, ignores the gulf which separated him from even the civilian Royalists. Unless his experience in 1643, and now the Scottish intervention, had drowned his desire for peace in a sense of the hopelessness of achieving it short of victory in the field, this notion cannot be the whole truth, or even the more important part of it. In addition to Hyde's own testimony to the fact, there is evidence provided even by one of the Westminster commissioners that in the Treaty of Uxbridge, subsequent to the events described, Hyde, as one of the King's commissioners for the treaty, worked hard to promote its success.[1] If he wanted negotiations throughout 1643, and, then again, keenly entered into them as soon as the Scots and the men at Westminster would permit them in 1645, it is hard to see how it can be maintained that he did not want them at the beginning of 1644. The fact that the King was materially much weaker at the time of the Uxbridge Treaty than at the beginning of 1644 does not bear upon the point save that Hyde had thought there was more chance of a successful negotiation when the King was strong than when he was weak.[2] If 1643 had shown him the weak side of that argument, nothing was better calculated to rectify the mis-application of the King's strength than the Oxford Parliament.

The Scots army was already on the move, and things had now gone so far that Hyde may easily have doubted of success. But at least the Oxford Parliament provided an answer in the affirmative to the questions which, in the absence of such an answer hitherto, had led Westminster to evoke the aid of the Scots. It was no longer possible to argue that the King did not want peace save through a crushing victory and that therefore negotiations were a waste of time. Nor was it possible to believe now that no treaty could bring security

[1] Whitelocke, *Memorials*, 1, p. 375.
[2] See the proclamation of 22 December, where it is stated that, 'the condition we are now in...is improved...to a better degree than we have enjoyed at any time since these distractions'.

to the men of Westminster,[1] for the King's pledge would now be supplemented by that of the great majority of the peers and by about a third of the original members of the House of Commons.[2] The Scottish alliance was an unpopular step even among the men of Westminster. The mistrust of the King in 1642 had derived in large part precisely from the suspicion that he planned to resort to foreign force. Moreover, everyone knew that the price demanded by the Scots was nothing less than the dictation of ecclesiastical legislation which few indeed would have wanted on its own merits. If the Oxford Parliament could provide the guarantees for want of which this drastic measure had been taken, it was believed that the Earl of Essex would be in favour of overtures, and it might not be too late to prevent developments of which none could foresee the outcome.

That was the attitude of the Oxford Parliament as soon as it met, and that was the attitude predicted of it before its meeting. In fact it was on this ground, amongst others, that the King was opposed to its being summoned. But though the Council told the King that he need have no fear that Westminster would receive overtures,[3] it is necessary to believe that Hyde, if he shared the views of his colleagues, was speaking here in terms of expectations rather than of hopes. Hyde and Culpepper were the only Privy Councillors who sat in the Commons and it was their function 'to prevent the running into any excesses of discourse';[4] in other words, to co-ordinate the desires of the House and the needs of the government in accordance with political tradition and necessity as Hyde saw it. It was Hyde's special responsibility to attend to the needs of the government in the matter of funds, but he showed no anxiety to curb the desire of the House for

[1] Clarendon, *History*, III, p. 295 (a part written in the second exile).
[2] For the numbers attending the Oxford Parliament, see Gardiner, *Civil War*, I, p. 352.
[3] Clarendon, *History*, III, p. 261 (from the *Life*).
[4] Ibid. III, p. 293.

the opening of negotiations. Hyde was at Oxford in 1644 in the position in which Pym had been at Westminster in 1642-3, and we may believe their respective attitudes and policies to have been very similar. The fact that preparations for peace and preparations for war were intermingled in neither case meant that there was no desire for peace. For though financial preparations were facilitated in that it was known that peace was being sought, peace itself had a dependence upon military strength. Moreover, it was imperative to provide for the possibility that the peace moves would fail. In addition, Hyde, though unlike Pym in 1642-3, was in the position of having to co-ordinate the attitude of the House of Commons not only with the House of Lords but with the King, who in this instance, as in 1643, preferred the prosecution of the war to any other course.

The action of Westminster was such as confirmed the assurances which had been given the King by his advisers before the convention of the members. First one overture for peace was made, and this was shortly followed by a second. The rejection of the second, as Hyde says, 'put a period to all men's hopes, who imagined that there might be any disposition in those councils to any possible and honest accommodation'.[1] Since Westminster refused to negotiate even in these new and more favourable circumstances, the Oxford Parliament issued a manifesto[2] which may be regarded as a comprehensive apology for non-violent parliamentarism and an exposition of its history and of its present position. The members at Oxford, the paper declares, had been called to advise the King, and the advice which they had given was that he should make peace. The results of their efforts were now plain for all to see.

God and the world must judge between us. In the mean time we must...tell these men [the men of Westminster] that most of us are too well known, even to themselves, to be

[1] Clarendon, *History*, III, p. 304.   [2] *Parl. Hist.* XIII, p. 86.

suspected to incline to be either papists or slaves.... And since the defence of the religion, laws, and liberties of the kingdom, seems to be (and in truth is on our part) the argument of this bloody contention; and that we are endeavouring all ways to destroy one another, in the behalf of that we all do, or all pretend to desire: we think ourselves obliged...to let the world know, that as we are much more tender of the religion, laws, and liberties of the kingdom, than of our lives and fortunes; so the uneasy condition wherein we are, and the heavy judgements and proscriptions imposed on us by our equals, have proceeded, and been caused, from that conscience, loyalty, and duty, in which we have been born and bred....'

The paper proceeds to point out that the Oxford members had shared and supported the work of the Revolution, and, in addition, had striven to procure an act 'for the ease of tender consciences in matters indifferent; which, if it had been accepted, would have prevented many of the miseries which have since befallen this poor kingdom'. It explained that the story of the destruction of the constitution, the story of the outbreak of the war and that of the proscription and ill treatment of the non-violent party were one and the same, and at the end of the account, asked whether it was the men of Westminster or the men of Oxford who had failed in their duty to the constitution and the peace. The men of Oxford, the argument ran, were no less members of Parliament than those who continued to sit at the place where Parliament had been first convened:

Yet we confess the place to be so material, that if there were that liberty and freedom which is due to the members, and indeed is the life of parliaments, the act of those in the House, being a lawful act, is the act of the House, though there were a greater number absent, who were all of another opinion: but in our case, when we are by force driven away, and by force kept away; and when nothing can be said to justify the actions which are done, but the reputation and number of the actors, we rely so much upon the understanding and honesty of our country-men that they will believe, when they see our concurrence and unanimity in resolutions and counsels for their peace, welfare, and security ...that it will be better for them to be advised by us at Oxford, than by those at Westminster; from whence we are absent only by reason of those outrages and violences offered to our persons or our consciences, which take away all freedom, and consequently all authority, from those councils.

Affronting the King, destroying the Church, and undermining the liberties of the subject, it was the men of Westminster alone who would not suffer their distracted country to be restored by a treaty 'to the benefit of a parliament, which would, with God's blessing, easily remove these miseries, and prevent the like for the time to come'. And since there was no freedom for all the members to meet at Westminster, all the acts, votes and orders which issued from the latter place were declared null and void, and the Lords and Commons who remained there denounced as traitors in respect of levying war against the King, of making a new Great Seal and of calling in the Scots. This denunciation, however, was immediately followed by a disclaimer of any intention to procure the dissolution of Parliament, or to violate any act which had been passed by it with the royal assent.

It is our grief in the behalf of the whole kingdom, that since the Parliament is not dissolved, the power thereof should, by the treason and violence of these men, be so far suspended, that the Kingdom should be without the fruit and benefit of a parliament; which cannot be reduced to any action or authority, till the freedom and liberty, due to the members, be restored and admitted; and they only who oppose this must be looked upon as the enemies to parliament; in the mean time we neither have or shall attempt any thing for the adjourning, dissolving, or proroguing thereof, otherwise than as it may stand with the act in that case provided.

Hyde's attitude to the war now, but only now, became what Pym's had been since the failure of the Treaty of Oxford. The opposing side had been proved incorrigible. The war must therefore be regarded as a war and no longer as the military aspect of negotiations for a compromise. Only at this point is it safe to say that Hyde has adopted a 'royalist' attitude to the conduct of the war. But lest it should be supposed that he had become royalist in any other sense, or in one that in any way abated his parliamentarism, it should be noticed that the war to the death is not against Parliamentarians as such, however incorrigibly opposed to peace, but against men whose incorrigibility took the form of a military alliance with the Scots. The war had become a war against foreign conquest and the imposition of foreign and barbarous laws. Secondly, Hyde has become royalist in his attitude towards the conduct of the war at the precise point at which he has become once more a Parliamentarian in the full institutional sense of the word. Hyde once more sits in, and leads a Parliament that preserves the inheritance of 1641, and, in addition, has surmounted the crisis in its relations with the King which up to now had not been resolved.

The terms of the manifesto written by him for the Oxford convention make it clear that there was indeed a legal difficulty and that Hyde was well aware of it. By the act of 1641, Parliament could not even be adjourned without its own consent. This difficulty was in part met by the view that the Parliament at Westminster was no longer free, and therefore was unable either to give or to withhold its consent in this matter.[1] But the behaviour of the members at Oxford was in keeping with the terms of their manifesto, and proves that Hyde was aware that the difficulty was met only in part. The preservation of constitutional purity, as such, had never been Hyde's objective. But now, as throughout the story up to now, the situation was such that constitutional purity

[1] See the proclamation of 20 June.

turned out to be the necessary result of the pursuit of the policy of reconciliation. No bishops sat at Oxford, since the Bill abolishing their parliamentary status had received the royal assent in 1642. There was no attempt made to seize the opportunity of giving consent to a dissolution. Out of regard for the possibility of peace with Westminster, the Oxford assembly did not claim full and exclusive parliamentary status. If anybody was inclined to look upon it as fully parliamentary, it would have been the King. For Hyde, it was a matter of some members being at Oxford and others at Westminster. Only both groups together constituted Parliament in the full sense.

Morally, however, the Oxford assembly had now a better right to be regarded as Parliament than the one at Westminster. That was the burden of the manifesto which followed the failure of the overtures for peace. In an important sense the efforts of Hyde which date back to the autumn of 1641 have been at last crowned with success. At the very moment when Hyde had become royalist in his attitude to the war, he had won a resounding success against Royalism at the very heart of its power. For full account must be taken of the magnitude of the exertions which must have been required to persuade the King to convoke the members.

But Hyde had succeeded in a sense which had now become irrelevant and which he recognized as such. It was just as if he had succeeded as against Pym in the autumn of 1641, and defeated the Grand Remonstrance, only to discover that agreement with the King was further away than ever. The success of the Oxford Parliament was morally and politically and, so far as possible, constitutionally complete within its limits, but outside those limits there raged an increasingly ferocious and apparently interminable war. And such qualities in the war were not solely the result of the intervention of the Scots, for that intervention was itself the consequence and the sign of the aggravation of the political and religious schism.

That Hyde indeed regarded his success as irrelevant is shown by the fact that even at the end of 1644 he was not prepared to agree with the King in denying, in an invitation to fresh negotiations, the title of Parliament to the assembly at Westminster, a denial which must have cut off at the outset all prospect of success. The King told the Queen that he would not have granted the title had two members of his Council been found to agree with him in refusing to do so. Only one was prepared to follow the King, and he was not Hyde, but Nicholas. Hyde's continued interest in peace negotiations is shown, also, in his conduct at the treaty which ensued at Uxbridge in the beginning of 1645, when he was the King's leading commissioner. The Treaty of Uxbridge differed from the Treaty of Oxford in that there was nothing in its circumstances which could have given Hyde the faintest expectation of a successful outcome. The King, weaker as against the Parliament than at the time of the Oxford treaty, and subjected to the pressure of the Oxford assembly, was at last willing to consider the expedient of bridge-appointments,[1] and the Queen was once again put out by the King's lack of resolution, as she defined that quality. She was afraid,[2] this time, of the effect which the King's willingness to treat would have upon the prospects of French aid. But she need not have worried. It was too late for successful treaties. It would have been too late even if, with the Oxford Parliament, the King had finally gone over to Hyde's policy. It was too late because the composition and purposes of the opposing party were now radically altered. This was the decisive thing.

It is true that the peace party leaders were represented at the Uxbridge negotiations; Northumberland, Pierpoint, Whitelocke, Holles. But there the resemblance to the Treaty of Oxford ended, for these men were flanked on the one hand by the Scottish commissioners and, on the other, by St John

[1] *Harleian Miscellany*, 1811, VII, p. 559.
[2] *Letters of Queen Henrietta Maria*, p. 276.

and Vane, who represented a type of violent parliamentarism, compared with which that of Pym had been only moderately violent, and which was marked off from the parliamentarism of Hyde by a difference that was more than one of method. That a negotiation was entered upon at all at the beginning of 1645 arose less from the relations existing between the King and his enemies than from the internal relations of the latter as a result of Pym's death. The treaty's success, if it succeeded, was envisaged by the Scots as a move on their part against the rising power of the Independents in Parliament and army: its failure was looked forward to by the latter as a move on their part against the Scots. The Scots sincerely desired peace and so did the remnants of the peace party who were now their allies, though reluctantly, and only out of fear of Cromwell and the Independents. But such sincerity had not the slightest bearing upon the possibility of a successful conclusion to the treaty. The Scots were in a sense the obvious allies of the King against the Independents since they wished to maintain the monarchical constitution. It was primarily their treaty, and, as has been said, they wanted a successful outcome. They intimated that if the King would give way on one point, they would support him on all the rest. But that one point involved the ecclesiastical issue. Peace had always depended upon keeping this issue in the background. But now it stood unavoidably in the foreground, and, what is more, took a form far more formidable than ever before. Not only was it hopeless to expect the King and the Anglican clergy to agree with the Scottish demand for full Presbyterianism in England and the acceptance of the Covenant; even liberal Anglicans were alienated. It was impossible, on the other hand, to build anything upon a joint Anglican–Peace party–Independent repugnance to the Scots and their Presbyterianism, for the peace party men were already so far apart from the Independents that they could not do without the Scots and Presbyterianism, and between the Independent

144

leaders and the King there was a gulf so wide that neither they nor Charles believed in the possibility of a mutual arrangement at all. The peace party men were far too weak to offer any hope, though it was evident that they preferred the men who were supposed to be their enemies to either of the groups who were formally their friends. Devices which Hyde had pressed at Oxford and which he was now empowered to employ were completely out of place. Hyde in his account[1] does not even mention this aspect of the negotiations. The best the peace party leaders could suggest was that if only the King would give way now on all points, they would help him back to his power at some later date. But that was fantastic. The King was already sufficiently distrusted. Moreover, such a dishonourable course would not have reckoned with the strength of the Independents, and if he had adopted it he would have given the latter a justifiably national cause. Whichever way, therefore, the King's commissioners turned, there was no possibility of breaking through on to ground which would support a compromise. But in this hopeless situation, and seeing clearly its full hopelessness, Hyde's desire for a settlement remained as strong and sincere as ever.

He never, he said, underwent so great fatigue in his life.[2] The direction of his efforts was what we should have expected. They were directed towards the English, not towards the Scots. At least there could be no question of a foreign solution to an English problem, and if an English solution was impossible, there could be no solution at all. The proposals of the English commissioners on the Church and on the militia were not put forward with any hope of eliciting agreement. It was suggested that bishops should exercise their power only with the consent of elected bodies of clergy, and that the ceremonial requirements of the Prayer Book should be relaxed in favour of tender consciences. On the

---

[1] Writing, that is, in the second exile, not in the period 1646–8.
[2] Clarendon, *History*, III, p. 501.

militia, it was proposed that the King and the Houses should jointly nominate the men to wield it and that these should do so for a period of three years, after which the military power should revert to the King. Such schemes, now stretched to the limit, were what Hyde had supported, or would have supported, at various junctures in the past. It was now too late for such things. They were put forward merely to show that the King's commissioners wished for peace and were willing to compromise in order to obtain it.

The Treaty of Uxbridge proved what was already clear enough before, that there was no longer anything to be hoped from negotiations. There was less and less to be hoped from the war either. Its course had turned against the King well before the Treaty of Uxbridge. Marston Moor, the joint victory of Scots and Independents, was fought on 2 July 1644. Naseby, less than a year later, concluded the business. The adherents of the King were soon to be a proscribed remnant with no alternatives but to make the best terms they could with the ruling powers or else to go into exile. Hyde went with the Prince of Wales to the West Country and, after a miserable experience of the final stages of the war in those parts, moved with the Prince to Scilly, and from thence to Jersey.

Jersey rounds off the story of the political phase of Hyde's activity and provides an epilogue to it. Hyde was more than a little inclined to view his time in Jersey in the same light. In Jersey had come to a head his opposition to the Queen's plan that the Prince of Wales should withdraw to France. With the entry of the Scots into the war, the King had tended more and more to break out from the uneasy synthesis of policy which he had effected between the ideas of Hyde and those of the Queen. He had looked increasingly towards Ireland and also towards France, seeking from the latter either mediation or military assistance. The project of sending the Prince to France was one which Hyde opposed with all his

strength as a deplorable example of this type of policy.[1] He
opposed it because he did not trust the French government.
He was convinced not only that the interest which it displayed was self-interest, but also that it was incompatible
with the interest of England. He feared the effect which the
removal of the Prince might have on English opinion and the
effect it might have upon the already non-existent prospects
of a negotiated peace.

With the Prince's departure for France and Hyde's refusal
to accompany him, his connexion with public affairs was
broken. He was now out of a game, which, as he said, had
been lost through their 'own gross folly and madness'[2] and
might have been longer played. But he reflected that no man
now underwent a worse condition than he had had reason to
expect when 'upon such infinite disadvantages' as had existed
in 1642 he first joined the King,[2] and, in March 1646, in a
mood less bitter than reflective, he started to write the *History*.
In the autumn of the same year, when he and his companions,
Hopton, Capel and Carteret, got wind of a plan of Jermyn's
to hand the island over to France in return for aid, they signed
a bond[3] to defend it, and agreed that if the plan were attempted they would call in the Parliament to protect the
island. This was a decision which confirms the assumptions
and ideas of Hyde about the nature of the late Civil War, as
we have interpreted them, as much as it reflects his patriotism.
In the spring of 1647, however, there was another kind of
alarm. It became known that there was reason to expect
a parliamentary attack upon the island. Hyde, therefore,
preparing for the worst, made his will. This included a 'short
protestation and declaration of and for myself, against any
unjust imputation'.[4] In this he declared that never during
his service in the House of Commons had he countenanced
'anything that in [his] conscience he thought inconvenient for

[1] *S.P. Clar.* II, p. 231.   [2] Ibid. p. 284.
[3] Ibid. p. 279.   [4] Ibid. p. 361.

the peace and happiness of the Kingdom, but desired (and never endeavoured other) that the frame and constitution of the Kingdom might be observed, and the known laws and bounds between the King's power and the Subjects' right'. This is no contradiction of the story of the outlook and the policy which has been unfolded. On the contrary, he mentions peace as a criterion of his action, and the emphasis is the one which the beginnings of his story must have received, given the occasion, and the purpose with which he was writing.

The very requirements, indeed, of self-justification and the direction in which it was addressed invited and resulted in a more explicit statement than can be found elsewhere of what had been the location of his efforts in 1641. The explanation of Hyde's 'conversion to royalism' contributed by his contemporary opponents, the violent party, into whose hands he now thought himself or his papers about to fall, was precisely the explanation which he as a historian gave to the conduct of the violent party leaders, namely ambition for power and place. The difference is that whereas, as he could not help making clear in his account, they trembled for their personal security unless they could fulfil their ambition, he himself, as his opponents viewed the matter, had deserted the cause of Parliament when in no personal danger whatever. For from their point of view he had been threatened with punishment in March 1642 and finally expelled in August of the same year as the consequence of a desertion perpetrated long before March 1642 and without provocation. Thomas May, historian of the violent party, Hyde's own counterpart in historiography, moralized at length on the matter, though without mentioning names.

It was no wonder, but very probable, that they were such men [the members of the House of Commons who deserted Parliament in 1642], and such as had, or thought they had, good parts enough to be looked upon by a prince: for those men (though we should esteem them all of equal honesty) were likeliest to fall off. There is a difference between wisdom and good parts, such as we count eloquence, wit, polite learning, and the like.[1]

Hyde's sensitiveness wherever in his writings he touched on his position with Charles I was pronounced.

That I had never the least thought, [he wrote in the present instance] by what I said or did in that House, to procure any recommendation to, or acceptance from his Majesty, being so far from any likelihood in reason of that, that those Persons to whom I had before always applied myself withdrawing themselves from their usual zeal to the King's service, and consequently losing much of that interest they had before in him. I had not the least knowledge of or relation to any man of esteem with his Majesty, more than what out of their own inclinations they vouchsafed to me, a stranger; so that I know not who they were who made the first good impressions in me with his majesty.

Hyde did not perish in the defence of Jersey. The men who had won the war did not attack the island, as had been expected. His personal winding-up was premature, and he lived to write in the spring of 1648 a reply to an important parliamentary declaration published in February of that year. Following the drafting of his own personal vindication, there appeared in *A full Answer to an infamous and traitorous Pamphlet entitled A declaration of the Commons of England expressing their reasons of passing the late Resolutions of no further addresses to the King*, the drafting of the vindication of the King himself. Nor was even this the end of the public issues which he had espoused, or of his connexion with them. As will be seen, it was merely the beginning of a new, quite different, and, in the end, much more successful phase. But it remains true that Jersey was the end of the story which began with the second

---

[1] May, *History*, p. 179.

session of the Long Parliament in the autumn of 1641, and that it was seen as such by Hyde.

Throughout the period from 1641 to the Treaty of Uxbridge, Hyde, as a public figure, had but one aim, to heal the breach between the King and the two Houses of Parliament which the earthquake of the Revolution of 1640–1 had created. Such an end came to imply, as a means, and even as part of itself, the reunion of a divided House of Lords and of a divided House of Commons. But, despite increasingly complex circumstances, bridge-building is the explanation of his thoughts and actions throughout this whole period. In that he had ideas deeper than those of a peace-maker as was certainly the case, he believed in the Revolution of 1640–1. If he had not believed in it, he could not have hoped to succeed. No compromise of the principles of the Revolution was involved in wishing to do so; none, even, was involved in adhering to the King when it came to civil war. It seems sometimes to be supposed that Hyde adopted a compromise between the principles of the Revolution and those of royalism, a compromise which can be called 'constitutional royalism'. That is not true, and the phrase is unsatisfactory. The kingship had been assumed both in the theory and also in the practice of the original Revolution. It was assumed even by the original violent party when well on their course. Between the latter and Hyde there was fundamentally no difference save one of method. It was the violent Parliamentarians and not the so-called 'constitutional royalists' who made a new departure, and who, despite their convictions and under the dictation of their own methods, concocted a hybrid constitutional standpoint which diluted the standards of 1640 with the type of argument from necessity and reason of State which had been used by the exponents of the absolute prerogative in the preceding eleven years, and which all the revolutionaries had wished to banish once and for all.

Gardiner states that Hyde took up a position between Strafford and Pym, and that while the ideas of the latter two were respectable, it was 'absolutely impossible' that Hyde's conception of the constitution could have been permanently adopted. That judgement is based upon a simplification in terms of later categories of the ideas of Strafford and of Pym. Strafford, Gardiner says, was prepared to solve the problem of sovereignty in one way, Pym in another.[1] But Strafford's picture always included Parliament, and Pym's always included the King, and neither thought in terms of sovereignty. Probably both of them, in so far as they could lift themselves above the stringent necessities of immediate situations and take a longer view, would have put more emphasis upon the need for collaboration between King and Parliament than upon the need for either to dominate the other.

The important point in the case of Strafford is that the King had listened to him only when the gulf between the government and the House of Commons was unbridgeable. But what Strafford as a member of Parliament had wished the King to accept in 1628 before the passing of the Petition of Right was precisely a policy designed to prevent the emergence of the unbridgeable gulf. The story of Charles's dealings with Hyde is a repetition of the story of his dealings with Strafford. In the one case, as in the other, the King listened to a voice from the House of Commons and accepted a new counsellor but only in a situation of a type it had been the cardinal purpose of the counsellor to forestall, namely an all but irreparable rift between the King and the Estates of the Realm. The difference between the story of Strafford and that of Hyde is that the one took place before, and the other after the constitutional Revolution of 1640–1. Whereas Strafford had sought to avert that Revolution by means of a legislative and constitutional compromise, Hyde as an enthusiast for the Revolution both before and after it had happened, had sought

[1] Gardiner, *History*, x, p. 169.

to consolidate it by means of a political union cemented by personalities between the King and the Houses of Parliament on the assumption that the King should accept the work of the Long Parliament.

As for Pym, the need for reconciliation would have been axiomatic with him from the start, and, no doubt, in the later stages also, in a theoretical sense. But all that can certainly be said of him from the second part of 1641 onwards, is that methods devised by him to meet contingencies as he assessed them carried him forward, creating a logic and a closed system of their own. Even if there had been no war, as Pym presumably counted that there would not be, this could never have reconciled a king and, instead, must have increasingly alienated him, and must, moreover, have too much resembled the system which had just been overthrown to satisfy the country. In this respect even if in no other the King accepted the Revolution and was able in this aspect of it, at least, to represent his subjects against the violent party. Hyde understood and feared Pym's system, and believed it could be broken, and tried again and again to do so. It is arguable, therefore, that Hyde had a clearer notion of an end to it all than Pym had. With Hyde there existed no contradiction between the means employed and the end in view as there did with Pym. Moreover it seems clear that not only Hyde's ends but also his methods represented the desires of the vast mass of those who were concerned and affected at the time.

Gardiner, as we have seen, says that it was absolutely impossible that Hyde's conception of the constitution could have been permanently adopted. Provided that we include the alternative way of stating the matter which was put forward by Falkland and Culpepper with their 'mixarchy', and if it is permissible to equate a period of over a century with permanence, it is true to say not only that Hyde's ends and means most probably represented what most men in his time desired and could approve but also that it was precisely Hyde's conception of the constitution rather than that of anybody else which did come to be permanently adopted. It is natural to stress the similarity between the logic of Pym's emergency procedure, his demand that government should be controlled by parliament in all respects, and the long-term logic of English constitutional history which in the end produced such a control, but if we wish to affirm the continuity of English history, as Gardiner himself did, it is necessary to point not to Pym but to Hyde. The true bridge between the non-resistance of the epoch of the Tudor rulers and the eighteenth-century constitution was the non-violent, the bridge-building parliamentarism of Hyde. The Tudor rulers in the sixteenth century had raised parliaments to administer, and so in the end to share their power. Now the non-violent party in the middle of the seventeenth century seeks to draw the King, already of course a true component part of parliament, into the working of a parliamentary constitution. What failed in the years which immediately succeeded 1640 was the attempt to do this by the distinctively parliamentary methods of discussion and compromise in an atmosphere of confidence.

It is indeed necessary to admit that Pym's estimate of the character of Charles I was neither unreasonable nor inexcusable, and that his realistic measures are far from unintelligible. But in this connexion, it must be recognized that Pym himself had a responsibility for the course taken by events, in that from the second session onwards he had adopted a policy which was so extremely provocative. The late seventeenth-century Huguenot historian Rapin de Thoyras, who was not prejudiced in favour of the Stuart dynasty, in a very acute discussion[1] of the point, shows that after what happened in the second session, the King, in the nature of the case, could not bring himself to believe that Pym's aims were not as aggressive as his methods. Finally, it should be stated that it

[1] Rapin de Thoyras, *The History of England*, 1733, II, p. 432.

is not reasonable to imply that Pym succeeded, and that his success rules out Hyde's alternative policy as historically insignificant in its own time. Pym did not succeed. The man who succeeded, and in his own life time, at the Restoration, was not Pym but Hyde.

Hyde did not change from a Parliamentarian into a Royalist or even into a Constitutional Royalist, on account of the Church, or on any other account. For he never made a change of this sort at all. Like Strafford, he did not apostatize, and in his case there is less justification for regarding him as having done so than there is in the case of Strafford. He was no less a Parliamentarian in Jersey in 1646 or 1648 than he had been in Westminster in 1640 or 1642, and no more a Royalist in those later years than at the outset.

What, then, is to be said of the *History*? Is not the *History* royalist? The epithet is not to be denied, but the explanation of the difference between Hyde the historian and Hyde the politician is not impossible to find. Apart from the angle and point of view from which he wrote, namely the angle and point of view of the King, there is an explanation and one which is of more consequence, since without it the changed angle of vision could not have been achieved. Although both his autobiographical and historical writings have been made to yield up a tale of non-royalist politics, the very intensity of those politics gave him the beginnings of an insight into the King's mind. He started at that point in the series of Declarations at which, in the cause of peace, he had sought to justify the King's past actions, the declaration, that is, of 21 March. But he proceeded as he fell away from the violent party and was driven into close proximity to the King, to a deepening understanding of a man faced, even though largely through his own failings, with a series of impossible predicaments which had ended by the time he wrote in a situation of acute distress. Hyde showed in his writing that he could always explain the King's action on any particular occasion, even though at the time he had deplored it. He came, for instance, entirely to understand the King's fatal withdrawal from Windsor in February 1642, though at the time he had taken as grave a view of that step as did the formal majority of his parliamentary colleagues. And there was more to Hyde's attitude than a deepening understanding, which might, after all, have been somewhat detached in character. It is clear that a strong bond of attachment was established between Hyde and the King. This dates, in all probability, from an early stage in his political association with Charles, though when in 'the protestation and declaration' of the Jersey period, he averred that one of his reasons for action in the early part of 1642 was a sense that the proceedings against the King were unjustifiable by the laws both of God and man, he may well have been antedating his feelings. That bond ensured that if Hyde was never a Royalist he early became a loyalist, and this fact was decisive for the *History*. Fired with this loyalty he became so good a historian in his exposition of the situations in which the King found himself, that he has misled his readers regarding his own attitude towards the events described at the time they were taking place. This misleading effect is heightened by the lack of sympathetic insight in Hyde's treatment of the parliamentary leaders. It has been argued here that despite what happened at the end of March 1642, with the threat to his personal safety, the first part of the war so far as Hyde was concerned was all of a piece with the preceding phases of his political activity, and that it was because he could so well enter into the mind of Westminster that he blamed the King so much in 1643. But the later stages of the war, the entrance of the Scots and the failure of the peace moves of the Oxford Parliament, produced a situation which brought it about that when Hyde, with his feeling for Charles, came to write the *History* he saw a King whose actions though always mistaken were always explicable, ranged over against men whose actions entitled them only to condemnation.

Close study of the *History*, however, reveals that Hyde went further towards a full historical explanation of the actions of the King's opponents in the war than is usually recognized: as far, indeed, as it was possible to go within the limitations which were now imposed. The conclusion which emerges from following Hyde's own argument is not that the events are to be explained in terms of the wickedness of men but that the wickedness of men is to be explained in terms of the events. The violent party, he shows, were impelled by the motive of self-preservation. What had originally been a desire for ministerial office, springing from a 'patriotism' which Hyde would have wished to describe in ironical terms only from his later and historical point of view, became, as distrust accumulated, a desire for office as the guarantee of personal security. Hyde originally approved the desire for office as a means to settlement. From the split between the violent and the non-violent parties there emerged the doctrine that the former had been inspired by malice and ambition from the start, and it receives explicit statement in the declarations which followed the decisively unaccommodating steps taken by Parliament in the middle of March 1642. This doctrine was not the inspiration of his action subsequent to that date, and the fact is reflected in and explains the fine quality of the *History*. It is responsible for the extent to which Hyde is able to give a truly historical explanation of the actions of the King's opponents. The doctrine, however, is certainly a doctrine of the *History*, as, of course, it is a doctrine of *A full Answer to an infamous and traitorous Pamphlet*, Hyde's answer to the Vote of No More Addresses. Personal sympathy for the King, and his own experience of the opposite party in the later stages of the war can reasonably be adduced to support the conclusion that the doctrine in question expressed a natural and a genuine personal feeling in Hyde. It must be understood, moreover, that whatever he felt, the universally accepted conventions of such a work as he was undertaking involved an artificial heightening and dramatization of the moral aspects of the story.

The *History* is royalist in that whereas self-preservation and reaction to provocation were allowed as motives in the case of the King and of his Royalist servants and were made to explain their mistakes and their crimes to the verge often of excusing them, such motives could not be allowed in the case of the parliamentary leaders. Hyde's own political career guaranteed to them the broad outline of an explanation, but they could hope to obtain no more. In *A full Answer to an infamous and traitorous Pamphlet*, Hyde's identification with the King is carried a stage further. Not only does the doctrine that the violent party were inexcusably wicked from the start dominate the picture to the exclusion of any kind of historical explanation of their conduct, but the extenuation of the King's actions springs into positive vindication. *A full Answer* is the most royalist of all Hyde's productions. But if his method is examined, it will be seen that in answer to the charges of the Parliament he usually either draws attention to those aspects of the King's policy which his own efforts had been able to affect, or else adopts the argument that the King's misdeeds have by now been dwarfed not only by the misdeeds of the violent party, but by misdeeds which were identical with those of which the King was accused. Thus, on the one hand, he disposes of the notion of a popish plot to overthrow English institutions foiled just in time by the resource of the violent party in taking up arms: he explains that what the King chiefly sought from abroad in the war was money and arms rather than armies: he maintains, correctly, that the King had never refused to the men of Westminster the title of Parliament, though he had denied that they were free: he expounds the truth about Waller's 'plot' and the Oxford Parliament ('there was neither real nor mock parliament set

157

up at Oxford'). On the other hand, not very subtly perhaps, but equally truthfully, he points out that if the King was charged with an evil church policy in the period before 1640, the violent party since that time had allowed the Church to be overwhelmed altogether in a fury of sectarianism: if the King had taxed illegally before 1640, since then Westminster had taxed at least as illegally and much more heavily. They claimed that the King had connived at plans to overawe Parliament in 1641 with an army, but they had themselves at a later date allowed Cromwell to do the same. If the King had tried unsuccessfully to arrest five members of the House of Commons, their own army had successfully ejected eleven. If the King were accused of plotting to introduce a foreign army, they had themselves introduced the Scots.

Such was Hyde's method in this his most royalist work and it implies nothing new: the purpose dictated the omissions. Moreover, that purpose was identical with the declarations of the later phase of 1642. In rebutting Parliament's reasons, he fought to reverse that decision to make no more addresses in support of which they had been adduced. He pleaded even now for a treaty which on the basis of the work of the Long Parliament should secure all interests and bring peace and settlement to the country.

PART II

HISTORIOGRAPHY

§ 1. *The Psalms and Machiavelli*

HYDE wrote the *History* because he had nothing else to do. He wrote it because events had brought the story which began in 1641 to an end, because the ideas and purposes of that period could no longer be applicable in the world of action. The outcome and the failure coloured his interpretation of the story of those years. He had understood that the system of the violent party depended as much upon the King's conduct as upon Pym's, and had believed that it could have been put an end to by appropriate action on the King's part. Since the King failed him, and since Pym succeeded in continuing on his course, the system of the latter is now elevated into a preconceived aim. What had been a notion thrown out in 1642 to discredit them—that the violent party had cut out the whole design from the start—now became an accepted principle of the *History*, and, drawn by affection and sympathy for the King now confronted with disaster, he looked at the story from his angle. He would show up the King's mistakes for the King's benefit. Those mistakes were no longer such as had helped to produce and to protract a calamity which at a number of points could have been averted. Entering into, and accepting the King's original fears and suspicions that the violent party were determined to destroy his Crown, his Church and his friends, the mistakes were now mistakes in the matter of crushing a premeditated and repeatedly attempted onslaught upon Church and State. It was a question, mostly, of the same actions and situations looked at from a different point of view. The new point of view was made possible because the King had in fact always acted in a resistant frame

159

of mind, and had actually refused concessions most of the time, and also because Hyde remembered his own declarations of 1642, which from that of 26 March had stood defiantly upon the King's constitutional rights. The consequences or the concomitants of these declarations were indeed startling enough to be remembered. The King's power when it came to hostilities had been such as no one in the earlier part of 1642 would have been able to predict.

But the new point of view necessarily entailed a complete reversal. It involved a neglect of the original purpose of the declarations, a peace which had never come, and a concentration, instead, upon their results in strengthening the King's position. In reality he had had successively to relate royalist means, royalist *faits accomplis*, to a parliamentary end. Now, however, it looks as if he was advocating and would in the past have advocated parliamentary means for the purpose of achieving a royalist end. As a result of this inversion, his view converges upon the view which had been pressed by the Queen in the months immediately preceding the Civil War. For example, whereas in 1642, from his knowledge of the attitude of men like Essex, he had upheld a policy of concession, and had believed that compromise on the militia could count for its success upon the support of such men, in the *History* and in the *Life*, Hyde says that Essex and many others began to waver in their opposition from the moment that the King stopped making concessions on the Queen's departure. The King's willingness to negotiate, the Queen had said, only encouraged the aggressiveness of Parliament. Hyde was now saying the same thing. 'Resolution' originally meant a resolution on the King's part that he should conduct himself as if he intended accommodation and peace rather than violence. Resistance had not come into the picture. Now, in retrospect, it meant a resolution to resist, but to resist not by resorting to force but by standing for the law:

...to shelter himself wholly under the law, to grant any thing that by the law he was obliged to grant, and to deny what by the law was in his own power and which he found inconvenient to consent to, and to oppose and punish any extravagant attempt by the force and power of the law; presuming that the King and the law together would have been strong enough for any encounter that could happen....[1]

Hyde still differs from the Queen. But it now seems more a question of method than of purpose.

In the exposition of the mistakes by which the disaster had come about there was intended to be a revelation of the method whereby it might be repaired.

And I have the more willingly induced myself to this unequal task out of the hope of contributing somewhat to that end: and though a piece of this nature (wherein the infirmities of some, and the malice of others, both things and persons, must be boldly looked upon and mentioned) is not likely to be published, (at least in the age in which it is writ,) yet it may serve to inform myself and some others what we are to do, as well as to comfort us in what we have done....[2]

Following the military collapse, the King and the Royalist leaders made their own attempts at repairing the disaster and resorted to negotiations with the victors, but Hyde expressed disapproval of what took place. He was opposed, as Firth points out,[3] to the Queen's policy of buying the support of the Scots by sacrificing the Church. 'He was equally hostile to her plans for restoring the King by French or foreign forces.' During the King's negotiations with the Parliament and army he was filled with suspicions. On the outbreak of the second Civil War which had been concerted with the aid of the Scots in 1648 he was summoned to attend the Queen and the Prince on the Continent, and so returned to public life. But he took the same line as before. He was against trusting the Scots and

[1] Clarendon, *History*, 1, p. 7, quoted by Firth in *D.N.B.*, who accepts the attitude of the *History* as that of 1642.
[2] Clarendon, *History*, 1, p. 2.   [3] *D.N.B.* xxviii, p. 374.

advised the Prince against doing so. The course of the negotiations at Newport after the second Civil War filled him with disgust and alarm. When the Prince became King on the death of his father, Charles retained, against the advice of his mother, his father's servants and the struggle went on. Hyde resisted the idea of restoration by means of accepting the terms of the Presbyterian Scots, and soon, reacting to an atmosphere of intense conflict in policy, he was happy to seize the chance afforded him in a mission to Madrid of absenting himself from the Council Chamber. At the end of 1651, when the French and Scottish designs of the Queen-mother lay in ruins, Charles II, having escaped from the catastrophe of Worcester, recalled Hyde from Spain. Hyde had not changed, and would not change in his judgement of the recent past, but from that time until the end of the exile in 1660 his ascendancy with Charles, though not unchallenged, was at least maintained.

If the interpretation which has been given of Hyde's attitude up to the Treaty of Uxbridge is correct, we seem from the end of the military operations of the first Civil War to be presented with a change more spectacular than any that has taken place up to date, a change more decisive than anything that happened to him either in the autumn of 1641 or the spring of 1642. For whereas he had been in favour of negotiations and compromise throughout all the foregoing period, he now seems to emerge as the champion of absolute intransigence. Throughout this later period, his correspondence bristles with appeals to high moral and political principles and to a Providence which would vindicate them, and resounds with emphatic assertions of the error of compromising an iota of the constitution in either Church or State. It would appear that reflection on the destruction and repair of a kingdom had ended in a no better policy to recommend than that of doing precisely nothing. So, at least, it seemed to the Royalists.

A figure emerges displaying features distinctly reminiscent of the strait-laced Hyde of historical legend. The difficulty in regard to the first phase, that which dissipated itself in and after the Treaty of Uxbridge, is the difficulty of working in the overwhelming shadow of Hyde's own historical and auto-biographical work. Hyde himself invited the hostile interpre-tation and the position taken up against him by, for instance, S. R. Gardiner. He himself implied that the ideas of the first phase were the same as those of the second. The difficulty in regard to the second phase is that in it Hyde's own letters provide contemporary evidence which suggest the truth of the legend. We are tempted to believe that the legend about Hyde's career, however wide of the mark so far as the first period is concerned, ceases to be legend and becomes the truth as the first period transforms itself into the second. But the fact of the matter is that, whereas the truth about Hyde's activity from 1641 to 1645 necessitates almost a reversal of the views which have been commonly held about it, the truth about the period which ended in 1660 necessitates not so much a reversal as an addition. The difference between an addition and a reversal will afford no extenuation of the legend, for the addition which must be made is such that it alters the picture of the second phase as radically as the reversal has altered the first.

The matter can be cleared up if the fact stated at the beginning of this second part is borne in mind. Hyde's reac-tion to the cataclysmic change of landscape involved in, and following upon the defeat of the King's armies was to become a historian. It seemed to him to be the only thing it was possible to be in the circumstances of political failure and military defeat. This reaction was decisive for the whole period which was governed by those circumstances, namely the period up to 1660. The change, therefore, deserves to be emphasized, but its true character must not be missed. In so far as he returned to political action within that period, he did so not only as a man who could write, and was writing history, but as a man in a historian's frame of mind and a man whose vision was now almost exclusively historical. The loyalism, the moralism, and the deep theological seriousness are undeniably present, and he planned, for inclusion in the *History*, though he failed to write it, a discourse on the constitution which would no doubt have been a classic of legalistic accuracy. These things are indisputable. They were the natural product and resort of a mind at a loss in a completely new political world where all the old landmarks had disappeared. But they are also aspects and concomitants of an attitude which was fundamentally and predominantly historical. They were the forms and categories of a historical interpretation.

The significance of this for the understanding of Hyde's position at this time should emerge if the difference which ought to exist between, on the one hand, a contemporary critic of Hyde's political recommendations, and on the other, the critical historian writing at a later time, is recognized to the extent which it deserves. The view of Hallam, for instance, was that Hyde was too sanguine and that he lacked the gift of practical statesmanship.[1] Hyde's only political principle, Hallam contended, was that 'nothing was to be receded from which had ever been desired'. Magnanimous such a principle might be, but it was hardly wise. 'No discussion could ever be settled if all men were to act upon it, or if all men were to expect that Providence would interfere to support what seemed to them the best, that is, their own cause.' But whereas the historian can appreciate that in the extremities and anxieties of failure and exile there was good reason why Hyde's point of view should exasperate adventurous minds, it remains possible for him to observe, as was not possible for the contemporary critic, not only that the constitution was

[1] [Henry] Hallam, [*Constitutional*] *History* [*of England*, Everyman's Library], II, p. 191 n.

restored, but that the manner of its restoration was an almost
complete vindication of Hyde's notions. If it be argued that
Hyde's responsibility in this was of a limited character, Hyde
himself would not have denied it. The second stage for him
was predominantly historical: it was a time of observation
and of reflection. But it will be seen that the strength of his
attitude and of the policy springing from it lay in the pro-
fundity of his analysis of the forces let loose by the English
Revolution in the midst of which he lived and played his part.
In regard to his confidence that Providence would interfere,
and that history was on his side, the answer to Hallam is that
the confidence proved to be overwhelmingly justified.

He wrote the *History* during the period 1646 to 1648. From
the same period dates the beginning of the *Contemplations and
Reflections upon the Psalms of David*. He broke off these works to
join the exiles on the Continent, and he lacked materials for
continuing the *History*. But while ambassador at the court of
Spain from 1649 to 1651 he took up again the work on the
Psalms. The series which had been carried as far as Psalm viii
in Jersey was not completed until the second period of exile
after the Restoration. But Hyde got as far as Psalm lxx while
at Madrid, and, at about the time when Hobbes was finishing
Leviathan, he committed to paper an exercise which, different
as it is in every other respect, has two points in common with
the third part of Hobbes's work. Hyde was determined like
Hobbes to restrict himself to the meaning of Scripture in the
simplest and most literal sense. The result was an essay 'in
captivating the understanding to the words of Scripture without any labouring to sift out a philosophical truth by logic',[1]
which was, within its limits, as thorough as the work of
Hobbes, though Hyde in place of Hobbes's stringent intel-

[1] [*A Brief View and*] *Survey* [*of the dangerous and pernicious errors to Church and
State in Mr Hobbes's book entitled Leviathan*. Oxford 1676], p. 202. Hyde is here
referring to and quoting Hobbes's words in the third paragraph of chapter 32
of *Leviathan*.

lectual discipline had nothing but a sense of history and a grasp of where he stood in relation to its contemporary processes. Secondly, the spirit of the work was almost as thoroughly political as Hobbes's exposition of the principles of a Christian Commonwealth. Hyde was later[1] to take exception to Hobbes's narrowly political conception of salvation, but the circumstances and the preoccupations of his mind in 1650 were as potent in making him susceptible to the predominantly this-worldly and matter-of-fact spirit of the Psalms as a particular philosophical outlook had done in the case of Hobbes. Hyde's version, it is true, was not at all exclusively political and mundane in the deliberate and systematic manner of Hobbes. His was a political salvationism in circumstances which seemed directly to sanction and to call for it. But he was only less bold than Hobbes in the way he wrested the divine oracles into the categories of political requirements.

Though Hyde stressed in writing on Psalm lxix that 'the entire scope and intention of the Scripture seems not more directed to any one particular, than to prevent and root out that opinion upon success, indeed to prepare men to expect it, and foresee that the endeavours of the worst men will be crowned with success to their hearts' desire, and that the just and faithful persons must look for trouble and oppression...',[2] notwithstanding this admission made in the course of the original meditations, he was to tell his children in the Prefatory Epistle to the completed *Contemplations*, dated February 1671, that the more he had read and revolved the subject-matter of the Psalms, 'the inevitable judgements pronounced upon prosperous wickedness, pride and oppression; and the protection and exaltation promised to those who suffer unjustly, and are not weary of their innocence, nor depart from

[1] *Survey*. In the remarks on Hobbes's chapter 38.
[2] *Contemplations* [*and Reflections on the Psalms of David. Miscellaneous Works of the Rt. Hon. Edward Earl of Clarendon*, 1751], p. 545.

it upon any temptation, I found cause enough to believe, that both the one and the other might possibly fall out, and come to pass in this world, as it must unavoidably do in the next.'[1] He saw so vivid a description of the condition of the cause which he had espoused and so many lively promises of assistance that he was driven to see the Psalms as prophetic: 'methoughts the future was so evident, that the present ought not to be submitted to without some cheerfulness.'[2] That this was Hyde's attitude at the time and not merely retrospectively is shown by the fact that a statement to exactly the same effect is to be found in the exercise on Psalm xxii, and he wrote to Secretary Nicholas from Madrid in August 1650 in the same terms. He deplored the transactions with the Scots, but expressed confidence that 'they who shall in spite of all evil examples continue honest and steady to their good principles, what distresses soever they may for a time suffer, will in the end find happiness even in this world...'.[3]

The pattern of prophecy which Hyde saw in the Psalms was simple enough. Under Psalm iii (that is, one of those on which he wrote while in Jersey) he stated the matter comprehensively in terms of a distinction between 'the mere moral man' and the man of rational faith. The latter, fixed upon 'the clearest principles of truth' begins by doing all he can 'by honest industry and dexterity' to forward the just cause—a description which may be applied to Hyde's first or political phase: 'laziness and inactivity, and a stupid reliance upon Providence, without using those parts or powers, which God hath given him...is not agreeable to the duty of a Christian.' But if the use of those parts and powers be unavailing, he does not surrender to despair or to unprincipled opportunism. He proceeds to consider 'what God's part is', going on to revolve 'all His promises and engagements for the protection, preservation and redemption of those, who having performed their parts according to the abilities He hath

[1] Ibid. p. 370.   [2] Ibid. p. 382.   [3] *S.P. Clar.* III, p. 22.

given them...rely...upon His immediate vindication and assistance'. Making an act of faith that does not contradict though it goes beyond reason, he becomes 'quiet and un-projecting, and even unconcerned to help himself; and believes that his being so advances his recovery; and that God would have no partnership in His own proper work'. Meditating the example of an ancient ruler, he remembers the rebellion raised against King David and how far it went in success, how his whole kingdom was possessed by the insurgents, and the hearts of the people stolen from the king, how his retire-ment was pursued with reviling and treachery: 'so that to human understanding, never any condition of a king appeared more deplorable or desperate.' He recalls how the king 'relied still on God, and waited his leisure and influence, to divide those councils, which his own policy could not frus-trate; and to recall and reform those hearts, which his own innocence could not retain; and by a full conviction of their error, to force them from those who had stolen them from the king; and resting quiet under this expectation and confidence, he quickly found, that he was sustained by a strength that could not fail him; and that the number of his enemies did but increase their own confusion'. When the man who was more than merely moral remembered all this, he composed himself, concluding, that however hopeless his position might appear, God would, if he continued innocent, 'as soon as it is fit, restore him to his right; and not only weaken his enemies, that they shall be able to do him no more hurt, but even humble them to sorrow and shame, for the injury they have done'.[1]

The belief in a divine judgement upon the violent party which would take the form of the bringing of divisions and confusions upon them, divisions and confusions which would, in their turn, work in favour of a reconstruction of the original order, is expressed also in the remarks upon Psalms xviii, xxxii,

[1] *Contemplations*, pp. 387, 388.

xxxvii, liv, lix and lxiii. But another aspect of the matter, a sense of a judgement that embraced not only the violent party but also the nation as a whole, including the King's adherents, is also in evidence. It is summed up in a passage, parallel with the *Contemplations*, in a letter written in March 1650. 'But I have long thought our nation will be either utterly extinguished under this great judgement, or be restored and preserved by such an extraordinary way, as we shall not be able to assume any part of it to our own wits and dexterity; for methinks, God Almighty exceedingly discountenances all the designs which our natural reason is apt to flatter us with.'[1] This passage brings out an idea which is deeply embedded in the *History*, the idea that the country as a whole had brought the Civil War upon itself, and, further, that the innocence of the King's adherents was deeply qualified both by their membership in the nation as a whole, and by their complicity in the origins of the troubles, and also by their innumerable deviations and delinquencies in the course of the war and in the subsequent diplomatic transactions with the victors. Not only was inactivity on the part of the King's adherents justified in so far as they were innocent, and so a privilege. It was required by past departures from that state, and so a punishment. The sword of judgement was two-edged. It smote the King's enemies, but it also smote his friends, and that was a consideration especially relevant to the situation, since the debacle had served to intensify Hyde's critical attitude to the Royalists.

A sense that there was no future, that the disaster was irreparable, is not surprising if the background against which Hyde was writing is appreciated. Charles I had been done to death. Everything for which Hyde had stood, whether or not the late king had agreed with him in standing for it also, lay now in ruins. He was on a distant and hopeless mission to an indifferent Court. The new King, after casting about, had

[1] *S.P. Clar.* II, p. 529.

committed himself to what Hyde regarded as a disastrous alliance with the Scots. It was far from certain that Charles would ever listen to Hyde, and he did not know that his part as councillor had not come to an end altogether.[1] For Hyde there was now nothing certainly left to do but to rejoice in a good conscience on his own account, and, when that event had taken place, to remark the judgement meted out to the Scots in their defeat at the hands of Cromwell. But it must be understood that the contemplation by Hyde of the possibility of ultimate irretrievable failure was not a lapse on his part into passive recognition that the entire scope and intention of the Scripture was to demonstrate that just causes had no right to expect this-worldly vindications. Instead, it was an implied criticism of a Royalist policy which could not, he was convinced, merit success. It must not be supposed that Hyde's reflexions on the Psalms can be dismissed as a train of pious truisms, in no significant relationship either with the *History* or with his judgement on contemporary events. As a matter of fact it was the latter, his judgement on contemporary events, which was primary and gave shape both to the *History* and the *Contemplations*. Fundamental to his attitude was his disapproval of Royalist policy, and the disapproval sprang from a sense of the long-term processes of English politics. Of these processes he remained incurably hopeful provided they were not incorrectly handled.

All the elements of the analysis were present in the period before he went to Madrid, and date, in fact, from the time he spent in Jersey. In November 1646 he had written:[2] 'truly I do not more believe that this odious rebellion hath brought all these calamities and miseries upon our poor country than I fear that the atheism of those that have heartily opposed the rebellion will continue, and increase those calamities and

---

[1] Hyde to Nicholas: 19 October 1650. *S.P. Clar.* III, p. 24.
[2] Hyde to Berkeley: Jersey, 21 November 1646. Clar. MSS. 28, 293. See also Hyde to Nicholas: 15 November 1646. *S.P. Clar.* II, p. 285.

miseries.' On the other hand he was declaring in the same period the inevitability of divisions amongst the victors: 'if those men of mettle quietly sit down and enjoy the fruits of their prosperous wickedness, I shall think Christianity itself suffers more than it hath done, since it was first planted'.[1] He announced that he was in favour of keeping both the Presbyterians and the Independents at arms' length, and that he expected 'no great good from either, till they have bettered their understandings, and reformed their consciences by drinking deep in each other's blood'.[2] 'I confess I have not skill or charity enough to know which of the two factions, Presbyterians or Independents, to pray for, but am very willing they should be let alone a while to convert one another, till they do both mend.'[3] Left alone, these parties would either destroy or convert one another to the point of view as yet held by neither and then 'whoever shall by God's blessing be able to preserve his conscience and his courage very few years, will find himself wished for again in his country, and may see good days again'.[2] Earlier still, it appears to have been an argument against the Prince of Wales going to France, that such an action would hinder the division between Presbyterians and Independents from taking effect.[4] Hyde made his point explicitly at the end of 1646 in a letter to Nicholas,[5] and again early in 1647 to Culpepper: 'And, to my understanding, it is much more natural to expect a restoration...from the faction, animosity and disunion between the Rebels upon their managery and disposition of the spoil,'[6] than from the King yielding to their demands in an attempt to reach a settlement. In the 'abortive declaration' drawn up early in 1649 in which Hyde had outlined a platform for Charles II to adopt after the death of his father, a platform which was rejected by the rest of the new King's

[1] Hyde to Cottington: 12 February 1647. Clar. MSS. 29, 103.
[2] S.P. Clar. II, p. 286.   [3] Clar. MSS. 29, 52.
[4] S.P. Clar. II, p. 276.   [5] Ibid. p. 308: 12 December 1646.
[6] Ibid. p. 326.

advisers, there is a trenchant statement of the proposition that the victors of the war agreed only in their opposition to the order overthrown, and that between them there was no 'union to settle any new form of government', and that this might 'appear some instance of [God's] future mercy and purpose'[1]. In March 1650 Hyde told Sir John Berkeley, who differed on the point, that the best thing to do was to 'sit still and expect some advantages by the enemy's distractions'.[2]

This conviction could not by itself have justified the position he had adopted. Together with the confident expectation of the benefits to be derived from the inevitable disunion between the violent parties who now dominated the scene in England, there lay in Hyde's mind another belief, a belief to which he gave expression as early as the former and which was indeed inseparable from it. In May 1646 he told Jermyn, in connexion with the projected voyage of the Prince to France, that 'the resurrection of the English loyalty and courage (wherever it may be encouraged by some neighbour, power, and strength) can only restore the King...'.[3] He repeated this statement to Nicholas at the end of the year, and went on to say that he comforted himself with the hope that the English would hereafter (though possibly he might be dead first) repair the breaches they had made, vindicate their loyalty and religion, and entertain their neighbours with the stories of their well-employed valour, as they did now with their romance of treason and rebellion.[4] To Culpepper in January 1647 he wrote in the same terms: the faction, animosity and disunion among the victors was one factor working to produce restoration, 'a resurrection of the English affection and loyalty'[5] was the other. In the operation of these two factors it is not too much to say that he continued to believe, not only in the years immediately following the defeat, but even after the

[1] *E.H.R.* VIII, p. 303.
[2] *S.P. Clar.* II, p. 522.
[3] Ibid. p. 234.
[4] Ibid. p. 307.
[5] Ibid. p. 326.

establishment of Cromwell's power and right up to the point
in 1660 when the belief was triumphantly vindicated.

In the first phase it had been Hyde's assumption that it was
only the threat of force by the King and then the misuse of it
which had enabled a suspension of loyalty to take place; in
other words, the outbreak and then the continuation of the
Civil War. As for the idea of the employment of foreign force,
such a prospect had been not only abhorrent to him, but
practically incredible from the days when the belief that the
King intended to use it against Parliament had been a factor
in the mistrust of him leading to Civil War, and whether he
was thinking of the importation of the Scots by the Parliamentary leaders or of the King's projects of relying on the
Irish or the French, his objection was one and the same and
unqualified. These views were based not on a sense of what
was politic but on the fact that he shared the sentiments which
such intentions or such actions outraged. His views on this
matter in the second phase were a continuation of those of
the first. If there were peace between France and Spain, and
they proceeded to unite to restore the King of England, 'Lord
have mercy upon poor England! for I do more fear a French
army than the Presbyterians and Independents...sure a
foreign aid (except of arms and money) will never reconcile
those hearts and affections to the King and his Posterity, without which he hath no hope of reigning'. There could never
be a resurrection of the loyalty of the English 'if they are made
a conquered people'.[1]

Hyde enlarged on this matter to John Earle, who had been
a fellow member of Falkland's circle of pre-war days. Earle
had suggested, apparently, that the greater part of men in
England could not be identified with that *Patria* towards which
Hyde was expressing his attachment. Yet 'even to those',
Hyde urged, 'there is a great proportion of compassion due.

[1] Hyde to Nicholas: Jersey, 12 December 1646. *S.P. Clar.* II, p. 307. Hyde
to Lord Bristol: 12 December 1646. Clar. MSS. 29, 3.

For if we have a natural affection and sympathy with the very air, climate, and situation, sure our affections ought not to be dead to the inhabitants, under any abstracted notions of good and bad, right and wrong, true and false.' 'And I pray God, the want even of this charity when we were in our country, of a due sense of our loss when we got most, hath not been in the number of those faults, for which He hath suffered us to be driven out of our country.' Moreover, the *Patria* was to be considered as inseparable from

the form, frame, and constitution of government to which all men owe their safety and subsistence; and any expedient that is in order to this, what destruction soever it is likely to bring to the opposers, ought to be seconded and assisted by all good men. Therefore if I have any pauses in their enterprises of foreign force, it is not out of tenderness to faulty persons, but out of apprehension that the frame of government would be more absolutely suppressed by those friends, than it is like to be by the other enemies, from whom it may be thought more capable of being redeemed by the experience, faction, and interest of themselves, than by the strength of a foreign un-concerned power'.[1]

And though in the 'abortive declaration' of 1649 he would have had the King publicly promise himself that he could count on the assistance of all Christian princes 'as in a joint quarrel and joint interest',[2] in a paper[3] on relations with the English parties delivered before his Spanish journey, he stressed nothing so much as the need of inculcating the belief that the King had no thought of conquering his subjects with foreign arms, and that nothing short of 'inevitable necessity' would drive him to such an expedient. The views expounded in this document, he said, were not the views of the men in whom the Queen-Mother was disposed to confide, but they were the views of a man not unacquainted with 'the humours

[1] *S.P. Clar.* II, p. 340.   [2] *E.H.R.* VIII, p. 306.
[3] [*The*] *Nicholas Papers*, [Camden Society, 1886,] I, p. 138. See also, *A full Answer*.

and tempers' which were involved, of a man not ill versed in the affairs of the King as they touched 'the nature of Englishmen'.[1]

'The rebellion and wickedness of a nation,' he wrote under Psalm xxxvii, 'may be so odious to God Almighty, that He will no more vouchsafe to give them a King to reign over them; and then both the Prince, and such subjects who continue faithful to him, must be involved in that punishment.'[2] He told a correspondent, as we have seen, that in his judgement the nation would either be 'utterly extinguished', or restoration would come in 'an extraordinary way' in which the action of the King's supporters would have no part. But if he had always possessed and contrived to maintain, as indeed he had done, this faith in the resurrection of loyalty, the scales were at once weighted on the side of the restoration, though in an extraordinary way. The punishment must fit the crime. If the nation as a whole, as distinct from certain individuals, had avoided extremes of depravity, and could be expected to demonstrate the fact in the future, it might be believed that the extreme penalty would be avoided and the old constitution restored. He was convinced (and he reiterated the conviction)[3] that the strength of both the Presbyterian and the Independent parties was based on the misguided concurrence with the leaders of men who were in themselves fundamentally honest and who wished 'the same peace the King himself doth'. Men joined the Presbyterians on the platform of their monarchic pretensions and out of fear of the subversive tenets of the Independents. On the other hand, men submitted to the Independent leaders from disapproval of Presbyterian Church doctrines and out of hostility to Scottish intervention in England. Both 'parties were made up of those who were

---

[1] *S.P. Clar.* III, p. 6.   [2] *Contemplations*, p. 468.
[3] Hyde to Nicholas: Jersey, 15 November 1646. *S.P. Clar.* II, p. 286. Hyde to Nicholas: Jersey, 12 December 1646. Ibid. p. 307. Hyde to Jermyn, 8 January 1647. Clar. MSS. 29, 52. *Nicholas Papers*, I, p. 143.

enemies to the principles of either'. The main body of each party would be happy to see their leaders hanged: 'the strength of either party consists principally of those who would be well enough contented to see the confusion of their own chief rulers... the body of both [parties] would be honestly applied.'

In so far as Hyde believed that there was nothing to choose between the alternatives which he put, and squarely contemplated 'utter extinction', he was guided by solid political judgement which was profound enough to be extraordinarily prophetic. As early as December 1646,[1] he was saying that the greatest danger in the future was that the Independents would resort to a conservative policy and, exploiting the traditionalism of the country, effect a restoration of destroyed or threatened institutions, though to the exclusion of the rightful dynasty. The concrete issue, therefore, was between a development of this kind and a resurrection of loyalty to the advantage of the King. Even the former assumed the vigour of the country's institutions and the continuity of its ideas, and such a development could hardly be described as the bringing of 'complete desolation' upon the country, a contingency he envisaged in the meditation on Psalm xxxvii. It would be a punishment more of the King and of the Royalists than of the nation—an appropriate consequence of their having allied themselves with Scottish Presbyterian invaders on the latter's terms, thereby harnessing English patriotism to the cause of the Independents.

It is clear, therefore, that Hyde brought to the exercise on the Psalms a pre-existing analysis of the political situation which slipped with the greatest of ease into the categories of the Psalmist. All that the latter did was to give to pre-existing ideas a simplicity and a tenacity which helped them to survive ten years of waiting. Hyde discerned, he said, 'that

---

[1] Hyde to Nicholas: 12 December 1646. *S.P. Clar.* II, p. 307. Hyde to Jermyn: 8 January 1647. Clar. MSS. 29, 52.

what I laboured and longed for, could not come to pass by any hand that held a sceptre upon earth; that He only who could pull down all other Kings, and bring desolation upon all other nations, could raise the low and miserable estate of my King and country; and I must confess the frequent reading of the Psalms of David gave me great hopes He would do it'.[1] Hyde believed at that time and continued to believe until it came to pass that the work would be done by Providence, by the necessities of history. Providence, he now held, having in the outbreak of the troubles and in the course which they took brought judgement upon the people's failings, would, under certain conditions which were themselves under its mastership, undo the destruction which had taken place. No principles of action could, he assumed, be effective which were not in conformity with a moral order which maintained itself in unshakable and relentless majesty. The King's opponents had committed themselves to evil courses. That they had done so would be proved by succeeding events, in the sense that succeeding events would punish them. But that did not mean that the Royalists could now hope to achieve their aims by political or military action. Most of what Hyde had had to say about them from the very outset of his career was critical, and he had begun the *History* in 1646 largely as a criticism, for the King's benefit, of royalist actions. After the war there was in his view too much activity which misconceived the aim, supposing that any kind of restoration of the King was admissible, and too much that was mistaken as to method.

Hyde was by no means unique in holding that the victors in the war would perish through their divisions. Indeed, the words addressed to his captors after the last battle by Sir Jacob Astley, 'You have now done your work, and may go play, unless you will fall out amongst yourselves', might have served as the inspiration of most subsequent royalist policy. Queen Henrietta Maria acted on the belief that they would

[1] *Contemplations*, p. 370.

fall out amongst themselves and so did Charles I. But it was precisely the fact that they acted which annulled in Hyde's eyes the effectiveness of their belief. The Queen, for instance, backed by Digby, would have had the King accept presbyterianism in 1646 at the time of the Newcastle propositions as a method of setting Presbyterians and Independents by the ears. That this was not what Hyde meant by relying on divisions amongst the victorious factions can be seen by his own comment upon the episode.

For the propositions, whoever understands them...cannot imagine that, being once consented unto, there are any seeds left for Monarchy to spring out of, and the stratagem of yielding to them to make the quarrel the more popular, and to divide the Presbyterians and Independents, is so far above my politics, that I am confident a general horror and infidelity will attend the person that submits to them, after the infamy of such a submission; and if I know anything of the King's heart or nature, he will not redeem the lives of his wife and children at the price, though he were sure they would not be consented unto when he had done.[1]

Hyde was correct about Charles I's attitude, but even Charles I, and indeed, since it was he who played the chief part on the scene till January 1649, Charles I most of all, offended by Hyde's standard. Charles believed his enemies would end by destroying one another. Indeed, he alone seems to have agreed with Hyde in thinking that it was possible to avoid ruin without surrendering either to the one party or to the other. He alone was as adamant and uncompromising at heart as Hyde presumably could have desired, but he still concurred with his wife and her advisers that the disintegration to which his enemies were self-condemned could be promoted by an active diplomacy. Preserving his conscience inviolate, as he held, and yet at the same time following the suggestions of the Queen, he was prepared again and again to negotiate on terms which he

[1] Hyde to Berkeley: 16 August 1646. Clar. MSS. 28, 178–9.

had no intention of accepting. Upon such conduct as upon all the rest there was a cumulative judgement or, in political language, of all this there were inevitable consequences in failure and disrepute, and even those who were not guilty must share in the judgement and suffer the consequences. 'Methinks God Almighty exceedingly discountenances all the designs which our natural reason is apt to flatter us with.'

Action from any side or by any party, Hyde held in the historical detachment which he had now achieved, necessarily produced in such circumstances as had come to prevail the opposite of what was intended. The violent parties in England must clash, and either destroy or weaken one another. Action by the Royalists with the assistance of forces sent by a European prince or combination of princes, supposing it were procurable (which Hyde generally held to be unlikely) and supposing it were successful, would defeat its end by enslaving the country and altering its institutions. Such a method was more likely to fail by rousing the whole nation to resist its application, cementing it against the old dynasty. Military action by the Royalists alone was almost certain to fail, and would only serve to counteract the natural working of fissiparous tendencies within the body of their opponents, intensify amongst the people the stupefaction already induced by the military success of the King's enemies, and pile new miseries upon his friends in England. Royalist enterprises in league with the Scots were either open to the same objections as expeditions from the Continent, or they must amount to a self-translation by the King from his own realm of immediate impotence into that of the long-term self-frustration of the English factions. The whole situation viewed from whatever angle had a curse on it. But the curse from its very comprehensiveness contained a promise of deliverance. No doubt the rebellious leaders 'will be very unwilling to declare that they have been all this time out of their wits, yet when they have turned round a little longer, they must upon the matter confess it and end where they began, without removing foundations...'.[1] Judgement would also be mercy. Providence would bring recovery in the face of every positive action for or against it.

The method of Providence in undoing the destruction was by placing from the outset limits upon the workings of the destructive forces. First, there was the conduct of the main body of Englishmen. Hyde never surrendered the conviction that the nation as a whole had not willed rebellion. Total national apostasy and corruption were not for him the explanation of what had happened. All his activity in the political phase had been based on a directly contrary conviction. Settlement on what he believed were universally acceptable principles, those of 1640–1, had always been just round the corner throughout that period, and had been frustrated only by the interaction of the King's mistakes and the skill of the violent party in Parliament. It was not now a question, therefore, of expecting Providence to restore the Kingdom to Israel in total despite of that nation. Completing, after the Restoration and in his final exile, the story begun in Jersey, and writing of the year 1645, he was anxious that the reader should not picture 'a universal corruption of the hearts of the whole nation'.[2] The lamentable events he described 'proceeded only from the folly and the frowardness, from the weakness and the wilfulness, the pride and the passion of particular persons'. He would not have the infamy of the few laid upon the age in which they had lived. In that age there was as much loyalty and integrity as there had been in the past. But this opinion is in conformity with views expressed closer to the events in question. Hyde opened[3] the original *History* with a similar statement of conviction. That 'less than a general combination,' and universal apostasy in the whole nation' could explain the rebellion and its success, was

---

[1] Hyde to Lady Dalkeith: 15 December 1646 (o.s.). Clar. MSS. 29, 11.
[2] Clarendon, *History*, IV, p. 2.   [3] Ibid. I, pp. 1, 2.

an opinion which though plausible he was determined to disprove. It is true that he had in mind chiefly that part of the nation that remained faithful after the defeat. Even so, the next paragraph indicates that the part allocated to the nation as a whole was to be infatuated and blinded. 'The poor people [were] furiously hurried' into complicity in actions of which they did not and perhaps could not see the import. Indeed, in a pamphlet[1] written in 1655, he went so far as to declare that to have escaped being deceived in the 'current of these last fifteen years' would have required a disposition so uncharitable and distrustful as could hardly be imagined. He had watched the process of deception at close quarters in the phase of his political activity.

In a famous passage of the *History* Hyde described the un-paralleled prosperity enjoyed by the kingdom on the very eve of the calamity of the Civil War. This recognition on his part of what is an indisputable fact so far at least as the gentry were concerned, itself had a history rooted in his own political experience. 'Could humanity', says Hume, 'ever attain happiness, the condition of the English gentry at this period might merit that appellation.' Those who had accepted the narrative part of the Grand Remonstrance, the interpretation of the preceding period put forward by the revolutionaries, would certainly not have agreed. Hyde had begun the process of adopting an interpretation which was nearer to the facts as they had affected his own class, and he had embarked on the rejection of an interpretation which was inaccurate save as it could be applied for demagogic reasons to the con-dition of the mass of the people which had indeed been much less satisfactory, because in the debate on the Grand Remon-

---

[1] *A letter [from a true and lawful member of Parliament, and one faithfully engaged with it from the beginning of the war to the end, to one of the Lords of his Highness' Council, upon occasion of the late Declaration showing the reasons of the proceedings for securing the peace of the Commonwealth, published on the 31st of October, 1655].* See *Calendar of the Clarendon State Papers preserved in the Bodleian Library*, III, 1876, p. 79.

strance he had been concerned to argue against looking too far back. He had meant that the interpretation of the reign given in the Remonstrance was unnecessarily offensive to the King. He had moved a step forward in his answer to the Remonstrance which had been adopted by Charles. In order to back the case that the King would accept the work of parliament, he had drawn attention to the peace and plenty of the previous period inferring that it reflected at least a measure of benevolence on the part of the King's earlier government. He had not denied at that time the arbitrary character of that government any more than he denied it now, but when in the late spring of 1642 he had turned against the violent party in the declarations, he had proclaimed that the system Pym was erecting was at least as arbitrary as the rule of the prerogative in the period before 1640 had been. He had soon found that he could truthfully say that the country had been better off in the 1630's that it was in 1642.

Led in this way to appreciate a fact, the appreciation of which was necessarily denied to the violent party, Hyde found that it assisted his own interpretation of the roots of the cataclysm. Such prosperity, he now explained, had itself been an introduction to folly: 'all these blessings could but enable, not compel, us to be happy: we wanted that sense, acknowledgement, and value of our own happiness which all but we had...'. The Court had been full of excess, idleness and luxury, and the country full of pride, mutiny and discontent; 'every man more troubled and perplexed at that they called the violation of one law, than delighted or pleased with the observation of all the rest of the charter: never imputing the increase of their receipts, revenue and plenty to the wisdom, virtue and merit of the Crown, but objecting every little trivial imposition to the exorbitancy and tyranny of the government...'.[1] If 'God sends the blessing of peace, and plenty, and reputation upon a kingdom and nation, that

[1] Clarendon, *History*, I, p. 96.

religion flourishes, and justice is well administered in it, that their affection and alliance is valued and desired by their neighbours, there are so many sharers in this transcendent prosperity, that scarce a particular man thinks it worth his particular acknowledgement....'[1]

Such states of mind provided the material out of which the minority of those inspired by malice and ambition, and so positively corrupt, were able to fabricate subversion. This material, however, would not have been malleable enough apart from the only too real 'distempers and exorbitances of government' for which the King's advisers were responsible, and 'which prepared the people to submit to the fury of the Parliament'. In religion, there were the indiscretions in the administrations of the two Archbishops, Abbott and Laud, to which had to be added the very unfortunate papal missions of Panzani, Con and Rossetti, missions of which Hyde took so grave a view that he declared them to have been analogous in the realm of religion to ship-money.[2] There were the offences against liberty and property, culminating in ship-money itself. There were the twin and inter-connected distempers of an excessive clerical influence in the civil government of the State, and of the bad blood between the clergy and the common lawyers. Hyde observed in his exercise on Psalm lix that 'since every sin is an opposition of His will and directions, it is God's usual method to punish sinners by others who are most opposite to the sins they practised'. Superstition and formalism in religion breed and are put down by their opposites, sacrilege and profanity. Rigidity and literalism in the administration of justice, divorced from 'a prudent consideration of the spirit and distemper of times', produce and are rectified by an overthrow of the whole principle of legality. An uncritical loyalism, confusing the fashions and excess of the court with the proper detachment of the council chamber, is corrected

[1] *Contemplations*, p. 493.   [2] *S.P. Clar.* II, p. 336.

by a licentious republicanism.[1] The important thing in Hyde's explanation is his insistence that the people were almost inevitably and almost guiltlessly led astray by those who created the violent party, given that they were already predisposed to err for one reason or another, and given what was in his judgement the worst of all the mistakes which had been committed in Charles I's earlier government, namely the mishandling and too hasty dissolution of, and too long intermissions between parliaments.

I cannot but let myself loose to say, that no man can show me a source from whence those waters of bitterness we now taste have more probably flowed, than from this unseasonable, unskilful and precipitate dissolution of parliaments; in which, by an unjust survey of the passion, isolence, and ambition of particular persons, the Court measured the temper and affection of the country; and by the same standard the people considered the honour, justice, and piety of the Court; and so usually parted, at those sad seasons, with no other respect and charity one toward the other than accompanies persons who never meant to meet but in their own defence.[2]

Hyde confessed himself amazed at the way the earlier parliaments had been handled by those who, like Buckingham and Weston, had advised the King. For though there had been 'several passages, and distempered speeches of particular persons' the bulk of the membership had throughout been 'very applicable to the public ends'. 'And whoever considers the acts of power and injustice in the intervals of parliaments, will not be much scandalised at the warmth and vivacity of those meetings.'[3] By protecting his servants from the threat of impeachment, Charles had merely increased the presupposition of their guilt. It would have been better to have let them stand their trial. In fact, Hyde said, not only had no innocent man suffered in those times by judgement of

[1] *Contemplations*, pp. 519–20. [2] Clarendon, *History* I, p. 5.
[3] Ibid. pp. 5, 6.

Parliament, but several guilty ones had been acquitted. 'But the course of exempting men from prosecution by dissolving of parliaments made the power of parliaments much more formidable, as conceived to be without limit.' The intermission of them, moreover, had encouraged in the royal ministers a sense of impunity. 'Whereas, if [parliaments] had been frequently summoned, and seasonably dissolved after their wisdom in applying medicines and cures, as well as their industry in discovering diseases, had been discerned, they would easily have been applied to the uses for which they were first instituted, and been of no less esteem with the crown than of veneration with the people.'[1]

The people had thus been made ready to submit to the final fury of the violent party, and it had to be understood that the main part in preparing them, above all in this last most important matter, had been a royalist part. The very violence, however, with which the pendulum had swung in the direction of an inflated and credulous parliamentarism was a guarantee that it would swing back again. The grim experiences following the King's defeat would bring people to their senses. 'Patience, John, and the scene will change', Hyde adjured Sir John Berkeley early in 1647:[2]

It is most demonstrable, that either no peace can be made, that the worst man discreetly can rely upon for his own interest, or it must be upon the old foundations of Government in Church and State, resuming such reformations as shall be thought reasonable to soberer times. And how ridiculous soever this seems, it will appear more necessary, the nearer men draw to the conclusion. And even they who are most peremptory against it now, will every day meet with somewhat in their journey, that will reform them.

'But that which works generally', he told the more sympathetic Hopton later in the same year,[3] 'is the experience,

[1] Ibid. pp. 9, 10. [2] S.P. Clar. II, p. 333.
[3] 9 June 1647. Ibid. p. 369.

that the alteration designed cannot be made without a long continued vast charge, and trouble of an army; and that that army cannot be kept with their security, and therefore they had rather things were as they have been, than pay so dear for the alteration.' In the 'abortive declaration' of 1649 after the execution of Charles I, in which the only offer to be made by the King was a free Parliament, a synod to settle the Church, and a free pardon for all but his father's murderers, Hyde had intended to point out that events should by now have demonstrated to the people the hollowness of the rebels' constitutional pretensions, that results achieved by the sword must be maintained thereby, and that the prospect now was nothing but 'a perpetual and everlasting war, though there should be no visible enemy to contend with'.[1] It was the ignorant passion of the people which had given the violent men their opportunity and their power. What they had made of it would encourage a revulsion of feeling equally strong, but, this time, wiser. In such terms, he wrote to Nicholas as late as July 1653.[2]

It was now, therefore, a doctrine to which Hyde explicitly subscribed that the only possible government for England, in the long view, was the old one as it had emerged purged and renovated in 1640–1, since that was the only one which accorded with the old-established habits and also with the recently accumulated experience of the nation. He did not regard himself as crying in the wilderness that he knew something which no one else knew or could know unless he told them. He was not proclaiming a political revelation as Hobbes was doing. It was part of the substance of his belief that others should hold it, and should hold it, not because he was there to explain it to them, but because experience would bring them to it of their own accord. He pointed to, and relied upon a process which would unfold its own argument.

[1] *E.H.R.* VIII, p. 302.
[2] 11 July. *S.P. Clar.* III, p. 178.

'Truly this genius and constitution of the Kingdom in which all Englishmen are jointly concerned, will be a trusty champion to recover all that is lost, if we have patience and constancy to rely on it.'[1] The genius and constitution of which he was speaking were nothing less than that law could not be changed by force, but only by consent, and men could not but come to see, he believed, that what the King had claimed to stand for in 1642, that he could not and should not be compelled to accept changes against his will, was as much their concern as his: 'the interest of him who hath plundered himself into an estate of a thousand pounds being as much concerned in that foundation, as his, who was born to £10,000 a year.'[2]

It was this same insight which lay behind Hyde's fears regarding the future conduct of the Independents. For

to think that those who have good fortunes and excellent understandings, have a design to dissolve monarchy and change the government which would carry away with it so much of the common law, as would shake their own property and every part of their condition, which made life pleasant to them, or that they are not themselves now more afraid of the people than ever they pretended to be of tyranny, is such an independency upon reason, as I believe no Independent of either House is guilty of, though they have no other way of keeping up their party than by conniving at all licence and opinion of equality which yet they restrain as far as is necessary to their business in hand.[3]

It would appear that Hyde had early taken into account the part which the interest of the propertied classes was playing in the politics of the Revolution. The royal government before the war had made as if it threatened property from above. But the Revolution threw up elements that questioned the land law and the existing system of property rights, threatening

[1] Hyde to Culpepper: 20 August 1648 (o.s.). *S.P. Clar.* ii, p. 411.
[2] Ibid.
[3] Hyde to Jermyn: 8 January 1647. Clar. MSS. 29, 52.

them from below. The fact that the assault upon the monarchy however limited in aim seemed as if it might start a landslide and carry away with it the very positions from which and on behalf of which the original attack had been launched was a fact of which Hyde was aware, and he seems to have counted on it to work to the King's advantage. The reciprocity for which Hyde had pleaded at the time of the Grand Remonstrance had contained an appeal to self-interest: and thereafter, in 1642, in the campaign of manifestos against the violent party, he had indicted them as constituting a worse threat to property rights than Strafford had done, and had sought to identify the cause of the property-owner with that of the King. In the war, it was often the well-to-do on the opposing side who were in favour of an accommodation with the King. Hyde's description of the negotiations at Oxford shows that he was aware of the fact.[1] Whether he was aware of it in 1643, it is impossible to say. But it is clear that at a time when the Levellers had become prominent he expected that the equation between the interest of property and the interest of the monarchy would not be hard to demonstrate.

Certainly the process of education which Hyde believed in might be a lengthy and a bitter one. The fact that men feared for their property rights at the hands of extremer elements meant that, however much they might chafe under military rule and the heavy taxation which it involved, they had still to regard the *de facto* government as affording some protection, and so requiring some support. Hyde committed himself to no estimate of the time the process would take to complete itself. 'Believe it Mr Secretary, it is not possible to see peace in England, till there be some great examples of God's justice and indignation upon the principal heads of this Rebellion; and I fear equal judgements upon the atheism of those, who have been enemies enough to the Rebellion.'[2] By 1647, for

[1] *Life*, III, p. 151.
[2] Hyde to Nicholas: 15 November 1646. *S.P. Clar.* II, p. 286.

instance, men had not had time to be convinced: 'it not being for God to wrap up the horrible impiety and inhumanity of the people in a sudden calm'.[1] Painful experience must be allowed to do its whole work. The conservative reaction noticeable after the first Civil War did not, Hyde thought, indicate a change of heart. Let it not, he said, in June 1647,[2] be overvalued 'as if it proceeded from the pure act of conscience upon a repentance of what they have done ill, and from the love and reverence to the old form of Government'. He hoped many were indeed converted, but feared it was too soon to expect it. He feared that at that stage the change had got as far only as a negative disapproval of the weight of the army and was not yet a positive approval of the old government. Nevertheless, he believed that general conversion would infallibly take place.

It was folly to rush in with a policy of constitutional compromise which would disband the army before the pathological aspects of parliamentarism had worked themselves out: 'you shall find the people so well satisfied with any alteration which shall lessen the power of the Crown', he told Hopton in connexion with the Newport negotiations, 'that it will never be possible to recover them; and the House of Peers shall be more grievous to the King than the House of Commons hath lately been'. Such action was unnecessary and would do great damage: 'Let me persuade you, as you have ventured your life and lost your fortune and your blood in the defence of your Country, so do not think you have preserved it when you have bartered away those fundamental rights, upon which the constitution of it is founded.'[3] It was not only that such action might be fatal to the monarchy considered in isolation. As a Parliamentarian he had repudiated in 1643, and still repudiated the old doctrine that a statute might be *ultra vires*.

---

[1] Hyde to Berkeley: 28 January 1647. Ibid. p. 333.
[2] Hyde to Hopton. Ibid. p. 369.
[3] Hyde to Hopton: 9 June 1647. Ibid. pp. 369–70.

There was nothing King and Parliament could not do between them. King and Parliament, together, 'may destroy foundations':[1] they had the constitutional right to work constitutional havoc. If the King made himself a party to such a settlement as was proposed he would seal and crystallize the distempers and disorders of the day. Whereas if he abstained, they would not only ultimately cure themselves, but his abstention would actually forward the cure.

Chaos and tyranny are the words which can be used to sum up Hyde's view of the Presbyterian and Independent parties, respectively. The original nucleus of the rebellion, Hyde always held, was a small one. Its political effectiveness was derived from the support of those who had put their own interpretation upon the claims of the violent party leaders or had thrown in their hands with them at different stages for a variety of reasons, some good, some bad, some public, some private. This fact he held to be true of rebellions in general, and an observation made in 1670 is in conformity with the attitude he adopted whilst the English upheavals were in progress and which he embodied in the *History*. 'The strength of rebellion consists in the private gloss which every man makes to himself upon the declared argument of it, not upon the reasons published and avowed, how specious and popular soever.'[2] He described the 'ridiculous lying, to win the affections and corrupt the understandings of the weak, and the bold scandals to confirm the wilful; the boundless promises they presented to the ambitious, and their gross, abject flatteries and applications to the vulgar-spirited....'[3] He showed how the violent party were concerned tactically to exploit the private gloss, to bolster ambiguities, and to dispense in the earlier stages with a too wholehearted con-

[1] Hyde to Earle: 12 February 1647. *S.P. Clar.* II, p. 338.
[2] *Essays* [*Moral and Entertaining on the various Faculties and Passions of the Human Mind.* 1815], I, p. 144.
[3] Clarendon, *History*, I, p. 430. See also p. 2.

currence with their own definite political aims.[1] But this original group, the violent party, now the Presbyterians, was itself lacking in that unity and positive character which could drive through and mould to its will the complexities of motives and interpretation upon which it had founded its initial strength. Consequently, it remained too much at the mercy of the situation and insufficiently endowed with constructive statesmanship. No other kind of party could in Hyde's view have achieved the disruption of a state as securely founded as that of England. It was inevitable that the inner counsels of a party which made such a disruption should itself have been marked in a pronounced degree by the presence of the private gloss. Thus it possessed strength to breach, but only to breach the unity of the State. The political distempers which had given Pym's leadership its chance dogged and remained engrained in the life of his party. It was this character which Hyde had himself tried to exploit in his political days, and which began to display itself after the war had begun to the detriment of the violent leaders.[2]

Hyde held that it was the tendency of rebellions to expire 'in a general detestation of the first promoters of them, by those who kept them company in the prosecution, and discover their ends to be very different from their profession'.[3] This was especially true of conditions in England. A natural phase of disintegration demanded a strength of leadership which especially after the death of Pym it was difficult to provide. The leaders lacked the equipment for dealing with a course of events which abated the original popular infatuation with parliaments. The support of ordinary men which Hyde held had been lost by the King through his own fault at the beginning of 1642 and which was gained by the violent party, afterwards became a liability to them. They lacked the energy to counteract centrifugal tendencies and they had been

[1] Cf. *Contemplations*, p. 411.   [2] Clarendon, *History*, II, pp. 495–6.
[3] *Essays*, I, p. 144.

and remained themselves a centrifugal group. 'Their councils', Hyde wrote, 'were most distracted and divided, being made up of many men whose humours and natures must be observed and complied with, and whose concurrence was necessary to the carrying on, though their inclinations did not concur in, the same designs.'[1] They lacked even the strong point of the Scottish Presbyterians. These, though they were chaotic, were nevertheless inspired by the fanaticism of the clergy. But the Scottish clergy were never in a position to bind the English Presbyterians with such cement. The English Presbyterians were and remained a loose association of grandees, gentry, clergy and townsfolk, an association held together by negatives.

But the nature of the Presbyterians and the nature of the situation engendered a second party and a second leadership as simple as the first had been confused, as strong as it had been weak. Looking back upon it, at a much later date, the government of Oliver Cromwell seemed to Hyde to have been conducted in accordance with the principles of Machiavelli in many, if not in all respects. Hyde held Machiavelli in high esteem as an exponent of the arts and processes of government. 'Machiavel was in the right, though he got an ill name by it with those who take what he says from the report of other men, or do not enough consider themselves what he says, and his method in speaking: he was as great an enemy to tyranny and injustice in any government as any man then was or now is'. But Machiavelli showed that once an insurrectionary government was set up, it 'must not think to prosecute' its tyranny 'by the rules of conscience, which was laid aside or subdued' before the first step was taken. The insurgents 'must make no scruple of doing all those impious things which are necessary to compass and support the impiety to which they have devoted themselves'.[2] Here, Hyde thought, the Presbyterians were at fault. They held that the means, first the

---

[1] Clarendon, *History*, IV, p. 303.   [2] Ibid. p. 304.

threat and then the resort to force, were justified by the end, but the end took for granted so much that was traditional that the rules of conscience and of legality were always impinging even in regard to means. Moreover, they took themselves too seriously in their part as a popular party, taking into account in advance what they thought would please the populace. Cromwell, on the other hand, as it seemed to Hyde, followed the full logic of the politics of usurpation. He went beyond the limited aims of the Presbyterians and was ready if necessary to effect a complete transformation. He abandoned the scruples and compromises of that party. Relying upon a tradition of success to dazzle the people and upon force to overawe opposition, he gave himself a greater freedom in the adjustment of means to ends. He had thus entered upon a new realm of thought and action. Hyde told Cottington in 1646 that the Independents were like butchers in a fence-school: he who used most skill against them would receive most knocks: 'So they that guess at the intentions of the other, by the rules of reason, or precedents in story, will be furthest from what they mean.'[1] The Independents thus escaped impaling their cause upon one of the horns of the dilemma of failure, that of being insufficiently thorough in their crimes, though they would not in the end escape the other. For, as he said in the same letter, they 'having the same pride, ambition, and avarice, that other men have, and not suffering any rules or bonds to be applied to either, will be sooner oppressed, by their own confusion, than by the power of their adversaries'.

Their adversaries, the Presbyterians, however, at least in Hyde's final summing up in the second exile, had been squarely affixed to both horns of the dilemma. First, they failed because they were wicked and in the nature of things the wicked must be 'ministers of each other's confusion'. 'If God would suffer a lasting union in any notorious wickedness, which He never

[1] Hyde to Cottington: 15 November 1646. *S.P. Clar.* ii, p. 291.

doth, the world itself would be shaken, and upon the matter overthrown.'[1] It was true that Plato's justice among thieves expressed a partial truth. Even criminals retained a sense of justice leading to unity in a degree. Nevertheless, their wickedness must result in division and strife amongst themselves, thus promoting in the end their collapse. But doomed to fail because they were an association in iniquity, they were doomed also because they were insufficiently iniquitous. The Earl of Manchester, Hyde wrote, lost his position when the Self-denying Ordinance was passed 'for no other reason but because he was not wicked enough'.[2] He and his party failed when tried by that standard of pure expediency which was the measure of the success of the Independents. 'He who hath drawn his sword against his Prince ought to throw away the scabbard never to think of sheathing it again.'

Hyde's application of Machiavellian categories to the course of English events was made, it is repeated, in that part of the *History* written after the second exile. The categories of the Psalms prevailed at the earlier time. But the later Machiavellian framework does not constitute a departure of any great significance from the earlier attitude.[3] His original interpretation of the aims and methods of Cromwell was similar on the whole to the final estimate. The protectoral government, he wrote in 1655, addressing the Council of State, 'pulls up all property and liberty by the roots, reduces all our law, common and statute, to the dictates of your own will, and all reason to that which you, and you alone, will call reason of state', and he mentioned in connexion with that government's activities 'Machiavel['s] *Prince*, Hobbes' *Leviathan*, and all other institutions of tyranny'.[4] Furthermore,

[1] *Contemplations*, p. 739.
[2] Clarendon, *History*, II, p. 545.
[3] Hyde has 'miscellaneous extracts and considerations' from (*inter alia*) Machiavelli's *Discorsi* in the commonplace book dating from 1646–7. Clar. MSS. 126.
[4] *A letter*.

even when writing at the later date, that is, in the final *History*, he did not say that the Presbyterians were any less wicked than the Independents. Their wickedness differed not in degree, but in kind, a distinction he pointed out in the letter of 1646 already quoted.[1] There can be no doubt that, while the events under discussion were taking place, he held the Presbyterian and Independent leaders in equal disapproval.

Against the background of such an interpretation of the English situation, Hyde believed that the King should stand firmly and clearly in any negotiations which he entered into and refuse to abandon the things for which he had stood in the war. Both the English and the Scottish Presbyterians had more need of him than he of them, since they were faced both with internal difficulties and with adversaries with whom they must inevitably come to blows. At the time of the discussions between Charles I and the army chiefs in 1647 he put forward the same argument. They must know how unpopular they were; 'and then to believe they can govern long by the power of the sword is ridiculous'; they would need the King and the Law, 'which it may be, they will sooner find themselves, than be taught by others'.[2] There was no need to give in to the demands of either Presbyterian or Independent, since the future belonged to neither of them. If he were to yield, he would succeed only in dangerously obstructing the processes which Hyde believed to be at work and which he said ought to be relied upon.

It was, for one thing, a matter of the tactics to be adopted in the circumstances of the King's material weakness, and Hyde drew attention to that aspect of the question: 'take heed', he besought Berkeley with respect to the negotiations with the army leaders, 'of removing landmarks, and destroying foundations; whilst you insist upon those, you have a place to fix your foot upon, but recede once from those, and they will

[1] Hyde to Cottington: 15 November 1646. *S.P. Clar.* II, p. 291.
[2] Hyde to Berkeley: 6 October 1647. Ibid. p. 379.

be too hard for you; by your own arguments and your own concessions'.[1] Depart from that position by one step only, and he had lost all justification for refusing to take two or three more: 'there is no judge of reason left, but plurality of voices and strength of hands; and that decision gives no security for what is last concluded'. If his opponents could move the King from his original position, they would have won not just one point but the whole match, and they would know that they had won it. Experience had proved this. 'I must say, that from the beginning of these contentions, unreasonable concessions always produced unreasonable demands.'

But fundamental to his recommendations in regard to tactics was his belief about the nature of the parties opposed to the King and about the movement of the historical scene as a whole. For after declaring, 'if they see you will not yield, they must', he went on; 'for sure they have as much or more need of the King, than he of them'.[1] Provided the King continued merely to stand for what he had stood for in the past, his opponents, so long as they were unable completely to satisfy and settle the kingdom, must for ever be playing into his hands. No matter if the parties failed to see that they needed him, no matter if negotiations broke down through his refusal to comply, and no matter how great his material weakness: he would remain secure in a reputation of enduring and ultimately decisive political significance, and one which nothing his opponents could do short of a resurrection of the constitution under a Cromwellian or some other dynasty could affect save to his advantage. If he gave way to them he would at once put an end to the existence of a clear alternative to the projects and plans of those in power. Instead of constituting as before a background against which every failure and every crime of his opponents must inevitably emphasize itself, his action in yielding would have the effect

[1] 6 October 1647. *S.P. Clar.* II, p. 379.

of magnifying every success they had achieved in the past and of making of their every project the main hope of settlement.

For if after all this, a real and essential alteration of Government in the Church or State be to be consented to, the people will believe that those at Westminster are more competent contrivers of such alteration than any other combination or society of men, how dexterous and prudent soever.[1]

Whilst we keep ourselves upon the old foundation of the established government, and the good known laws, how weak soever we are in power, we shall be strong in reputation; whereas, when we are devising alterations, others' judgements will be submitted to before ours, and we shall only have the infamy of being unfortunate projectors.[2]

The old contention of 1642 that the King was not to be compelled by superior force to anything contrary to his conscience, honour and judgement: 'and that the people may not be compelled to submit to any determinations, contrary to the laws established which have not his Royal assent', was all that was needed to give the King in the present circumstances a remarkably creative part in English politics. The violent party had proved nothing but that they could win a war. 'Believe it', he told the restive Berkeley, '(and you will find it true after I am dead) though a war may be carried on by a new model, a firm peace can never be established but by the old.'[3] The point of Hyde's doctrine in respect of these matters was the essentially reconstitutive function of the mere existence of the King. Conversely, nothing that the King's opponents could do could be so destructive as what he had it in his power to do. 'God hath trusted the King with a Kingdom rarely and admirably moulded and constituted, which

---

[1] Hyde to Culpepper: 30 August 1648 (N.S.). *S.P. Clar.* II, p. 411.
[2] Hyde to Digby: 30 November 1648 (N.S.). Ibid. p. 459.
[3] 6 October 1647. Ibid. p. 379. See also *A full Answer*.

cannot be exposed to perfect and irreparable ruin, but by his own concurrence and consent.'[1]

The main difference after Cromwell's rise to power was that it became less possible for the King to exercise his unique prerogative of destruction, and all the easier, therefore, for the King and for those of his followers who were in exile to follow the right course.[2] The 'wilderness of prudential motives and expedients' of which Hyde complained in 1648[3] had become a simpler, if a not less uncomfortable place. Nor, in Hyde's view, so long as Cromwell was unable to secure the Crown, would the right course be any less politically effective. However, the limiting condition was a matter for great concern. Hyde's optimism had never been facile. Up to and including the Madrid period he had been filled with a sense that the situation in England was out of hand and uncontrollable by politics, that things must be worse before they were better and that the storm must be allowed to blow itself out. On the return from Spain and with the ascendancy of the Independents, the situation though simpler became more exacting. The liquidation of the Presbyterians at the hands of rivals cleverer than they had rounded off what was being accomplished by the internal disintegration of that party. But in the case of the Independents, though there could hardly be a more effective voucher for eventual failure than was afforded by the magnitude of their crimes, the forms nevertheless which their wickedness took seemed capable of indefinitely delaying its consequences. Their power and skill seemed to put them beyond the reach of all rivals either inside or outside the country, and a veritable genius of evil tirelessly worked to

[1] Hyde to Culpepper: 8 January 1647. *S.P. Clar.* II, p. 326.
[2] Hyde to the King: 10 November 1651 (N.S.). Ibid. p. 572. 'Your Majesty's own fate and that of your three Kingdoms depends now purely upon your own virtue.' Hyde was congratulating Charles II on his escape after the battle of Worcester.
[3] Hyde to Digby: 30 November 1648 (N.S.). Ibid. p. 459.

maintain unity and solidity within the recesses of the party itself and so to counteract the type of weakness from which the Presbyterians had suffered. Moreover, that same genius played upon the people as a whole to prolong an astonishing tale and reputation of success.

Hyde, in his new role as historian and connoisseur of the political art, developed a high respect for the Independents and for Cromwell. Independency as represented by Cromwell embodied for him the extreme of political intelligence, an intelligence, which, since it was entirely divorced from morality, must ultimately fail, was nevertheless unerringly and uncannily correct in its technique. 'I have not', he wrote as early as the end of 1646,[1] 'the same opinion, and contempt of the Independents, that other men have, from the opinion of their abhorring Rules of Government. I find they admit as strict Government as is necessary for their purposes.' There was no independency permitted in their military organization. 'Are not the Heads of the party the best Heads of the pack?' It seemed to him that they were well enough aware of the inconstancy and fury of the rabble. 'Believe it, they do as well know what they would have; as what they would not have; only they find it easier to pull down than build up', and, until they were ready, they found it politic to let the people believe what they liked of them. Freer principles made the best tactic for winning the support of all discontented men against the Presbyterians. But once victorious, Hyde expected that they might change their methods. They would have no revolutionary change in institutions: 'they are too wise men to think to live to see a submission from the people in peace to another government than what they have been acquainted with.' Hyde prayed he might be wrong but feared that he might be right when he said that they would keep up monarchy 'to the height, and probably improve it', and, being conscious of unforgivable

[1] Hyde to Nicholas: 12 December 1646. Ibid. p. 307-8.

14-2

offences, change the monarch and his line. They would see, as clearly as Hyde himself saw, that the period of disorders would increase the general attachment to the old forms. Consequently the restoration of them would become a policy all the more desirable to pursue. There was a possibility that England would recover the externals of the old laws, but with the monarchy raised towards absolutism and the rightful line excluded.

Accordingly, there are to be seen two threads running through Hyde's comments on English affairs after his return from Spain; the thread of hope and the thread of fear, the one pursued as he considered the wickedness of Cromwell's success, and the other, as he perceived the success of his wickedness. In December 1652 he wrote for the last time expressing confidence in the mutual destructiveness of Presbyterians and Independents.[1] From then on, Cromwell dominates the scene. On 9 May 1653, Hyde told a correspondent in Rome that it was a strange thing that princes abroad should be so much terrified with the power of the English rulers since they were so distracted amongst themselves that they would be ruined without an enemy.[2] On the same day he wrote to Nicholas that he was apprehensive of an elective monarchy with Cromwell on the throne.[3] A little later, the news that the latter had dissolved the Rump, that 'accursed assembly of rogues', was 'glorious' in one sense, but frightening in another, for such an action could not but endear him with his countrymen.[4] At the end of the month he declared that he had more hope from the confusion in England than from any order or method of their own; if the nation had been united there would have been no hope of prevailing.[5] In June, however, he was damping his cherished expectations of divisions

---

[1] Hyde to Nicholas. *S.P. Clar.* III, p. 125.
[2] Hyde to Wilford. Clar. MSS. 45, 330.
[3] *S.P. Clar.* III, p. 165.
[4] Hyde to Nicholas: 16 May 1653. Ibid. p. 167.
[5] Hyde to Newcastle: 30 May. Clar. MSS. 45, 409.

in the army.[1] 'Truly for my part I think he hath power enough to compass anything he desires, and I cannot imagine that his modesty will retain him from being a King', though he went more slowly towards that objective than Hyde expected.[2]

Later in the same month, he was reiterating the doctrine of 1650: that it was a question either of complete destruction or of a recovery independent of their own actions, and that the right course was to sit still.[3] On 11 July he was on the same tack: 'in truth I do not expect the confusion of these men from a just indignation of Princes...but from the same cause which gave them opportunity and power to do all their mischief, the rage and jealousy of the people which at some time will destroy them.'[4] On the 25th he said that he thought that the fate of John Lilburne, the Leveller, would be a test of the extent of Cromwell's mastery of civil and military divisions: 'infallibly...one will hang the other.'[5] In September he declared he was 'still so mad as to expect' some good turn 'rather from England than from foreign princes'.[6] In October letters were stopped, which he hoped meant that there were disorders in London.[7] In November, on the other hand, he was resisting the temptation of giving too much credit to reports of divisions in the army. Cromwell, he believed, was too wise a man to proceed as he did were he not sure of his control over it. And yet, and this was in the very same letter, there must surely be many officers resentful and jealous of him. 'And if I did not assuredly believe that...from that fountain of pride and madness, they will at last determine the confusion and be each other's executioners I should be very melancholic.' He had 'really more hope' from that and from

[1] Hyde to Nicholas: 6 June. *S.P. Clar.* III, p. 170.
[2] Hyde to Rochester: 13 June. Ibid. p. 172.
[3] Hyde to Nicholas: 20 June. Clar. MSS. 45, 488.
[4] Hyde to Nicholas: 11 July 1653. *S.P. Clar.* III, p. 178.
[5] Hyde to Nicholas: 25 July. Ibid. p. 182.
[6] Hyde to Wentworth: 7 September 1653. Clar. MSS. 46, 215.
[7] Hyde to Wentworth: 17 October. Ibid. 46, 322.

'old acquaintance in poor England' than from all Nicholas's plans for fleets and armies from abroad.[1]

The following week the two threads were more closely intertwined. The confusion was great in England, Hyde reported, but it was probably heightened by Cromwell of set purpose to make the country glad of the order he could impose and thus prepare the way for his assumption of the crown early in the following year.[2] Hyde said in December that he dreaded Cromwell becoming King, or even Protector, more than anything that could happen, but that he still would not despaii.[3] Early in 1654, however, he wrote that there seemed better evidence of a powerful party in the army opposed to any such a project on his part.[4] Hyde was to be disappointed. The protectorship was achieved, but Cromwell would, Hyde thought, have trouble with Parliament. 'God Almighty hath somewhat in His hidden purposes which He will bring to pass by ways we cannot think of.'[5] On 6 March he was writing that Cromwell had a plan to change the title of Protector into that of King 'since he finds the odium as great, and the power and security less', but that there seemed yet to be disunion enough in England and Cromwell's 'greatness to be threatened by many; and without doubt, if the supine compliance and submission of foreign states do not give him great countenance and support, he will sink under the weight'.[6] Hyde was prepared to allow him every refinement of political skill. He committed men to prison that he might be thought to have discovered more plots than he had in fact succeeded in doing. 'He endeavours by all imaginable dexterity to incline considerable persons of all factions to a conjunction with him and his interest',

---

[1] Hyde to Nicholas: 21 November. *S.P. Clar.* III, p. 198.
[2] Hyde to Nicholas: 28 November. Ibid. p. 200.
[3] Hyde to Rochester: 5 December. Clar. MSS. 47, 115.
[4] Hyde to Nicholas: 2 January 1654. *S.P. Clar.* III, p. 208.
[5] Hyde to Nicholas: 9 January 1654. Ibid. p. 210.
[6] Hyde to Clement: 6 March. Ibid. p. 223.

whether they were Presbyterians, Cavaliers or Roman Catholics. 'He makes not that haste was expected into state and lustre.' On account of the opposition from the army he would try stealing into monarchy by degrees.[1] But how was he to transfer the basis of his power from the army to something resembling the law? For that was the significance of any plan to take the crown.

Cromwell stood to lose the army and so perhaps to jeopardize his own safety if he took the crown. But if he did not take it, his power could never be embodied in a regular settlement. It was a problem which could not be evaded, but one which as time passed Cromwell was not able to solve. Hyde remained afraid that he would become King or even Emperor. In July 1654, with Cromwell in alliance with France, he admitted to a correspondent that he was now as high as to human understanding he could be, and the King as low.[2] But on the whole Hyde's confidence held its own against his fears. At the end of October 1654, he wondered that Cromwell was so much feared abroad, when at home he was subject to more fear himself than he was able to inspire in others.[3] In November, he was referring to the disaffection both of officers and of Parliament; so it was hoped his reign was drawing to an end.[4] Cromwell's success ran on. But could he carry it over into the dimensions of a secure and settled authority? If he could, there was no hope. But perhaps he could not do so. 'To govern according to law', as a historian writing of the Protector later than Hyde has put it, 'may sometimes be an usurper's wish, but can seldom be in his power.'[5] Perhaps this was the way judgement was to strike.

[1] Hyde to Clement: 13 March 1654. Ibid. p. 223.
[2] Hyde to Taylor: 8 July 1654. Clar. MSS. 48, 315. See also Hyde to Kent: 2 September. Ibid. 49, 20.
[3] Hyde to Taylor: 28 October. Ibid. 49, 89.
[4] Hyde to Bellenden: 27 November. Ibid. 49, 182.
[5] Hallam, *History*, II, p. 230.

§ 2. *Historical Politics*

'The Marquis of Ormonde and the Chancellor believed that the King had nothing at this time to do but to be quiet, and that all his activity was to consist in careful avoiding to do anything that might do him hurt, and to expect some blessed conjuncture from the amity of Christian Princes, or some such revolution of affairs in England by their own discontents and divisions amongst themselves, as might make it seasonable for His Majesty again to show himself.'[1] So, at a later time, and with accuracy, Hyde summarized the only attitude which in his view it was right or possible to adopt during the ascendancy of Cromwell, but it is to be understood that the attitude and the assumptions behind it are the same as had been maintained as far back as the Jersey period.

A blessed conjuncture from the amity of Christian princes seemed about to arise as it became apparent that Cromwell would go to war with Spain. In the summer of 1655 Hyde was anxious that the Spanish ministers should see the advantage of joint action with the King of England.[2] 'You are very ill informed of the reputation, power, and interest of the enemies of the King, my Master, if you do not believe, that a small countenance from a powerful friend, will give such life to those who only attend such a conjuncture, that we cannot expect too much from it.'[3] In other words, a 'small countenance' was all that was necessary to produce a 'revolution of affairs in England', even if it could not take place without it. The Spanish authorities were slow to be convinced. The King's representative was told to stress the fact that Cromwell was held in universal detestation, and that the heads of the factions in England knew that they could not

---

[1] Clarendon, *History*, v, p. 240.
[2] Thomas Carte, *A Collection of Original Letters and Papers*, 1739, II, p. 53.
[3] Hyde to Don Luis de Haro: 31 August. *S.P. Clar.* III, p. 275.

overthrow him without the King's help.[1] The Spaniards
eventually fell in with such suggestions, and a treaty was signed
in April 1656. The Spaniards, in return for certain under-
takings on Charles's part to be performed when he should be
restored, consented to provide four thousand foot and two
thousand horse, with arms and ammunition, for an expedition to England.[2] Hyde said it was the most cheerful news he
had had for seven years.[3] But the business moved slowly. In
November he drafted a paper for the Earl of Bristol to be
communicated by him to Don Juan, containing definite statements of the King's prospects and plans, and making inquiries
about Spanish co-operation. Each of the English factions, it
was pointed out, was applying to the King, and his own party
had instructions to join with whichever of them would first
oppose Cromwell. The King intended to go over to England
before Christmas and to use the regiments composed of his
own subjects which he had succeeded in forming on the
Continent.[4]

Meanwhile, the idea of a mutually profitable connexion
between the internal and the external enemies of the Protector was being considered in another quarter. Colonel
Sexby, a leader of the Levellers, was in Spain in 1655 to ask
for help. Naturally there were difficulties in combining three
such interests into a workable plan, but attempts were made
to surmount them. Sexby told Don Juan that if the Spaniards
preferred that the King's party should begin the movement
against Cromwell, he and his party would do what they
could to help, but that if they preferred the Levellers to begin,
Cavaliers who took arms conjointly with them must do so
simply in the name of the liberty of the country and without

[1] Hyde to Sir Henry de Vic: 17 December. Clar. MSS. 50, 49; Hyde to
Lord Norwich: 21 December. Ibid. 50, 225; the King's Instructions for de
Vic: 11 February 1656. Ibid. 51, 64.
[2] 12 April 1656. Ibid. 51, 147.
[3] Hyde to the King: April 21. Ibid. 51, 175.
[4] Statement sent to the Earl of Bristol: 13 November 1656. Ibid. 53, 25.

mentioning the King. He asked for a thousand foot and five hundred horse, the former to be Irish.[1] The King's counter-proposals, drafted by Hyde, were to the effect that he agreed to the support of a Leveller rising by the King's party without mention of the King, but preferred that the rising of the Levellers and that of the Cavaliers should be simultaneous. If the Levellers acted first, and succeeded, it was feared that the King would merely have exchanged a new enemy for an old one. If they failed, Cromwell's reputation would be still further enhanced, and the people still further disheartened. The Levellers were the more likely to fail if they took the lead in that, as Hyde pointed out, their unity was based on common dislikes rather than on common aims of a positive character. Such aims existed, but they were divergent and mutually incompatible. The King's party, on the other hand, was united by a single positive aim and would provide the coherence which was needed, consisting as it did of 'persons of all the considerable fortunes and families in the kingdom'.[2]

This episode is remarkable for the exactitude with which the King's plan as traced out by Hyde coincides with the principles he had laid down in 1649. In the paper[3] of that year he laid it down that the King would enter into relations with any party in England simply on the basis of common action against the prevailing power. It was to be understood that there were to be no constitutional discussions or promises beyond that of a general pardon, a free Parliament and a national synod to settle the Church.[4] This had been the platform of the Oxford Parliament[5] with the difference that the

---

[1] 14 December *S.P. Clar.* III, p. 315.
[2] 16 December. Clar. MSS. 53, 107. *S.P. Clar.* III, p. 315.
[3] *Nicholas Papers*, I, p. 138.
[4] The synod had not originally been Hyde's policy, but he seems to have accepted it from the start of the civil war.
[5] 'The humble petition of the Lords and Commons of Parliament assembled at Oxford according to your majesty's proclamation.' *Parl. Hist.* XIII, p. 114.

late King's murderers were now exempted from the pardon and that in Hyde's view the Long Parliament had been dissolved by the death of Charles I. Above all it must be understood that the party in question, whichever it happened to be, must agree to act with the old party of the King without any reservation. Hyde stressed that it was a matter of indifference which party was concerned, but went so far as to suggest that it was the Levellers who might be most worth while considering. They had, he pointed out, opposed Parliament's rule, and as enemies to arbitrary government would be the more easily reduced to a reverence for the laws. Separated both in time and also in social status from the original violent party, they would be less hostile to the men who had fought for the King. Their purposes were less closely linked with personal interest than the purposes of the Presbyterians, and being impracticable would evaporate of themselves. As military men they would be of more service than the Presbyterians and they represented the possibility of a split in the Cromwellian army.

Once again, Hyde's judgement proved strikingly prophetic, as prophetic as it had been in the matter of the type of policy which the Independent leaders might in the long run be expected to adopt. The one respect in which the policy of 1656 seems to differ from that of 1649 is the complacency with which at the later date Hyde appeared to regard the help of foreign troops. But it must be remembered that he had never rejected out of hand the idea of a julep. When the help of the Scots had been under discussion ten years before, he had allowed the possibility of a 'Julep from the North', provided too heavy a price were not paid for it.[1] The point both of the aid of the Scots and of the Spaniards was to set in train a native opposition which Hyde always believed was potentially decisive. He certainly viewed Spanish aid with more equanimity than he had done that of the Scots. But the

---

[1] Hyde to Nicholas: 12 December 1646. *S.P. Clar.* II, p. 307.

former was the more necessary in that, notwithstanding 'the universal detestation' in which the Protector was held, his political finesse and military strength seemed capable of indefinitely postponing the reckoning. But just because it was only those qualities which protected him, the movement against him when it came could not help being an overwhelmingly native one. None the less, it is probable that Hyde had misgivings, and it is perhaps significant that there is more stress in Hyde's papers on money and ammunition than on troops. It had been mainly money he was after when he had been ambassador in Spain.

Still more significant for the understanding of Hyde's mind at this time is the fact that *A letter from a true and lawful member of Parliament* was composed in the very period when there was a greater possibility of continental military assistance than at any other time. In October 1655, the Protector had published a declaration denouncing cavalier conspiracies and arguing, not only that these necessitated the raising of new forces, but that the cost of them should be met by a special tax on the Cavaliers. It was this which called forth from Hyde for circulation in England *A letter from a true and lawful member of Parliament*. This is an exercise, a historical exercise, in putting himself in the place of an imaginary parliamentarian who had remained at Westminster during the Civil War, only to be expelled by Colonel Pride at the end of 1648, and who, through Hyde, now speaks his mind about this latest step of the government. There is nothing remarkable about the paper as a historical exercise in that part of it in which Hyde sketches the story from 1642. Here, he was merely summarizing the changing appearance of events from the non-violent parliamentarian standpoint, that is, from his own, save that in this case his vision had to be that of a man who had stayed with Pym. What is remarkable and important in the present connexion is his interpretation of the reaction to Cromwell's latest step. He makes his parliament-man explain the reasons why the Protectorate had been accepted so quietly by men like himself. Those reasons, as he gives them, were the prospect of order after so much turmoil, the notion that Cromwell's rule would be temporary, and the hope of a free parliament. In fact, however, the Protectorate had turned out to be a government contrary to the principles of the Long Parliament and the ends fought for in the Civil War. For that reason it was accepted now only because it could not be overthrown. But for that reason, so runs the argument, the case of the now proscribed Cavaliers was the case of all Englishmen, and particularly the case of a member of the Long Parliament. All the Cavaliers, whether or not they had taken part in the late risings, and on the mere assumption that they were disaffected, were now to be subjected to punitive taxation. Disaffection was far wider than the Cavalier party. The conclusion must therefore be that the whole framework of law and constitutional government was now in principle overthrown : and what was the system now established in England but 'that arbitrary power we have so long inveighed against, made so many men odious with the reproach of, made but the endeavour to set up an arbitrary government the abridgement of all treason, against which we first took up arms, and for the rooting out of which we have shed and lost so much blood?'

This contention was not far-fetched. It was a precise anticipation of the argument relentlessly pressed against the government by the second Parliament to be held under the *Instrument of Government.* It was an exact expression of the type of consideration which lay behind the *Humble Petition and Advice,* the movement to persuade Cromwell to take the crown. Hyde had exactly gauged the prevailing current in England. If he could put himself in the place of a member of Parliament under Cromwell, this was no more remarkable than the fact that Cromwell's Parliament identified its cause with that of the oppressed Cavaliers. Provided Cromwell could not surmount the dilemma which the question of the Crown pressed upon him, there was no extravagance in the expression of the hope by Hyde at the end of *A letter* that the nation under Providence would free itself without foreign help from the miserable condition in which it found itself. Cromwell himself spoke much of Providence, but let him, said Hyde's parliamentarian, look again. He could indeed tell an astonishing tale of success, but yet 'your perplexity and insecurity remains greater than before; you have no enemy in the three Kingdoms, who stands in opposition to your power, or who indeed is owner of a sword to resist you, and yet you avow and discover such a proportion of fear, that new armies must be raised for your defence: you have gotten all the wealth of the three Kingdoms into your hands, and enjoy none, your wants and necessities being so great; when you had little credit and less interest to do good or harm, you had many friends, and few who hated you, and now it is in your power to make great whom you please, and so destroy all whom you are angry with, your friends leave and forsake you': 'all your safety is in the army, and yet you fear it'.

So far as his enemies outside the country were concerned, Cromwell was saved not by his own exertions but by the internal collapse of the schemes laid against him. The Leveller movement became concentrated upon a plot to assassinate the Protector which failed. The Spaniards postponed action until the project petered out. By May 1657, Hyde was reiterating to Nicholas his fundamental doctrine. 'Indeed (Mr Secretary) when I have been most sanguine towards our business, it hath been only upon the contemplation of the horrible wickedness and transcendent villainy of those rogues, which I am confident God Almighty will punish with exemplary judgments in this world, and it is that hope still that keeps up my spirits, not any dependence upon our own invention, or the assistance of powerful friends, which humanly speaking will be too weak to go through our work; and yet it may be we are nearer our deliverance than we can reasonably expect.'[1] It was soon apparent that the pattern of deadlock so manifest in earlier years had reimposed itself, if indeed it had ever been absent. Sir Henry Bennett wrote from Madrid to say that the trouble with the Spaniards was due not to want of goodwill on their part but to a general failing in all their affairs.[2] Hyde, in September, noted[3] that the temper of the King's party in England was such that 'all that can be expected from here will not do our work'; if the King were to land tomorrow with as good an army as it was reasonable to hope for, he would be overwhelmed as at Worcester, 'whilst all men sit still, and look for the effect of the first battle'. The King's party must be roused from such a condition, otherwise foreign help would be useless. But whereas at this time Hyde wrote that nothing but weakness held the Spaniards back, Bennett, some weeks later, was writing[4] to say that the Spaniards would not move until something was begun in England. He feared that in the contest on the question who was to begin the King would fall between two stools.

There was, thus, reason enough for Hyde to write as he had written in May of the year to Nicholas. But there was reason to do so in more senses than one. For at the time he was writing that letter and repeating his fundamental beliefs the Protector's death was but fifteen months in the future. A somewhat but not much longer period was to separate the Protector's death from the restoration of King and constitution. Hyde's personal position in politics had been easier after Cromwell's rise to power. But that was only because the scope for the expedients pursued by Royalists in the antecedent period was now limited. After Cromwell's death, the

[1] Hyde to Nicholas: 28 May. *S.P. Clar.* III, p. 342.
[2] Sir H. Bennett to the King: 23 August. Clar. MSS. 55, 302.
[3] Hyde to Rumbold: 12 September 1657. *S.P. Clar.* III, p. 364.
[4] Sir H. Bennett to the King: 24 October. Clar. MSS. 56, 166. Sir H. Bennett to Hyde: 14 November. Ibid. 56, 198.

211

possibilities which had existed before his establishment opened out once more.

Hyde in his successful opposition to the new outbreak of royalist expedients in the time which remained did not oppose or refrain from all 'inventions' any more than he had done in the preceding years. The point was that the action taken must conform with the movement of events as he interpreted it, and this was important in his view for no less a reason than that it was his belief that the greater part of the work would be done by the movement itself. He could want a no more striking vindication than the fact that whereas the rising of 1659 against a much weaker government than that of Cromwell failed, this was followed in 1660 by a restoration of the whole constitution which was totally non-violent in its character.

In Hyde's early bouts with Royalist opportunists, each accused the other of a lack of realism. The latter charged Hyde with unwillingness to adopt handy expedients for reasons which they either did not understand or did not consider relevant. They felt that Hyde's weakness was that he was burdened with ecclesiastical preoccupations. They argued that the King could not afford profound and rigorous principles; that the only principle was to obtain the Crown by any means to hand; that in any case action was preferable to inactivity. Sir John Berkeley had frankly told Hyde in connexion with the negotiations with the Scots commissioners at Breda in 1650 that 'conscience' was a word the Anglicans were in danger of misusing as the Papists misused 'infallibility' and the Puritans 'the Spirit', and that they were as blameworthy as either if they used it as a bolt-hole when pressed by rational arguments. Rather, it should be a matter of conscience 'not to suffer a glorious and flourishing Church and State for ever to perish, rather than it should be recovered by those, against whom we have passionately engaged ourselves'.[1] Hyde, for his part, was aware of the contempt to which his attitude laid itself open, 'as if it were a senseless expectation of miracles.'[2] 'I know that...the fixing upon honest principles...is reproached and laughed at, as delighting in metaphysical notions and imaginary speculations.'[3] He was conscious that he would be thought 'fitter for a monastery, than a court'.[4] He knew that he was branded as 'an enemy to peace',[5] and 'an enemy to moderate Counsels'.[6] 'I know, I shall be thought too scrupulous, if not superstitious.'[7] But he threw back the charges in the face of his critics: 'there must go more miracles to the prospering' such 'poor abject composition'[8] as theirs, than were necessary for the success of his own recommendations. 'You seem to think', he told Berkeley, 'that a man who rejects one expedient is bound to propose another for action; which, under your pardon, I think is not just; for there may be visible mischief in one, and the condition so low that no other can be proposed, but to sit still and expect some advantages by the enemies' distractions, or some other way than yet appears.'[9] The political outlook to which Hyde's critics subscribed saw the whole story in terms of the existing circumstances. It magnified and pushed to the front immediate events. Historical faith, on the other hand, as the foundation of political reasoning, declared the expedient-mongers to be superficial. The immediate circumstances were viewed in terms of the whole story, looking far back and far forward. But Hyde was never in a position to prevent an extension of opportunist thinking among the Royalists at least as marked as that which was to be seen in

[1] 22 March, 1649. *S.P. Clar.* II, p. 530.
[2] Hyde to Culpepper: 8 January 1647. Ibid. p. 326.
[3] Hyde to Lady Dalkeith: 24 October 1646. Ibid. p. 284.
[4] Hyde to Digby: 30 November 1648 (N.S.). Ibid. p. 459.
[5] Hyde to Morley: 18 March 1650. Ibid. p. 518.
[6] Hyde to Nicholas: 18 March 1650. Ibid. p. 525.
[7] Hyde to Berkeley: 18 March 1650. Ibid. p. 522.
[8] Hyde to Culpepper: 8 January 1647. Ibid. p. 326.
[9] Hyde to Berkeley: 18 March 1650. Ibid. p. 521. Also *Essays*, I, p. 96.

the parties on the stage in England, and whereas opportunism in the latter was what he expected and what he desired, opportunism amongst the King's adherents was precisely that which would in his view prevent the faults of the English factions from working to the country's advantage and that of the King.

The last thing that can be said of Hyde's position is that it was a theological or moral idealism arrived at and sustained independently of a sense of political circumstance. On the contrary, though he trusted in Providence, the force and persistence of his belief were indistinguishable from a grasp of the sweep of events which was both penetrating and comprehensive, and which, furthermore, was very far from ignoring the less ideal aspects of politics. He held that the King's case must be based on conscience, but he hastened to show that it would be all the more effective for that reason: 'believe it, in the end, it will be found good husbandry as well as good Religion.'[1] He expected self-interest to show itself before conscience in the process of the education of his countrymen back to constitutionalism, but it was possible to count on its operation only if the King's position was outside and above the immediate play of English interests and in that sense was based on principle. He was convinced that the policy of his critics could not succeed, that the application of such remedies as they supported would only discredit the physician and impair the patient.[2] But there was no fanaticism in his opposition and he remained on good terms with those from whom he differed. He knew that intrigues, impatience, and bitter differences were inevitable in a 'necessitous, unfortunate Court'. There would be unity once the tide turned. As has been seen, he was far from dogmatic about when that could be expected to happen. His view of the course and meaning of events was clear, but it was not rigid. He told

---

[1] Hyde to Culpepper: 30 August (N.S.). *S.P. Clar.* II, p. 411.
[2] Hyde to Berkeley: 26 December 1646. Ibid. p. 315.

Nicholas in 1657 that he was glad Charles II's alliance with the Scots had been tried, now that it was possible to look back upon it. If Charles had not gone to Scotland, 'he would have been thought to have overslipped an opportunity to have recovered his three Kingdoms'.[1] Nor could Hyde's attitude be justly charged with being a predominantly ecclesiastical one. He was anxious that the King and his family should maintain a reputation for Protestantism. If they failed to do this, enemies in England would exploit the fact to the King's disadvantage, and be quick to infuse new life into the frenzied misconceptions of the days before the Civil War. Some of the schemes for restoration were objectionable because they meant coming too close to Roman Catholicism. A restoration by composition with the Presbyterians was objectionable because it could not be made save at the expense of the anglican episcopate. But both courses were sufficiently objectionable for other reasons, reasons which have been discussed and which were not ecclesiastical.

Hyde's opponents tended to be both too easy and too hard with the English victors. In that they were prepared to make large-scale constitutional deals with them, they took more seriously than Hyde did both their power and their ideas. On the other hand, in that they regarded them as rebels, who, if only the King had the power, merited suppression, their attitude to them as individuals tended to be less humane than his. Following his political phase, Hyde refused to grant the Presbyterians special status as monarchists, and refused to admit that they were in that respect nearer than the Independents to the King's interests. The rank and file had been drawn into complicity and would see the error of their ways. Only the leaders had distinctive ideas, but these were subsidiary to 'private and digested ends'.[2] These men, if they survived, were convertible. The very fact that they were an

[1] Hyde to Nicholas: 8 October 1657. Ibid. III, p. 372.
[2] *Nicholas Papers*, I, p. 144.

15-2

amorphous party in comparison with the Independents supported this conviction. Further, the existence and strength of an extremer party tended to make them draw closer to the King. Presbyterians started making approaches to the King soon after Cromwell had achieved his ascendancy. 'The wise men...' he wrote in 1656, 'know well the impossibility of prevailing for their party, which is no otherwise united amongst themselves than in pulling down in negations, that will not have this and that, without any determination what they would have established, and therefore they are using all dexterity in their application to his Majesty for their own particular conveniences....'[1] But the Independents, for their part, were not irredeemable either, provided they had not been accomplices in the death of Charles I. The bulk of them, as in the case of the Presbyterians, had been misled and dragged along by circumstances. Some of them, moreover, precisely because they were furthest in time and spirit from the original circumstances of tl e Revolution were in that respect more accessible than the Presbyterians. Hyde wrote in a commonplace book in these terms:[2] 'They shall be unreasonably accused of affection for Independency who believe that Independents are more likely to be converted to allegiance and loyalty than the Presbyterians; those for want of logic and a natural disposition not understanding the necessity, and so not valuing them; these having corrupted the pure metal of government with such an alloy as may pervert it on all occasions to their own corrupt and profane and impious purposes.' Hyde was thinking, presumably, of the extreme wing of the Independents, and what he says here is to be compared with statements elsewhere about the Levellers.

None of the parties, as such, possessed in Hyde's view any principle of permanence. All were founded on sand, though admittedly on sand of different qualities. The Presbyterians

---

[1] *S.P. Clar.* III, p. 316.   [2] Clar. MSS. 126, p. 55.

were incapable of success even if the protracted character of
their failure was as galling at one stage as the brisk success of
the Independents was later to be. The Independents were
capable of success, but only of a success which, though
brilliant, must ultimately, he was convinced, be transitory.
The Levellers pursued aims which were merely absurd. The
parties were inherently contradictory and mutually destructive, for even though Independency had overthrown the
Presbyterians and the Levellers as effective parties, it weakened
its own basis by driving, in its very triumph, Presbyterians
and Levellers back towards the King. The parties could live
as parties only if the King compromised with them as such,
or if, through his active opposition to them in circumstances
adverse to himself, he put new life into them. The King said
that he was supported in all his afflictions by the belief that
many honest men who had been deceived would one day, when
undeceived, be the principal means of the confusion of their
seducers. So ran the King's answer to an approach by the
Levellers in 1656,[1] but it exactly represents Hyde's attitude
to all the English parties throughout the period. In 1646 he
had ridiculed the high democratic and egalitarian pretensions
of the Independents. They would, he said, set up a new
monarchy, in a new dynasty, but one which must needs possess 'a more unlimited sovereignty than any King hath enjoyed
since the Conqueror himself'.[2] As for the Presbyterians, with
their limited monarchy, they wished to keep the old line and
the old institutions, but aspired to have the King govern under
their own control and in their own interests.[3] That was why,
as Hyde said, they would rely on the perpetuity of the Long
Parliament (which Hyde maintained had been legally dissolved by Charles I's death), and why they were more interested in suppressing the King's party than in anything else.[4]

[1] The King to Will. Howard: 14 July 1656. Ibid. 52, 77.
[2] Hyde to Jermyn: 8 January 1647. Clar. MSS. 29, 52.
[3] S.P. Clar. II, p. 308, and Clar. MSS. 29, 52.
[4] Nicholas Papers, I, p. 141.

The Levellers were the 'lunatic rabble',[1] whose notions, even though sincerely held, would 'for the most part fall of themselves'.[2] Their ideas were a function of political breakdown and would subside as soon as the rule of law was re-established. Hyde was unimpressed by the political and constitutional ideas that flickered upon the scene of events. He preferred to trace the logic of political necessity and to hold fast to the abiding facts of social interest.

Staunch as he was throughout, however, against compliance with parties as such, in England, he never minimized the value of making contacts and conducting negotiations with their membership irrespective of party affiliations. This is the explanation of the fact, which is easily ignored, that from 1646 he had always expressed the greatest satisfaction when the King entered into negotiations, and hoped well of them. It was compromise he was opposed to, not contacts. He advocated that the King should exert himself to disentangle individuals from the web of circumstance in which they found themselves. This was 'a way that in no civil war, which has arrived to any vigour and power of contending, ought to be declined'. 'Let not the landmarks be removed, no pillars, upon which the fabric relies, be taken away', he wrote in connexion with negotiations in 1646-7 with the Scots, but 'let them have all circumstantial temporary concessions.'[3] 'In God's name, distribute as many personal obligations as can be expected, but take heed of removing landmarks and destroying foundations,'[4] he declared in connexion with contacts with the army leaders. Hyde was disappointed with the latter 'from whom I expected such a proceeding, as, with reference to their own interests, appeared to me to be best for them'. But he added in respect of new contacts with the Scots: 'I do confess it is the office of wise men to find ex-

[1] Hyde to Jermyn: 8 Jan. 1647. Clar. MSS. 29, 52.
[2] Nicholas Papers, i, p. 141.
[3] Hyde to Culpepper: 8 January 1647. *S.P. Clar.* ii, p. 326.
[4] Hyde to Berkeley: 6 October 1647. Ibid. p. 379.

pedients to reform and reconcile the affections of distempered men, but it must be still to reduce them to just and true principles.'[1] The King would remember, he wrote in 1648 in *A full Answer*, 'only by whose fidelity he hath recovered what he had lost, and not by whose fault he had lost it'. Extraordinary care must be taken, he explained in 1649,[2] 'to separate these men from their companions...and the King must really receive, and his party cordially join (without the least reproaching or remembering what is past) with, all who will now bear their parts towards the enthroning his Majesty...'. In 1656 Hyde explained[3] to Ormonde that in treating with the Levellers the method was 'to make such particular promises to particular men of advantage to themselves as shall go farther than any concessions to their satisfaction'.

The idea of securing individual conversions must indeed carry little weight unless the King was sufficiently powerful to be convincing. Even this species of action was denied him until events themselves made it possible. But once their movement was demonstrably under way, it was a method which began to be extremely effective. The more the King was given by events through the shortcomings of those in power in England and the reaction of the country as a whole against them, the more desirable it became for prudent men to make their peace with the King and, if possible, to be of service to him. The more he was able to exploit this desire, the more widespread would the desire become: that again would make it easier to exploit. After the death of Cromwell, the method of personal contacts and assurances began to demonstrate what it could not do before, its superiority over party compromises. This is the policy which reached its culmination in the weeks before the Restoration in the decisive contact with General Monk

---

[1] Hyde to Ld. H.: 6 February 1648. Ibid. III, p. 1.
[2] *Nicholas Papers*, I, p. 143.
[3] Hyde to Ormonde: 17 March 1656. *S.P. Clar.* III, p. 289.

who was the creature of circumstance in so high a degree that he could speak in the end for all. This is the policy which in the Declaration of Breda resulting from the conversion of Monk generalized for the whole country the assurances of personal security and reward which had previously been extended individually, while avoiding any constitutional rearrangements. This is the policy which finally embodied the provisions of the Declaration of Breda in the statutory Indemnity and Oblivion of the Restoration Settlement itself.

Such a course was the practice in politics of that duty of abstaining from revenge, which he afterwards preached in the *Essays*. By keeping the King from becoming 'a property to either party, out of animosity to the other', he might, Hyde had said long before, 'at some time give the law to both'.[1] The King's adherents, he wrote in *A full Answer*, should understand the prime duty of charity. By relying on the course of events and by dealing with people as personalities only, and not as party men, Hyde could hope for a restoration which would be of the same order and quality as that peace for which he had hoped and worked in the political phase. To negotiate, even successfully, with parties as they had become, and to take their principles seriously could result only in temporary equilibrium. There could by that method be no mutual confidence between the King and the people: rather, the monarchy would be situated over against the people in a strained contractual relationship. A constitutional bargain would be as bad as a state of affairs where the rightful ruler was imposed on the nation as conqueror and autocrat. Hyde did not want a restoration which should place the King either over and above the people by force, or over against them by contract. He desired the King so to act, and prevailed with him so to act, that the people would return freely to him, and only the method of personal assurances against a background of the working of broad political forces freely and

[1] 6 February 1648. *S.P. Clar.* III, p. 3.

patiently accepted and unobstructed could be congruent with such a design.

Hobbes stood at an opposite extreme from Hyde in all these matters, and the difference between them may be taken as representing in its acutest form the issue at stake between Hyde and his royalist critics. In the first place, Hobbes gave his support, for instance in the discussion in *Leviathan* of the question of ship-money, to what was a distinctively royalist principle of action throughout the whole period. His only criticism of ship-money was directed against the grounds on which it had been justified, namely the resort by the judges to the distinction between the rules of law and the rules of necessity or reason of State. Such a distinction he would not allow. Necessity, as interpreted by the Prince, was the one and only standard both in law and politics. Hobbes seemed to stand for the direct method of asserting the King's authority, and in this he was expounding, though with theoretical constitutional implications which they did not, of course, necessarily share, an attitude which was to all intents and purposes identical with the one which was acted upon by Digby and the Queen and their successors from the time of the attempt on the Five Members onwards. For them it was a question of suppressing a rebellion by force. Having lost the first Civil War, the idea of starting another with the aid of foreign armies was not only acted upon in the second Civil War but was never afterwards abandoned. Hobbes himself, of course, returned to England to live under the usurper, expounding 'the new maxim that protection and subjection are relatives and cease together,' which as Hyde had put it, 'was neither divinity nor law seven years since'.[1] Cromwell not only indisputably provided *de facto* government but better exemplified direct or 'violent' methods than anyone else in Europe.

Hyde's whole course of action, on the other hand, was a living commentary upon a phrase in one of his 1642 declarations.

[1] Hyde to Berkeley: 21 November 1646. Clar. MSS. 28, 293.

It is impossible for the King, he wrote, 'to subsist without the affections of his people, and...those affections cannot possibly be preserved or made use of but by parliaments....'.[1] His entire political career in the first phase after the passing of the Grand Remonstrance had been devoted to explaining to the King that the royalist method could not possibly succeed and must, if persevered with, infallibly deprive the Crown of its authority by undermining men's affections and destroying their confidence, and in the second phase he had directed the same argument against the schemes for conquest with foreign armies. Hyde's argument, indeed, was exactly the one put forward in a speech which Pym made to the House of Lords in 1628 at the impeachment of Manwaring, the court preacher who had advocated compliance with the Forced Loan.[2] Anybody, Pym said, who attempted to assert or to maintain the royal authority by measures which terrified his subjects or made them justifiably resentful was an enemy and not a friend of the King. The only difference between Hyde and Pym in this respect was that, unlike Pym, Hyde declined to allow himself to be caught up in the vicious circle which such action, as Pym had explained, necessarily precipitated, and had sought instead, from different points on the arc of the circle to arrest the procession of reactions. In the book on Hobbes, which he wrote after the Restoration, the elaboration of what was essentially Pym's point in opposition to Hobbes's contentions on taxation and other matters made up a large part of Hyde's thesis, and he was preeminently qualified to elaborate it. It may be added that the discourse on the constitution which was planned for but omitted from the *History* can thus be dispensed with. For Hyde's conception of the English constitution was matured in the universe of his own political experience. Indeed, the frequent references to the finely tempered legal relationships of English institutions and the political reciprocity which he

[1] Clarendon, *History*, II, p. 202. [2] J. Rushworth (1682), 1618–29, p. 595.

believed that they promoted as between King and people, can best be understood as describing his own contribution to policy-making both in the political and in the historical phase in the setting of the Revolution of 1640–1.

Secondly, though it is perhaps possible to accuse Hyde of underestimating the part played by theoretical ideas in the course of English events, Hobbes must be charged with having exaggerated it. Hobbes had all the doctrinaire's respect for the ideas of other people. He rated highly what he regarded as erroneous notions as a cause of the disruptions; in particular, as a pre-disposing factor, the prevailing ideas about the limited and mixed nature of governmental authority; and, as a source of weakness to the King on the eve of the war, the cherishing of such ideas by the King's parliamentary advisers. He believed that such notions predisposed them to accommodation with Parliament lest the King should acquire too much power[1]. Here he was criticizing Hyde himself, and identifying himself in effect with the view which was taken by the Queen when she had argued that to appear accommodating only made Parliament the more aggressive.

It must be admitted that in terms of Hobbes's theory of sovereignty the distinction between Hyde's view and the theory of the mixed state disappeared, and Hyde's own view had indeed been enough to predispose him at any time after the King's recovery of strength at the end of 1642 to seek a settlement with Parliament lest royalism should endanger the constitution. Hobbes was nevertheless wrong in his indiscriminate charge against the King's advisers that they had promoted the doctrine of mixed monarchy. Hyde, it has already been stated, did not subscribe to this doctrine, neither writing nor approving the answer to the Nineteen Propositions in which it had been expounded from the King's side. He adhered instead to a more traditional notion of limited kingship, though without, of course, accepting the

[1] *Behemoth*, pp. 112, 114.

223

absolute prerogative which he in common with the men of 1640 regarded as a recent usurpation. He implied this ancient doctrine in *A full Answer*, quoting the case of the *Post-Nati*, Egerton, Dyer and Bracton, and he expounded it in the attack[1] on *Leviathan* which he delivered after the Restoration. For Hyde the monarchy was limited by law to act within a system of institutions which it could not itself change or even, now that the absolute prerogative was disallowed, in any circumstances transcend or evade. But it was nevertheless a true monarchy still and not a mixture of monarchy, aristocracy and democracy, since Lords and Commons shared not the authority of the State but merely in the exercise of it. Moreover, all his political experience led him to stress not the division of authority and checks and balances but co-operation, and his particular constitutional idiom was much less the cause than the consequence of his political activity.

Hobbes's prescription for the cure of all political ills was to change men's political and constitutional ideas by the inculcation of his own. Hobbes can hardly be said to represent the typical royalist attitude in so far as the latter was anything but doctrinaire. But in the realm of practice the attitude of Hobbes and that of the Royalists were not so far removed from one another. As has been seen, the Royalists took the ideas of their opponents seriously at least in the important sense that in the type of negotiation they were disposed to conduct, they paid such ideas the compliment of accepting them as irreducible facts. The contrary extreme to Hobbes, as it is found in Hyde, at least had the merit of allowing for the fact that most men's ideas are at the mercy of social circumstances and of political events. In so far as circumstances and events had created doctrines, they would also break them. Hyde's sense of the deeper causes of English events was superior as political thinking to that of Hobbes precisely because he was thinking historically. Moreover, in the matter of recovery, his

[1] *Survey*, pp. 54, 122, 124, 164.

sense of the operations of providence is in marked contrast with the positivism of Hobbes, which was, indeed, on the same level as the 'over activity',[1] the 'activism' of the Royalists. From Hyde's point of view they were equally atheistic.

It should by now be clear that Hyde's position was as widely separated from the typical royalist one in this second phase as it had been in the first or political phase. Moreover, it is now possible to see more clearly the sense in which, and the extent to which the writing of the *History* marks a turning point. Once again, as in the autumn of 1641, and in the spring of 1642, that turning point was more an external one than an internal one, and was primarily a change in the course of events. What had happened was that the course of events had put a decisive end to that line of policy which Hyde had pursued. There was a break and a change more catastrophic than any that had occurred so far; and in that catastrophe the *History* was conceived and written. The catastrophe had been great enough to make him put an interpretation upon past events which was different from what it had been while he had lived and acted in their midst. In view of the misunderstanding which it has created regarding the true nature of Hyde's part in those events, there is no call to minimize the change. Nevertheless, it is clear that Hyde's attitude to the contemporary scene in the second phase is in direct continuity with his attitude in the first one. The ideas and recommendations of 1646 onwards are nothing but those of the previous period in a completely different setting. While working for settlement, and later for peace, he had, as an enthusiast for the Revolution of 1640–1, assumed the desirability and the possibility of an accommodation in terms of that Revolution. When he now opposed compromise, it was because the world in which he had previously worked for it had collapsed: 'I would not...buy a peace at a dearer price

[1] *Life*, II, p. 80.

than was offered at Uxbridge; and I am persuaded. . .if ever it shall be purchased at a more dishonourable or impious price, it will be more unpleasant and fatal to those who shall have their hands in making the bargain, than the war hath been.'[1] In other words, he would not have a peace at a dearer price, because he could not conceive that it would be peace.

But the context which he had previously assumed, he now, because it had dissolved into universal confusion, proceeded to emphasize. Whereas, and also because, in the earlier time, he had relied upon a general satisfaction with the purposes and achievements of 1640–1 and the general desire for peace, as the basis for a policy of settlement, he now lauded that satisfaction and that desire in themselves, and drew attention to their underlying presence. If he spoke of old English loyalty and in a spirit of conservatism, it must be remembered not only that the Revolution of 1640–1 was at the time it took place almost universally conceived of as a restoration of the constitutional past, but also, that against the background of all that had since happened in Church and State, the revolutionary objectives of 1640–1 now stood out as a happy and moderate traditionalism. Further, all that had happened since 1641 must not only, he believed, strengthen those factors and operate towards their institutional re-embodiment, but would also, provided the King stood firm on the platform now suggested, which was that of 1642 transformed, solve in the long term the problem which the Revolution itself had failed to solve, the problem of institutional compatibility, of mutual confidence between King and Parliament. But while that platform in 1642 had been a platform for intense and delicate political action, and Hyde had, at that time, regarded activity as of the utmost importance, after the war, on the other hand, the platform required only to be stood upon, and action therefrom tended to do more harm than good. It was one thing, for instance, to trust that the divisions in England would work

[1] Hyde to Nicholas: 1 June 1646. *S.P. Clar.* II, p. 237.

to the King's advantage, and quite another to attempt to promote them by diplomacy. Thus, Hyde now believed that history itself could do and would do what his politics in the previous phase had failed to do. He could not but observe that despite all the frustrations and the failures, his own and the King's, there were more men favourable to the King in 1646 than in 1642;[1] and, what is more, that between these frustrations and failures, so far as they were the King's, and the increase in the number of his supporters, there was not lacking a relationship of cause and effect. The weaker the King was, the less opportunity there was for him to alienate possible supporters. Accordingly, we see that what he had previously opposed as obnoxious from the point of view of the achievement of settlement—deviations from law as it stood after the first session of the Long Parliament, and attempts to reassert authority through force alone whether native or foreign—he now opposed as impediments to the historical process.

Even the enthusiasm for negotiations with opponents and the principle of bridge-appointments are carried over into the second and historical phase. In terms of the principle of bridge-appointments, indeed, the whole of the story of Hyde's recommendations can be told. With the Great Patriots, in the beginning, he had wished to bridge the gulf between King and Parliament from the Parliament's side. With the appointment of Falkland and Culpepper, the King had at last sufficiently resorted to the principle to place Hyde and his colleagues in a mediatorial position which might enable them to build a bridge over the gulf. But because the King had done this late in the day, and because he did other things too, they were left in mid-air and were under the necessity of bridge-building in both directions. There Hyde had remained suspended until the failure of the militia negotiations. Thereafter, from the King's side, he had pressed for the maintenance of bridges in

[1] *S.P. Clar.* II, p. 284. See also *A full Answer.*

the cases of Essex and Holland and Littleton, and for their extension in the cases of Northumberland at the Treaty of Oxford, of the Earls later in 1643, and of the by then eclipsed peace party leaders at Uxbridge. When the chasm itself disappeared and a new and unrecognizable landscape emerged, as it was beginning to do at Uxbridge, the principle remained and was embodied in personal contacts, whether upon the scenes of formal negotiations for settlements with which he could have no sympathy, or at any opportunity which might present itself. The purpose of the application of the principle in the new circumstances was to encourage a historical process in its working towards constitutional reconstruction and political reconciliation. At the Restoration it was to be crowned with success.

The truth is that in this second phase Hyde had become a strikingly penetrating and successful exponent of the art of contemporary historical analysis, and better as a historian than he had been as a politician. And yet it must be observed that the historian's analysis stems directly from the assumptions, the actions and the experiences of the original political phase. His historical insight could have had no other foundation than the work he had done in terms of, and on behalf of, an original non-violent parliamentarism.

As for the actual *History* itself, it has been conceded that it reveals Hyde as a Royalist at least in his capacity as a historian. But that is but an aspect of the truth that the *History* is the retelling of the past in terms of the ideas and the recommendations of Hyde's second or historical phase. It is the furnishing of a background to his interpretation of the movement of the contemporary scene, though that contemporary interpretation is itself the product of historical reflexion on past political experience.

If I were now to die, I can impute the ill success of the King's affairs in these contentions to no one thing more (drink excepted) than that supine temper in many honest men, of endeavouring expedients to satisfy those, who were confessedly, wickedly in the wrong, and breaking the quarrel into pieces. This particular [a point of Church government at that time under negotiation with the Scots] was not worth a war. . . . There ought to have been no other matter in issue on the King's part, than that they would compel His Majesty by arms to consent to laws and acts, which it was in his power lawfully to refuse; this was, and is in truth, the quarrel; and when you change it, you will have a worse; yield to one thing, you justify the demand of another; and it is an even lay, there will be more reason to demand the second than the first, you having by that yielded and receded from the best argument you had to deny.[1]

This was not the doctrine of 1642 when he had set himself against the unconciliatory attitude of the King as much as against that of the violent party, attitudes which between them had led to war. It was the doctrine of 1646–8, when the King's outlook which he had opposed had passed into history and it was not only necessary to make the best of it, but entirely possible and indeed inevitable emotionally that he should have done so. It was a doctrine and a recommendation arising from the contemplation of the existing scene as the irreversible outcome of the years which were past. The mental continuity of the second with the first phase explains the fact that it has been possible to use the *History* and the *Life* in the reconstruction of the first phase. But the great break in the train of events which preceded the writing of the original *History*, together with the relationship with the King which had become so important to him, explain why the criteria retrospectively employed by the writer are different from what he would have employed at the time the events described were taking place.

It can hardly be denied that the interpretation of the first phase which is involved in Hyde's work is grossly misleading if his own attitude during that phase is under consideration.

[1] Hyde to Lord H.: 6 February 1648. *S.P. Clar.* III, pp. 2.

Indeed, Hyde himself in the early period was wrong by the standards he was now employing: but he still contrives to imply that it was he who was right and the King who was wrong. Certain facts lessened the violence of the transition where his own standing was concerned. It had never in the first phase been a question of recommending a compromise involving a radical change of the King's constitutional position as defined by the legislation of the first session of the Long Parliament, since that constitutional position had naturally been assumed by him to provide the setting for reconciliation. The King would certainly have accepted no further modification and the revolutionaries, including himself, would never have accepted less. Secondly, and more important, he had penned for the King the declarations of the late spring and summer of 1642, and these, though in a context different from that now assumed by Hyde, had certainly embodied in striking form and with striking results the sentiment of 'thus far and no further'.

But such considerations will not account for the fact that the *History* is not a confession of past political error on Hyde's part, nor an admission that the King had been right after all. By the new standard the King may have been right to have been so unco-operative and unconciliatory in his attitude to the insurgents and Hyde may have been wrong to have worked for reconciliation between Charles and his opponents: but it was still Hyde who had been right and the King who had been wrong because the King's intransigence towards the rebels was not only not the whole story: it had not even been the main burden of it. Though he can explain the factors which extenuated and excused it, the King's worst fault in the story as Hyde now unfolded it had been his lack of confidence in his own judgement and the consequently erratic and inconstant character of his policy. With a fundamental and insurmountable distrust of the violent party and an honourable determination to defend the Church and the rights of the Crown against their attack, qualities which Hyde now capitalized as his chief political virtue, Charles, Hyde shows, had nevertheless and with the most disastrous results oscillated between or attempted to fuse together two incompatible courses of action, that recommended by himself and that recommended by the Queen and the Royalists. Hyde shows that his own policy had been wrong only because it had been applied in alternation with or in combination with that of the Queen, and we are to infer that without the latter element the combination of his own policy and the attitude of the King would have resulted in a policy which was right.

There was and there remained as Hyde looked back upon the past, indeed there remains even today, a possible doubt about the interpretation which ought to be put upon the King's attitude to the Revolution, and if it is a doubt which from one point of view justifies the conduct of Pym from the second session of the Long Parliament onwards, from another it justifies the conduct of Hyde in the same period and also the attitude which he now adopted as a historian. The *History* is a paradox only if we choose to see in it the spectacle of an enthusiast for the Revolution of 1640–1 arguing, however critically, the cause of the King who had never intended to accept it. In that case Hyde would be like Harrington, the republican theorist of *Oceana*, an instance of a man who, though moving in a different and incompatible world of thought, nevertheless fell under a Stuart spell. But Hyde for all his criticism never took such a view of Charles I. Such a view was the view of Pym. Nor was Hyde likely to make a worse estimate of the King's intentions in retrospect than he had done in the period when the events he now described had taken place. For he himself now agreed with what had apparently been Charles's belief at the outset, that the violent party were incorrigible and could never have been accommodated. The drastic actions, therefore, which he might originally have feared as anti-parliamentary in their fundamental bearing, he could, if not by any means condone, at least understand now as having arisen from temptations which were natural and difficult to resist.

Put into strictly constitutional terms the questionable point was whether Charles accepted the conviction of the men of 1640 that they had abolished the absolute prerogative. The difficulty here was that by definition the Crown's absolute prerogative was inseparable: it could not be abolished even by the King himself, and it followed that the Bills which seemed to have abolished it could be held to be *ultra vires* even though Charles had given his assent to them. In the King's favour, it can be pointed out that despite some hesitation in 1643, he had never acted on such a doctrine after the Revolution, and Hyde evidently did not now entertain grave doubts about the King under this head. Because he entertained no such grave doubts even the Queen's views on the Revolution, whatever they may have been and whatever he had in the past thought about them, did not now matter save in that they had represented a disastrously mistaken method. They represented not only a method which had been evil in itself, the method of force, but a method which when combined as a result of the King's uncertainty with concessions and attempts at settlement had merely strengthened the arguments of the violent party and increased their influence and their power.

Hyde went further even than this and implied that it was the Queen and not himself who in 1642 had represented the policy of concession. He did not blame her for the attempted compromise on the militia since it had been his own policy, but he was under no necessity of blaming himself, for it had never taken place. He did not mean, of course, that the Queen had entertained any sincere desire for compromise or that she had vacillated between concessions and the policy of forceful repression as the King had done: he meant that concession had been used in politic combination with the policy of force. Such an interpretation was not unnatural. He may not have initiated, as has been seen, even though he had emphatically supported the King's message to Parliament of 20 January 1642, and at least there had been one surrender, important in the event, which he had not recommended and for which he thought the Queen had been responsible, namely the surrender in the matter of the Bishops' Exclusion Bill.

By 1646 Hyde's failures which had been so largely due to the King were swallowed up in the failure of the King himself. Historical imagination induced by sympathy for Charles in his misfortunes and his own personal alienation from the violent party which produced an actual identification of Hyde's present mind with the King's past intransigence towards them, took the edge off his criticisms and formed the starting point for the second phase and the setting for the *History*. Perhaps now at least he could suppose that Charles had learnt from his failures. The *History* was an undertaking to write from the royal point of view and for the royal benefit and it makes him, though retrospectively only, into a Royalist. Hyde was now, in writing the *History*, actually taking the position which the King had taken in 1641–2 which had been royalist in that it had been based on the distinction between loyalists and rebels, King and Parliament. But he assumed that that point of view could also have been a parliamentarian one in that resistant and intransigent form which he himself had now adopted, and he postulated a royal benefit which would have flowed from an unqualified acceptance of the Revolution.

In the second phase, however, when Hyde stood for intransigence, the King and most of his adherents were inclined for compromise or at least, as in the case of Charles I, pretended in the pursuit of positive diplomatic objectives that they were. This statement, it has been explained, is misleading in regard to the continuity (in the sense not of the development but of the identity) of Hyde's mind and the bearing of the action which he now proposed, but it brings out the fact that he remained as far removed as before from the ordinary currents of royalism, and it has been seen that from his new standpoint the present attitude of the Royalists is projected back into the past so that it obliterates the true sense in which compromise, namely his own policy, had been an alternative, and completely reverses the parts as between himself and the Queen. In the months before the war and during the war he had been compelled to adopt royalist positions when, and because, the Royalists had moved a stage further on, and he had done so from a motive of parliamentarism and settlement. Now, when it is over, he has incorporated entire the unbending mentality which had characterized the King throughout the whole period from 1641 to the end of hostilities. The process with which he had had to contend from the outset had now repeated itself and on a spectacular scale, and he is left as isolated as before. The second phase, as a system of ends and means, recommended for contemporary application, was essentially as much an example of non-violent parliamentarism as the system of the first phase had been. The difference now between Hyde and the Royalists in the realm of method is still so great because it still involves a difference of purpose. As a politician, in the early period, his parliamentarism had included, as a matter of course, an element which is misleadingly termed royalism. As a historian, in the later one, he distilled a royalism which, as soon as he looked up from his manuscript to regard the contemporary scene, became, as a matter of course, nothing but a means to something which it is in no way misleading to term parliamentarism. The stories spread about him by Royalists, that he had planned to deliver the Prince of Wales to Parliament in the Jersey period, and later, that he had been in correspondence with Cromwell, though completely wide of the mark, are not without a symbolic significance in this connexion.

It should also be noticed that the ideas and recommendations of the second phase were superior as historical thinking when applied to contemporary events than they were when applied to the past and embodied in the actual *History*. The latter is vitiated as history by the doctrine of the original malignancy of the parliamentary leaders. The *History's* great merit lies in the inwardness which Hyde achieves in his presentation of the King's mind, and in its sustained sense of all-embracing and interacting movement, a quality which, because the doctrine of the original malignancy of the parliamentary leaders was artificial in the sense that he had not believed or at least had not acted upon it in the period he now describes, to a considerable extent survives the imposition of that doctrine upon it. On the other hand, it was a doctrine which in no way affected the quality of Hyde's contemporary historical analysis. On the contrary, it served to add dramatic point and pungency to the terms in which he made it. The *History*, therefore, not only misleads in the matter of Hyde's quality as a politician, it fails also to do full justice to him as a historian. The true justice to him in this latter capacity was done in his contemporary interpretations, the sufficient accuracy of which was demonstrated by events as they unfolded. It is true that Hyde was a Royalist only when he was writing the *History*. But he is a better historian outside his own *History* than in it, and outside it he is no more Royalist than before.

The late Sir Charles Firth maintains[1] that Hyde's account of the close of the upheavals and the Restoration contrasts with his account of their beginning; that in the latter he had exaggerated the importance of individual actions and dispositions, while in the former it is 'the current of human affairs which guides men's acts, whither they know not, whether they will or not. The individual actor, even when he seems to

[1] *E.H.R.* xix, p. 483.

direct the course of events, is in reality their creature.' Firth was thinking in particular of Hyde's treatment of General Monk. The General's contemporary biographers, he points out, agree in putting forward the view that Monk from the time[1] that he declared against the army's usurpation of the government had decided to restore the King, and so make him the hero of the Restoration. Hyde, on the other hand, declared that the General's behaviour was entirely moulded by events, by the 'accidents which fell out'.

It was the King's great happiness that he never had it in his purpose to serve him till it fell out to be in his power, and indeed till he had nothing else in his power to do. If he had resolved it sooner, he had been destroyed himself, the whole machine being so infinitely above his strength that it could only be moved by a divine hand; and it is glory enough to his memory that he was instrumental in bringing these mighty things to pass, which he had neither wisdom to foresee, nor courage to attempt, nor understanding to contrive.[2]

This was not mere spite on Hyde's part against Monk, and essentially, as Firth says, the view is correct. Firth also testifies to the high quality of the last book of the final *History*, and to its general consistency with Hyde's views and policy during the period[3] therein described. He shows that, while denying credit for the achievement of the Restoration to Monk or to anybody else in England, he also attributed nothing to himself, though he might very legitimately have done so.

These judgements by one of the greatest modern authorities are important. But it should be pointed out that in so far as a contrast between the earlier and the later work exists, it is due to the notion that the parliamentary leaders had cut out all their work from the beginning, and to his attempt in the earlier work to show what the King could and should have done to frustrate them. But even the original *History* written

---

[1] October, 1659. [2] Clarendon, *History*, VI, p. 164.
[3] September, 1659–May, 1660.

after Hyde's efforts as a politician had failed embodies a deep
sense of a process embracing and transcending human action.
Once Hyde had dropped, as he did in the later work, his
didactic purpose, that sense had uninterrupted play. There
is, therefore, no real contradiction between the earlier and
the later work. The profounder view entrenched itself throughout the historical phase, during and after the writing of the
original *History*, as he contemplated actions of the violent
party and their successors which could only be negative and
destructive, and as he criticized the royalist expedients which
must be impotent to effect the end desired. It is possible,
therefore, to understand the high quality of the last book of
the final *History*, written as it was at a time when the didactic
purpose had been abandoned and when Hyde had merely to
recapitulate what had turned out to be a correct contemporary
historical analysis. As Firth points out, the Restoration represents not only a triumph for Hyde's interpretation, but a
triumph for his policy, a vindication of its practicability
against all others. On the one hand, the sense of Providence,
of a creative process in events, presided in his mind: on the
other, the sense of the critical importance of the action of the
individual. He himself first devised, and then directed a policy
for the King which was based on historical insight into that
process, and we have seen how much emphasis he put upon
the importance of adhering to that policy. It was individual
wickedness and error which caused the Civil War, unleashing
gigantic necessities which must play themselves out. But they
would play themselves out in the end and to the advantage
of King and country, provided the King stood by the best of
his own personal past and that of his father and refused
altogether to handle the consequences of combined or contrary individual actions which had embodied themselves in
transient parties, doctrines and institutions. The action of the
first phase failed. That of the second succeeded, and largely
because the King was in a position to do so much less harm

to himself in the second phase than he had been in the first. Nor does it appear that this was a fact of which Hyde was unaware.

The final result was indeed paradoxical. The Restoration of King, of Parliament, and of Church was a triumph of statecraft, a proof of the superior practicability of Hyde's views to those of the 'mere moral man', and, at the same time, a supreme example of that transcendental element in politics which Hyde was later to defend and urge against Hobbes, an element which made politics irreducible to the positivism of *Leviathan*. This Restoration was not merely providential in the sense that all events were so: it was 'such a prodigious act of Providence as God hath scarce vouchsafed to any nation since he led his own Chosen People through the Red Sea':[1] it was effected 'by such an extraordinary influence of divine providence, that there appears no footsteps of human power in the deliverance'.[2] For 'no man living had of himself either wisdom enough to foresee, or understanding to contrive, or courage to attempt and execute it'. It was accomplished 'by a union of contradictions, by a concurrence of causes which never desired the same effects; making those the instruments of our recovery who had destroyed us...'.[3] Hyde was too modest. If there were no footsteps of human power, there were vestiges of human wisdom, and none other than his own; and if no one contrived, attempted or executed it, he at least in one sense foresaw it, peering far enough and confidently enough into the mechanics of that union of contradictions and that concurrence of discrepant causes and effects to enable him to find the method of co-operating with Providence. But to have admitted this would not have entailed the denial of the miraculous character of the Restoration. He could see into the mechanism: to do so was a duty of statesmanship. But the spectacular character of its operation, 'the

---

[1] Clarendon, *History*, VI, p. 143, and *Contemplations*, p. 744.
[2] *Contemplations*, p. 596.   [3] Ibid. pp. 582 et seq.

incredible expedition', facility and dexterity and, above all, its achievement without bloodshed of what must by all expectations on the natural plane have entailed it, these things were completely inscrutable. A Roman Catholic critic, Cressy, maintained that the distractions and eclipse of the English[1] Church were divine punishment for its political character. It was fitting that a Church so intimately involved in political interests should perish in a political upheaval. He also disputed the claims of Anglicanism on the ground that, unlike the Roman Catholic Church, it could boast of no miracles. Hyde disposed of both points at once. The Restoration was not only a divine attestation of the English Church, it was an attestation miraculous in such a degree that it dwarfed all the miracles of Rome, and stood on a level with the dry-shod passage of the Israelites through the Red Sea.

[1] *Exomologesis [or a Faithful narration of the occasion and motives of the conversion unto Catholic unity of Hugh-Paulin de Cressy, lately Dean of Laghlin etc. in Ireland, and Prebend of Windsor in England. Printed at Paris. Ann. Dom. 1647]*, pp. 108, 109.

PART III

RELIGION

§ 1. *The Tew Circle*

IN the first or political phase of Hyde's activity, ecclesiastical partisanship has no predominating place. It was not an ecclesiastical motive which made him change sides: for he did not change sides. He did not desert the Revolution in order to save the Church, for he did not desert the Revolution. And it is easier to say that he worked to heal the breach between King and Parliament at the expense of the Church than it is to say that he did so in order to save it, for his concern seems to have been to save the Revolution. The most it has been possible to say so far is that in and for the pursuit of that purpose his anglicanism had placed him in a favourable position. Moreover, the second or historical phase is explicable, and would seem best explained, apart from any such ecclesiastical preoccupations as have been attributed to him.

But such preoccupations have been ascribed to him because he ascribed them to himself. When, long afterwards, he wrote about these events from an autobiographical angle, he emphasized his churchmanship, describing himself as having been an anglican stalwart from the beginning, and making of that fact a fundamental in the explanation of his conduct. He says that he was a friend of Laud:[1] that he opposed the bill to exclude the bishops from the House of Lords even in the first session of the Long Parliament, and when Falkland supported it: that he was made chairman of the committee on the Root-and-Branch Bill in order that his opposition to it might be muzzled, but that he contrived to impede the Bill in that position: that it was his conspicuous churchmanship which

[1] *Life*, I, p. 56–7.

240

brought him to the King's notice: and that he was opposed to the royal assent being given to the Bishops' Exclusion Bill in February 1642. He tells the story[1] of a conversation with Edmund Verney on the eve of hostilities which brings out his conscientious anglicanism, and relates also how he defended the Church at the Uxbridge negotiations and was praised by the King for doing so.[2]

This picture was one which Hyde drew in the last exile. There is no warrant for supposing, on that account, that any one of these details is fictitious. But the impression created by them as a series penetrating and promoting his activities has been rejected in this study. It is not, of course, to be inferred that Hyde deliberately set out to create a false impression. On the contrary, and in all good faith, the story would have tended naturally to take such a shape when looked back upon, and even from the point of view adopted for the writing of the original *History*.

In the first place there was an emotional factor. Hyde had been moved to an intense feeling for Charles I. Charles had been a great churchman and seems always to have thought of Hyde in the same light. Hyde, of course, knew and rejoiced in this when he came to write, and his awareness would be well to the front in his record of a story which was so much concerned with his connexion with the King. But just because it was Hyde's Anglicanism which had originally attracted Charles's notice and so was the cause of their relationship, the special intensity of the Anglican fervour displayed in the *History* need not have been more than the consequence of Hyde's recollection of his relationship with the King. It is in itself no evidence for the quality or the significance of his original churchmanship.

Secondly, as has already been stressed, Hyde on looking back from the hither side of the Civil War, was impressed by the advantage which had accrued to the King on the occasions

[1] Ibid. II, p. 134–5.   [2] Ibid. III, p. 184.

when he had stood firm, and by the profit to his enemies when he had yielded on the points in controversy. It was Hyde's belief, expressed in 1648, that the King's stand for the Church had drawn more men to him in the last resort than any other circumstance.[1] Such a consideration could not possibly have informed Hyde's own policy before the Civil War. What we have here was, in fact, a distillation from reflecting upon the astonishing circumstances of the outbreak of war and the extraordinary way in which, after the events of early 1642, the King had acquired a party. Hyde's own literary activity in the manifestos which followed the rupture of the militia negotiations involving as it did a stand for the Church in addition to the stand for the King's constitutional rights, played a notable part in this, and that fact, though originally part of a story of failure and not of success, formed the bridge over which, urged by the now unalterable facts of the past and a quite new situation in the present, he passed from the original to the final attitude. From that final angle, it was natural not only to antedate his own adoption of the more rigid policy, but also to distort its original motive and purpose. To understand how natural it was that this should have happened, it is only necessary to recall that the doctrine of the *History*, when it ultimately came to express itself in autobiographical form, had behind it the overwhelming vindication provided by the Restoration. A modern scholar, however, has shown[2] that even at the Restoration Hyde's policy was not as rigidly and consistently anglican as he afterwards made it out to have been.

The question arises whether Hyde's ecclesiastical emphasis is to be dismissed as of a mainly conventional character. But it would be rash to conclude that the considerations mentioned above justify such summary procedure. It has been pointed out, and very rightly, that 'when seventeenth-century writers profess religious motives they are to be believed unless

[1] *S.P. Clar.* III, p. 3. [2] Keith Feiling, *E.H.R.* XLII, p. 407; XLIV, p. 289.

there is evidence to the contrary'. Lord Acton, speaking of Hyde, went so far as to say that he 'had reflected more deeply than any man then living on the problem of Church and State'.[1] In the absence of overwhelming evidence to the contrary, it is proper to allow that the religious opinions and ecclesiastical policy of Hyde constitute questions in themselves. If it is necessary to throw doubt upon his own suggestion that his action in the first phase sprang from High Church views and attachments, that fact does not preclude the possibility that formed convictions but of another pattern had some part to play.

In examining this matter, it is necessary to investigate the relationship which existed between Hyde and Falkland, for both the facts and also Hyde's interpretation of them, are bound up with that relationship. Hyde was critical of Falkland. He makes himself out to have been superior to Falkland as a champion of the Church. But evidence which he himself provides, indicates that in certain respects which were of fundamental importance, Hyde's own opinions in matters of the Church were identical with those of Falkland.

Hyde describes in the *Life* the wide circle of friends in London, with whom as a young man he spent his time, and how he was obliged to withdraw somewhat from this company to meet the call of professional legal studies; from all, that is, except Selden for whom he had a special devotion, and who, of course, would assist rather than impede his studies in the law. But he goes on that he had 'then another conjunction and communication',[2] an inner circle of friends from which no studies could draw him, implying that here was a connexion as important and influential with him as his professional ties. He was often heard to say, he wrote, 'that if he had any thing good in him, in his humour, or in his manners, he owed it to the example, and the information he had

[1] *Lectures on Modern History*, 1930, p. 209.　　[2] *Life*, I, p. 34.

received in, and from that company, with most of whom he had an entire friendship.'[1] These persons were Lucius Cary, later Lord Falkland, Francis Wenman, Sidney Godolphin, Edmund Waller, Gilbert Sheldon, George Morley, John Earle, John Hales and William Chillingworth. Of these, for Hyde, Falkland was easily the chief. He describes with famous charm and skill the circumstances and character of Falkland, and how 'his house where he usually resided (Tew, or Burford, in Oxfordshire) being within ten or twelve miles of the university, looked like the university itself, by the company that was always found there'.[2] Falkland himself, residing at one or other of these country houses, was the centre of the inner circle of Hyde's friends. This circle developed a strong theological colour. 'Here Mr Chillingworth wrote, and formed, and modelled, his excellent book[3] against the learned Jesuit Mr Knott, after frequent debates upon the most important particulars; in many of which, he suffered himself to be overruled by the judgement of his friends....'[4] Chillingworth was the leading intellect, and Falkland was very close to him in his sympathies and outlook. John Hales, a close friend but less frequent visitor made a third contributor, and between them these three gave the circle of Tew the character of a theological group with distinctive tenets.

Its intellectual setting was formed, in the wider sense, by the impact of the Counter-Reformation upon the heritage of the Reformation, and, in particular, by the nature of religious controversy in England. The Counter-Reformation had sharpened and intensified such controversy in Europe beyond all bounds. From the beginning, it had passed the limits of verbal war. Germany and France had already suffered civil wars, and now a climax seemed to have come in a new German war which threatened in the supposed

---

[1] *Life*, 1, p. 34.   [2] Ibid. p. 39.
[3] *The Religion of Protestants* [*a Safe Way to Salvation; or, an answer to a book entitled Mercy and Truth, or Charity maintained by Catholics,* 1638.]   [4] *Life*, 1, p. 40.

interests of religion to engulf the whole of Western Christendom. England had as yet escaped civil war, and its Stuart rulers had declined to commit the country to a Protestant crusade at the request of the Puritans. But what was lacking in this respect was in some degree balanced by a peculiarly complicated situation. For not only was there, as in Germany and the United Provinces, a split in the Protestant ranks which made the struggle a three-cornered one, there was also a development in the aims and methods of the dominant party which itself perplexed and exacerbated controversy.

The Roman Church had consistently argued that the Fathers and Councils of antiquity were on its side. This, of itself, was a standing invitation to its opponents to shift the dispute into mainly historical channels, and pride of scholarship with the improved critical apparatus of the age reinforced the reasons rooted in religious conviction for accepting the challenge. But the Church of England had from the beginning been especially susceptible. In the first place, temperamental conservatism in such leaders as Cranmer and Parker, when added to political motives, had left it with a stronger connexion with tradition than any other reformed Church. In the second place, such men as these were small men with eclectic minds, and there had been no leader of sufficient eminence to bind the Church as a body to himself as a contemporary source of interpretation. This had left it relatively free. In the third place, to the many who were conscious of a vacuum and wished to fill it by adopting the system of Calvin and thereby carry the Reformation a stage further, their opponents found that the best replies could be found in the armoury of antiquity. But lastly, the anglicans came to the conclusion that in their lack of a Luther or a Calvin they inherited a blessing in disguise. Not only did they not want such a leader, they rejoiced in his absence, for it left them free to stress the implications of the traditional nature of their settlement. In the revival and reconstruction which was under way in the early seventeenth century, a negative conservatism was turned into a positive and constructive one. No longer was the existence of a vacuum to be denied and the Calvinists to be kept at bay with weapons drawn from the primitive Church, the vacuum was to be by implication admitted and filled from the source which had previously only provided arguments against change. Mere arguments from antiquity became, under such men as Bancroft, Andrewes, Overall, and Laud, the advocacy of the ideals and practices of antiquity. The Christianity of the English Church was to be the Christianity of the early Fathers and Councils

Among the consequences of the new historical theology there were two which were important in the present connexion. Controversy in the first place, was increased in range and complexity, and, consequently, in inconclusiveness. On the one hand, there would be superficial knowledge and the exercise of ingenuity for which there was only too much opportunity, and, on the other, serious scholarship suffering from bewilderment for which there was only too much cause. Secondly, the threat from the Counter-Reformation was aggravated. A Protestantism which committed itself to such difficult terms of reference, and, while requiring authority in excess of the Bible, committed itself to finding it in so obscure and confusing a medium as antiquity, was an easier prey to Rome than the earlier Protestantism had been. Moreover, on many specific doctrinal points antiquity seemed to favour the claims of the Roman Church. Chillingworth himself, in listing the reasons which weighed with him, when, for a brief period, he became a Roman Catholic, placed among them the consensus in Rome's favour on the part of the primitive Church and Fathers. Isaac Casaubon, the foremost scholar of the age, was very hard pressed by Cardinal du Perron on this matter, and might have had to admit defeat, had not a timely remove to England placed him in the company of like-minded but unshaken Anglicans of the new school. Whether it was because Andrewes was a better scholar than Casaubon or whether it was because he was a worse one, or whether it was because he had the freedom and the standing of the English State establishment which kept the Romanists at a safe distance, the fact remained that Andrewes was not to be shaken. But the very steadiness of the school of Andrewes and Laud as against Rome worked in another way to increase the menace from that quarter. For though not strong enough to divide the forces of the Counter-Reformation, the new Anglicanism was strong enough, and especially with the convinced and devoted adherence and support of Charles I, to constitute a Counter-Reformation within Protestantism itself.

'Hobbes of Malmesbury would often say that he [Chillingworth] was like a lusty fighting fellow, that did drive his enemies before him, but would often give his own party smart back blows.'[1] The men of the Tew circle roused themselves against the Counter-Reformation, but attacked it from a position so placed that their missiles inevitably struck the High Anglicans as well. That circumstance followed from the fact that they attacked controversy in itself as then conducted. There would have been nothing profound or unusual about that. To deplore controversy was common form with every controversialist. Moreover, the exasperation of the laity in the face of endless ecclesiastical dissensions was already observable in many forms. But these men represented something more than either ecclesiastical commonplace or lay exasperation. They represented a revival, in circumstances which made it even more apposite than before, of the critical humanism of such men as Erasmus and Acontius. It was a view which was not only critical in regard to the consequences of controversy, but deeply sceptical in regard to the factors which produced it and gave it its importance in the eyes of those who conducted it.

[1] *Athenae Oxonienses*, 1692, II, p. 22.

17-2

Such a view involved much more than attacking any one Church. For it was the destruction of the hegemony of the Church of Rome and the consequent and continuing process of dissolution within the new churches which presented the problem which faced them. The greater part of controversy was precisely on the question of the authority for settling differences and the question of the criteria of orthodoxy. In a united Christendom, these had not been questions at all, or, at least, they had not been problems, for every one knew the answer. In a divided Christendom, and here the Tew circle took up their argument, the trouble arose because all parties tended to assume that these questions were not two questions but one question. But that was an error. The two questions had different answers. The answer to the first was that there was, in the usual sense of the term, no authority by which differences should be settled. The answer to the second was that the criteria of othodoxy were furnished by the Bible. The great Protestant parties would have considered that they were in agreement with this latter statement. But they would have been mistaken, for this rationalizing school taught that orthodoxy consisted of that part of the content of Holy Scripture upon which all Christians, despite their differences, were agreed, the part, in other words, which was plain and clear and upon which controversy was therefore impossible. The Protestants certainly took the Bible as their starting-point, but the Tew argument was to the effect that it was a starting-point when it should have been a stopping-point. In the person of a Luther or a Calvin, who, it was assumed, interpreted the truth of the Bible with self-evident cogency, they committed themselves to a system of doctrine from which dissent was impermissible, and maintained that Scripture itself implied a system of doctrine or discipline or worship which was universally binding. Such procedure, according to this school, stultified the Biblical criterion, and not only assimilated the Protestants to the Papists, who, after all, appeared to erect their own structure upon a text, but put them at a disadvantage in that the Papists claimed an infallibility which the Protestants had in principle eschewed. In the super-structures of Protestant and Catholic alike, orthodoxy, the basic Christian truth, the faith necessary to salvation, was not at stake, and this was proved by the fact that they were not universally accepted. Only that which all Christian men agreed in believing was necessary to be believed. As for those things on which they were divided, they were not of vital consequence and Christian men should agree to differ. If this were true, as these men urged it to be, all the urgency was drawn from controversy as it was then waged. It was no longer a matter of eternal consequence that men should be persuaded, and still less forced, to accept the whole system of Rome, for instance, or the whole system of Geneva. Plenty of room for contending there undoubtedly was, and it was not necessary to give up doing so. But it must be understood that nobody's salvation was at stake, and that unity in diversity through charity must be maintained.

Controversy as commonly conducted was unnecessary. There was no need to stress that it was bad for that, at bottom, was the starting-point of the Tew argument. 'Nothing troubled him more than the brawls which were grown from religion', wrote Hyde of Hales,[1] and it was equally true of the others. But in addition to being unnecessary and bad, controversy was also to a large extent vain. This was not only because people refused to be convinced by argument, a fact which these men, because of their rationalist strain, were not inclined to stress, but also, and chiefly, because the authorities upon which so many of the disputes between Papist and Protestant, and *a fortiori*, between Protestants, turned were inherently unsound. They pointed out that the Scriptures were useless *in foro contentioso*. Chillingworth[2] held that there

[1] *Life*, I, p. 50.
[2] Chillingworth, *The Religion of Protestants*, 1845, p. 201.

was a distinction in the Scriptures between what was revealed because it was necessary and what was necessary because it was revealed, and he would not have allowed the Calvinists, for instance, with their biblical schemes for the government of the Church, to assert that the distinction was not an important one. He maintained, in common with Falkland and Hales, that the function of Scripture was to impart a revelation which was of its very nature, and of necessity, indisputable, and that it had, and could have, no other function. What, on the other hand, was necessary because it was revealed was only necessary to those who could understand it, in that it was revealed only to that class of persons. It was impossible that all should understand everything that was revealed. Where it was not plain, Scripture produced controversy, it could not cure it.

Nor were unwritten tradition and 'traditive interpretations of Scripture',[1] which the Romanists quoted and the traditionalist Protestants quoted, any better. It was not that the Tew circle repudiated the ancient maxim that a tradition universally and always held must be true. It was rather that it seemed to them that no tradition could survive the test. The only sure traditions were first, the Bible itself and secondly, the belief regarding its nature and significance. Certain things which seemed to have been universally held in early times were now universally repudiated.

It was the same with the ancient Fathers and Councils, the authority which the Romanists were accustomed to urge and which the new school of Protestants in England had adopted to the increment of controversy and the advantage at worst of Rome and at best of what appeared to many to be a new and retrograde Protestantism. Falkland, wrote Hyde,[2] 'had read all the Greek and Latin Fathers...for in religion he thought too careful and too curious an enquiry could not be

---

[1] Chillingworth, *The Religion of Protestants*, p. 461.
[2] *Life*, I, p. 40.

made, amongst those, whose purity was not questioned, and whose authority was constantly and confidently urged, by men who were furthest from being of one mind amongst themselves; and for the mutual support of their several opinions, in which they most contradicted each other'. In this aspect of the matter Chillingworth, Falkland and Hales were assisted by the appearance in 1631 of Jean Daillé's *Traicté de l'employ des saincts peres, pour le jugement des differends, qui sont aujourd'hui en la religion.* This book, written by a French Protestant of deep learning, was devoted to showing that inquiry into the doctrines of the early Fathers was 'of such vast and almost infinite labour, that it made him very much doubt whether or not we could be ever able to attain a full and certain assurance what the positive sense of the ancients had been, on the whole body of controversies now debated in this age';[1] and secondly, that though these Fathers were indeed 'very able and excellent men', they were, notwithstanding, 'still men, subject to error, and who had not always the good fortune to light upon what was true and sound'.[2] These arguments were driven home with such comprehensiveness and force that there was little left to be said provided the reader was predisposed to agree with the thesis. Daillé provided the Tew circle with an admirable critical demonstration of the point that it was useless to appeal to antiquity. Falkland called him the Protestant Perron.[3] The appeal to antiquity had multiplied the inconclusiveness of controversy and generated a fog from which only those with minds already made up were able to emerge. The Tew theologians declared that the resort to the Fathers necessarily produced obscurity. Falkland wrote of them[4] that 'many are lost, many not lost

[1] English translation of *Traicté* by T. Smith, re-edited and amended by G. Jekyll, 1843, p. 168.   [2] Ibid. p. 225.
[3] [*Sir Lucius Cary, Late Lord Viscount of*] *Falkland,* [*His Discourse of Infallibility, with an Answer to it: And his Lordships Reply. Never before published. Together with Mr Walter Mountague's Letter concerning the changing his Religion. Answered by my Lord of Falkland.* 1651,] p. 202.   [4] Ibid. p. 280.

not to be gotten, many uncertain whether Fathers or no Fathers, and these, which we have, and know, being too many for almost any industry to read over, and absolutely for any memory to remember...'. Chillingworth, no longer a Papist and writing *The Religion of Protestants*, peered back into the past and could see only 'some Fathers against others, the same Fathers against themselves, a consent of Fathers of one age against a consent of Fathers of another age...'.[1]

In Daillé and the Tew theologians there is to be seen a further stage in the development of criticism. The expansion of patristic learning in Catholic and Protestant alike had at first gone with the exaltation of the Fathers as a standard of reference. But now the most learned in this field, including certain Roman scholars, discovered that the difficulties outweighed the advantages. A more relentless historical criticism now corrected what had been an excessively historical drift of mind. The discovery of the inconclusive results of patristic study was naturally encouraged by the presuppositions of the main contending parties. Rome, believing that the Church of every age was equally inspired, must necessarily have admitted in the last resort that the Fathers were only to be heard in so far as they agreed with the Church. Conventional Protestants as represented for instance by Daillé, the Huguenot, had all along believed that the corruption of historical Christianity dated from the first days, and, consequently, that the Fathers could by no means be said to be incorrupt. In fact, Daillé said that one of the right uses of them was precisely to show how soon and how extensively the corruption had spread. Protestants of this conventional type were interested only in the age of the Gospel and in its recovery in their own time. The school of Tew were not mainly concerned to agree with Daillé in stressing that all Christianity had been darkness between St Paul and Luther, or that all the darkness had been dispelled at the Reformation and,

[1] Chillingworth, *The Religion of Protestants*, p. 461.

consequently, that the Reformers were incomparably more reliable than the Fathers. Falkland explained[1] that the Reformation had been tentative and that it was not final, that its instincts were sounder in what it denied than in what it affirmed, and that many of its leaders had gone astray into a dogmatism as noxious as the one they had abandoned. But neither could the Tew circle recognize any special virtue in the age of the Fathers. It was difficult to discover what the Fathers taught, and their opinions even if they were discoverable did not necessarily bear upon the disputes of an age so different from their own.

The High Churchmen, however, while agreeing with Tew in the relative detachment with which they regarded the Reformation, were different in their attitude to the Fathers. As has been shown, this school, not content with using the Fathers in argument, a practice which was unsatisfactory because of its difficulty, actually took them for their point of departure and standard of reference in ecclesiastical reconstruction. Rome and the older Protestants could afford to be encouraged by the latest drift of scholarship. But the High Anglicans were committed to a vested interest in the intelligibility and in the compelling authority of the Fathers. The patristic ages were the ages of an undivided and, it was held, of an uncorrupted Christianity. Casaubon, for instance, took the first six centuries with special emphasis on the epoch after Constantine. '*Hoc saeculum*', Casaubon wrote of the age of Constantine, '*cum duobus sequentibus*, ἀκμὴ τῆς ἐκκλησίας, *flos ipse ecclesiae et aetas illius aurea queat nuncupari.*'[2] Upholding the primacy of Scripture, the High Anglicans, nevertheless maintained that its revelation must have been most accurately apprehended at a period near enough to the age of Christ and the Apostles to escape corruption, but far enough away from that age for its implications to have been adequately apprehended. Of

[1] *Falkland*, p. 138.
[2] *Introduction to the Literature of Europe, in the fifteenth, sixteenth, and seventeenth centuries*, Henry Hallam, 1839, III, p. 56 n.

the over-systematic elaborations of later times they were almost as chary as they were of medieval superstitions. Accordingly, in all matters of doctrine, government and practice, both disciplinary and liturgical, resort was to be had to this golden period as to a tribunal without appeal.

It might be that in the pursuit of this ideal the High Anglicans might get the better of Rome, since Rome was engaged not so much to discover what the Fathers said as to square their teaching with its own. Andrewes and Laud were less burdened in their inquiry. But even allowing that Daillé had overstated his case, was the appeal to the Fathers necessary? 'Those things', asked John Hales,[1] 'which we reverence for antiquity, what were they at their first birth? Were they false? Time cannot make them true. ... The circumstance ... of time ... is merely impertinent.' The fact of the matter was that the Tew theologians were not committed to a vested interest in any particular age at all. In this respect they were at one with the Roman Catholics. Certainly the ages of a Bible closed through ignorance or policy were bad. But whatever else it did, the Church had taught the fundamentals of faith. Salvation did not depend upon correct doctrine, but rather upon making the best of what was available. Salvation was relative to circumstances. Tew and Rome were agreed that 'the circumstance of time is merely impertinent'. But whereas Rome maintained that this was true because there was always the Church teaching an unchanging orthodoxy, the theologians of Tew did so because there was always the unchanging Deity, a Deity who did not demand the impossible. The knowledge of multiple truth was required only of those who possessed the capacity and the opportunity for acquiring it, and only the simplest beliefs were necessary to salvation. Similar teaching, no doubt, could be found among the Romanists, but what was part of casuistry for the latter, was made by the Tew circle into the central and solitary pro-

[1] Hales, *Of Enquiry and private judgment in Religion. Works*, 1765, III, p. 163.

position of apologetics. These men were determined to separate saving truth from correct theology, from merely human articulations. In respect of the latter, indeed, the facts seemed to them to tell heavily against antiquity and indeed against all ages except the present. In respect of knowledge in itself, as opposed to knowledge unto salvation, they had indeed a vested interest in a particular time, in the age of the Revival of Learning, which was their own. Falkland said that he could not see why the Fathers 'should weigh more than so many of the now learned, who having more helps from Arts, and no fewer from Nature, are not worse searchers into what is truth, though less capable [than the Fathers] of being witnesses to what was tradition'.[1]

The men of the Tew circle belonged to the Renaissance rather than to the Reformation. They went back beyond Calvin and Luther to Erasmus, whom Falkland frequently quoted. They would have agreed that in the distinctive products of the Reformers there had been a frustration of other ideals, and that new systems of dogmatics had cancelled an original and laudable ambition to loosen through critical reasoning the encrustations of late medieval thought. It is not to be forgotten that the High Anglicans also embodied much of this spirit as against both the Counter-Reformation and the by now well-hardened structures of orthodox Protestantism. But with them it was a different strand, the strand which imitated rather than the strand which sought emancipation from antiquity. Compared with the idea of Tew, even the liberalized and purified system of Andrewes and Laud, watched over by an adequately critical spirit, was still too like a religion encumbered with human thoughts and traditions. Controversy, the symbol and symptom of a disintegrated Christianity, could not for the Tew circle be made innocuous by the Laudian programme. It was only by proving that controversy was unnecessary that it could be

[1] *Falkland*, p. 294.

hoped to put an end to the damage which it caused. This could be done only by emphasizing the distinction between essentials and inessentials. Essentials, they urged, were so simple and so few that it was impossible to quarrel about them. Once this was recognized, the Churches which now 'persecuted, burned, cursed and damned'[1] one another would see that the gulfs between them were unreal, and that they were all by this test in the way of salvation and consequently as united as they needed to be. The recognition of this already present unity and of its implications in charity and accommodation was more important than the prosecution of the existing disputes and the attempt to achieve an unnecessary unity of opinion.

The Tew theologians wished to divert energies from the present channels of doctrinal disputation into those of practical and moral improvement. They did not identify Christianity with ethics, but they indicated that it should be concerned more with correct action than with correct thought. This might be a truism, but the present state of affairs made it necessary to stress it. Their humanism urged them in the same direction. Lutherans and Calvinists and powerful elements in the Roman Church, stressing the depravity of human nature, were committed to emphasizing a correct saving theology. But the men of the Tew circle preferred the Gospel narratives to the theology of St Paul and saw the completion of Christianity in the moral life. Chillingworth, wrote Hyde,[2] was of 'so rare a temper in debate that...it was impossible to provoke him into any passion': 'in all those controversies', he wrote[3] of Falkland, 'he had so dispassioned a consideration, such a candour in his nature, and so profound a charity in his conscience, that in those points, in which he was in his own judgement most clear, he never thought the worse, or in any degree declined the familiarity, of those who were of

---

[1] Chillingworth, *The Religion of Protestants*, p. 283.
[2] *Life*, I, p. 52.   [3] Ibid. pp. 40–1.

another mind; which, without question, is an excellent temper for the propagation and advancement of Christianity'.

Any other approach would merely, according to this view, accumulate evils. With a freedom from doctrinal preoccupations which was almost rationalism in the case of Hales, with a moral refinement which in that of Falkland bordered upon scrupulosity, and with a critical spirit which with Chillingworth verged on scepticism, the Tew circle were able to throw into high relief the anatomy and pedigree of evil in the intellectual history of Christianity. Falkland's Roman antagonist argued that for errors to have been able to enter ecclesiastical tradition, it was necessary to postulate a greater degree of wickedness than was easily credible. That, Falkland denied: 'neither see I any such unspeakableness in the contriving, but that ordinary understandings by several degrees, in a long tract of many ignorant negligent ages, egged on by ambition, cloaked over by hypocrisy, assisted by false miracles and maintained by tyranny, might easily both induce and establish them'.[1] Falkland and his associates pointed to the connexion between clerical vested interest and the doctrinal disputes which seemed to have made up the greater part of the history of the Church. Church history for Hales was one long story of 'the factionating and tumultuating of great and potent bishops',[2] and Falkland saw dubious motives at work almost everywhere in the working of ecclesiastical institutions. They could see little merit in General Councils, a point of view which put them at odds with the High Anglican party in that the latter reverenced the Councils of antiquity and professed to hope for a new Council to dispel the dissensions of Christendom. Hales's whole train of thought seems to have been started by his disgust with the Synod of Dort at whose deliberations he was present; leaving, as Hyde wrote,[3] 'the best

[1] *Falkland*, p. 189.
[2] Hales, *A Tract concerning Schism and Schismatics. Works*, I, p. 128.
[3] *Life*, I, p. 49.

memorial behind him, of the ignorance, and passion, and animosity, and injustice of that convention'. Of Councils in general, Hales wrote that they 'not only may and have erred, but considering the means how they are managed, it were a great marvel if they did not err...'[1] To him truth attained by the counting of heads seemed to be a self-evident absurdity. Councils were merely the *foci* at which clerical power and dogmatic system grew and spawned together, each producing and expanding the other. 'But I doubt', wrote Falkland,[2] 'whether Councils are fit deciders of questions; for such they cannot be if they beget more, and men are in greater doubts afterwards (none of the former being diminished) than they were at first.' The Reformation, the breach of continuity which should have exposed and ended all this, seemed only to have made the situation worse. Each new Church set out upon the path upon which the old one was already so far advanced, and proceeded to conduct incessant hostilities with its rivals. '...pride and passion, more than conscience, were the cause of all separation from each other's communion.'[3]

In the face of these evils, Tew declared that religion must be sharply distinguished from intellectual and political systems, even though the former might call themselves theological, and the latter, ecclesiastical. If only this distinction could be accepted and this liberty granted they believed that the peace and progress of Christendom would be assured.

For, seeing falsehood and error could not long stand against the power of truth, were they not supported by tyranny and worldly advantages, he that could assert Christians to that liberty which Christ and his apostles left them, must needs do truth a most heroical service. And, seeing the over-valuing of the differences among Christians is one of the greatest maintainers of the schism of Christendom, he that could demonstrate that only these points of belief are simply neces-

[1] Hales, *A Tract on the Sacrament of the Lord's Supper. Works*, I, p. 65.
[2] *Falkland*, p. 7.
[3] *Life*, I, p. 50.

sary to salvation wherein Christians generally agree, should he not lay a very fair and firm foundation of the peace of Christendom?[1]

Let those leave claiming infallibility that have no title to it; and let them that in their words disclaim it, disclaim it likewise in their actions; in a word take away tyranny...and restore Christians to their just and full liberty of captivating their understanding to Scripture only: and as rivers, when they have a free passage, run all to the ocean, so it may well be hoped, by God's blessing, that universal liberty, thus moderated, may quickly reduce Christendom to truth and unity.[2]

Falkland wrote in a similar strain hoping that if liberty were generally allowed and 'if particular interests were trod wholly underfoot', and if 'such spirits as those of Cassander and Melanchthon were more common, no considerable things would in a short time be left, but all would flow again in the same channel'.[3] Speaking more particularly of Protestantism, he was confident 'that all who receive the Scripture for the only rule, and believe what is there plain to be only necessary, would if they truly believed what they profess, and were not led aside either by prejudice, or private ends, or some popish relics of holding what they have long been taught, or following the authority of some by them much esteemed, persons either alive or dead, soon agree in as much as is necessary' and conclude 'no necessity of agreeing in more...'[4]

Reason as applied to the Bible, and the facts of history showed that God's promises to the Church had been misconstrued. It was the Divine Word which would not pass away, not ecclesiastical authority which would never fail. It was not true that a succession of apostolic ministers had preserved the truth intact, or even that it had maintained an unchanging doctrine. At no time, further, did it seem that

[1] Chillingworth, *The Religion of Protestants*, p. 280.
[2] Ibid. p. 284.   [3] *Falkland*, p. 139.
[4] Ibid. p. 235.

there had existed a unity of doctrine. When it seemed that there had, the observer was assuming on insufficient evidence something which was inherently unlikely. On the other hand, the fundamentals of religion had subsisted throughout all differences and in all circumstances. It was only necessary to admit this, and act upon the implications. Only what all agreed upon was necessary to be believed. Falkland went so far as to envisage a situation where 'some may convey some truths, and others another, out of which, by comparing their doctrine with the Scripture, men may draw forth a whole and perfect body of truth'.[1] This was the doctrine of Tew at its most optimistic, but it remains true that the ideas of the school as a whole were a reassertion of the spirit of Erasmus and an attempt in the circumstances of the Counter-Reformation and of the later developments of Protestantism to do what Erasmus had tried to do at an earlier period. 'Their pillars', wrote Falkland of Rome, and the words carry his criticism of all the other systems as well, 'are too weak to hold up any building, be it never so light, and their building is too heavy to be held up by any pillars, be they never so strong...'.[2]

In the speech[3] which Falkland delivered in the House of Commons in February 1641 the latent difference between the Tew position and the ideas of the Laudian regime flared into the open in vehement criticism, the burden of which was that the ecclesiastical government in obliterating the distinction between essentials and inessentials had made intolerable inroads upon religion and liberty. The Laudian clergy, he said, had tithed mint and anise and had left undone the weightier works of the Law. Moreover, in the sphere of what even they admitted to be one of opinion, namely the points of Predestination and Free-will, they had put the whole weight of the administration of the Church behind the advocates of one side

[1] *Falkland*, p. 287.
[2] Ibid. p. 298.   [3] J. Rushworth, 1692, pt. III, vol. I, p. 184.

of the question and against the advocates of the other. They had openly preached tenets conducive to clericalism. Episcopacy was not, Falkland declared, *jure divino*. Bishops were neither necessary nor unlawful. It was a question of convenience. It was convenient to retain the order, but its present power and policy were worse than inconvenient. Furthermore, he was in favour of an easing of the law in the matter of ceremonies.

The ideas of the men of the Tew circle have been described, not because they have not been adequately explained before, but because they were the ideas of the men who were Hyde's friends in early life and who on his own confession greatly influenced him. If he for his part imbibed them, there would be no cause for surprise. The men of Tew did not invent these ideas or preserve any monopoly of them. An even more potent contemporary example of such thinking as this is to be found in Episcopius, and in the Arminian movement in the Netherlands. Then there were the rationalistic Socinians, who, though often regarded as disreputable, were not lacking in influence. The discussion of the possibilities of ecclesiastical reunion which occupied men like John Dury often involved similar notions. Nor were they limited in their appeal to strictly theological minds. Indeed, they may be said to have carried a special appeal to minds which were not predominantly theological. There was the increasing exasperation of the laity, to which reference has already been made, and which in reaction to the political consequences of theological divisions tended to move in similar trains of thought. Bacon, Lord Herbert of Cherbury, Sir Henry Wotton, Hobbes and John Selden, though differing widely can be mentioned in this connexion. It is noticeable that ideas of this type seemed especially attractive to the political mind. The closed systems, both Protestant and Catholic, were sufficiently potent, and also sufficiently weak, to produce in all the quarters which

RELIGION

did not embrace them without reserve a mentality peculiarly
receptive to the kind of argument of which the Tew circle had
made themselves the masters.

Intimate as Hyde was with this circle, however, it is not to
be immediately presumed that he shared its opinions. He
described with great accuracy and sympathy the convictions
and the spirit of the Tew circle. But it can no more be assumed
that he shared Falkland's views because he wrote so inwardly
of them than that he shared the outlook and the judgements
of Charles I, because he succeeded in describing them so sympathetically. Hyde must not be allowed to suffer on account
of his excellence as a historian in the one case any more than
in the other. The inner circle, moreover, as Hyde described
it, included Sheldon and Morley, divines who, whatever the
nature of their opinions before 1640, came to represent points
of view different from the outlook which was shared by Falkland, Chillingworth and Hales, and Hyde may easily have
done the same. Even if he were originally closer to Falkland,
Chillingworth and Hales than the men who were to govern
the Restoration Church, there is nothing inherently improbable in his having outgrown an early standpoint. His
acutely sympathetic accounts of the spirit which informed the
gatherings at Tew may be little more than the product of a
tender memory of friends and influences which had long
passed away. There was, however, a sequel to these early
connexions, and the sequel shows that the reason he wrote so
sympathetically about the ideas of Tew was that they were
the ideas to which he himself still subscribed.

In the last year before the Civil War there appears to have
belonged to the close acquaintance and circle of Falkland and
of Hyde a clergyman called Hugh Cressy. Falkland had been
his patron, and had obtained for him in the year of the outbreak of the Civil War a canonry at Windsor. There is evidence of the closeness of the personal relationship, and evidence
provided by Cressy himself that he was under the intellectual

262

influence of the school of Tew.[1] But the doctrine of the men whom Cressy called the Chillingworthians was very well for him so long as the outward frame of the English Church subsisted. When it dissolved in the melting-pot of Civil War and defeat, he found that such a doctrine as theirs no longer convinced. Moreover, he would appear always to have set more store by the ideas of hieratic succession and priestly authority than the Chillingworthians could countenance, and was easily led to repudiate their attitude towards antiquity. The story of his conversion[2] to the Roman Church is told in *Exomologesis*, a book which is an extremely effective and damaging attack on the doctrine of Tew. He explicitly admits his roots in that school, and the great potency which *The Religion of Protestants* had with him. He declares that Chillingworth's book alone was the principal influence which held up his conversion. The admission is borne out by the fact that the book is in certain respects a new departure in Roman Catholic apologetic, one which was necessitated by Chillingworth's onslaught, and also by the fact that even in his Romanism certain strains of the old attitude remain. *Exomologesis* became an influential book and its author a leading defender of the Roman Church.

About a decade after the Restoration a distinguished anglican divine made a number of serious charges against the Church of Rome, including that of fanaticism, and Cressy hurried to its defence. That divine was Edward Stillingfleet. He was a man who as author of *The Irenicum*, a book of pronouncedly latitudinarian and liberal tone, could be termed a follower of Chillingworth. Cressy, in his reply, seized upon this fact, and calling his pamphlet *Fanaticism fanatically imputed to the Catholic Church*, proceeded to throw

---

[1] *S.P. Clar.* ii, p. 322. Also *Fanaticism fanatically imputed to the Catholic Church,* [*by Dr Stillingfleet, and the imputation refuted and retorted*, 1672], p. 165, where Cressy speaks of 'My noble dear Lord Falkland'. For Cressy's relations with Chillingworth, see *Exomologesis*, p. 141.

[2] Cressy entered the Benedictine Order, taking the name Serenus.

18-2

back in Stillingfleet's teeth the charge of fanaticism. He
argued that Stillingfleet's principles were not those of the
true and original English Church, that they had been introduced by the Tew circle, and that they were no better in the
last analysis than the ideas of the Church's enemies who had
overthrown it in the Civil War. He went so far as to assert
that he himself was not guiltless in respect of their genesis,
claiming to have introduced Daillé's book to Tew, and maintaining that this work had turned his friends from the patristic
studies which might have saved them from a doctrine which
in its rationalistic individualism was ultimately indistinguishable from Socinianism. He declared that the English Church
should lose no time in publicly repudiating 'all the Discourses of Mr Chillingworth, My Lord Falkland...Dr Stillingfleet and several other doctors...who all exalt their single
judgements above her Authority'.[1] No such repudiation was
made by the Anglican bishops. Instead, there appeared in
1673 a pamphlet defending the Chillingworthians written by
'a person of honour'. The name of the person of honour was
Hyde, at that time Lord Clarendon, and now in exile. The
name of Cressy probably sufficed to make him read the book.
The name of Falkland would have been enough to make him
write one in reply.

Hyde was concerned to rebut Cressy's contention 'that his
old friends' religion is new, that they have no reverence for
antiquity, no regard for the authority of the Fathers, and only
make use of their natural reason to find out a new religion for
themselves'.[2] If it were true, he said, that the Chillingworthian position was indistinguishable from the fanaticism
of the Puritans, it was odd that the latter should have failed
to recognize their friends in the camp of the enemy.[3] He
argued that the rationalism of Tew was not Socinianism and

[1] *Fanaticism fanatically imputed to the Catholic Church,* p. 169.
[2] *Animadversions [upon a Book entitled Fanaticism fanatically imputed to the Catholic Church by Dr Stillingfleet etc.* 1673 and 1674], p. 188.
[3] Ibid. p. 197.

that his friends had been true sons of the English Church, since its authority was one which allowed a place to the play of individual reason. As for tradition, there was, he maintained, no difference between the Church of England and the Church of Rome 'in any particular that relates to tradition, where the tradition is as universal or as manifest as it is in that of the Scripture'.[1]

It is clear nevertheless from Hyde's line of argument that he had assimilated the ideas of Tew. He proceeds, in fact, to expound them. Having declared that the Anglicans even exceeded Rome in the respect paid to the Fathers,[2] he could not forbear to add that neither the one Church nor the other, nor any Church in the world 'submit or concur in all that the Fathers have taught, who were never all of one mind, and therefore may very lawfully have their reasons examined by the reasons of other men'.[2] Moreover, the remark quoted in the preceding paragraph about tradition is essentially a Chillingworthian remark. He is saying that Scripture, its existence and its authority, is precisely the only certain part of tradition. It was impossible, he wrote, to be 'guided and governed' by tradition, that is by tradition other than that of the Scriptures, 'by reason of the incertainty of it'.[3] He cited the primitive controversy about the date of Easter, declaring that it would never have arisen had tradition been a reliable standard; 'and if tradition was so doubtful a guide in those primitive times, when so few years had run out, what must it be now, when five times as many are since expired'.[4] He declared that the attempt to end controversies by appealing to Fathers, to Councils or to Scripture had in 'near two hundred years' proved ineffectual,[5] and, as the Chillingworthians had done before him, indicated that it must necessarily do so. Of a future General Council, an authority

[1] Ibid. p. 174.   [2] Ibid. p. 189.
[3] Ibid. pp. 63–4. See also, *Contemplations*, p. 582.
[4] *Animadversions*, pp. 64–5.   [5] Ibid. p. 255.

recognized by the High Anglicans, he was as emphatic in a sense opposite to theirs. It was morally impossible, he said,[1] for such a Council ever to meet not only because the Pope would prevent it except on his own terms, but also for a reason which would have surprised more ecclesiastical minds: 'when the whole world is converted...it will be very hard for the greatest geographer to assign a place for the meeting, where the bishops from all parts may reasonably hope to live to be present there, and to return from thence with the resolutions of the Councils into [their] own country.' Even in the matter of recognizing contemporary Church authority, he chose to repel the charge of Socinianism, not by emphasizing an Anglican authority, but by exalting, in the fashion of the Tew circle, the place of reason in religion. Reason was the highest faculty with which mankind had been endowed: it was not to be laid aside because some things were out of its reach; 'and yet even when that is true (for it is often thought to be true, when it is not, and that some things are above reason which are not) reason shall contribute more to that obedience that is requisite than any stupid resignation to... authority...'.[2]

Hyde took this stand, because he, like the others in the circle of Tew, held that all that was necessary in Christianity was so simple that nobody could mistake it, and that these 'essential principles'[3] were to be found in the passages of the New Testament which it was impossible to misunderstand. He developed this theme at length in the pamphlet, doing so in his own terms and style. He explained that the apostolic witnesses had written 'with that plainness in what is necessary, that there remains no difficulty'.[3] 'If an exact knowledge in all particulars contained in Scripture were required from us, or if it had been in any great degree necessary', the writers, in that they were inspired, would have defined those things,

[1] *Animadversions*, pp. 148-9.
[2] Ibid. p. 205.   [3] Ibid. p. 111.

'in defining and determining whereof so much time hath been since spent, and so much uncharitableness infused into the hearts of men, so that instead of learning more of what Christ would have us know, we have almost unlearned all that He would have us do.'[1] Christ himself, who must have foreseen the contentions which would arise, nevertheless took no pains to explain doctrinal points 'or indeed to institute anything of speculative doctrine in his Sermon upon the Mount, which comprehends all Christianity, but to resolve all into practice'.[2] The Apostles had issued a warning that there was much in religion which could never be settled, and advised men to be satisfied with what was easily and plainly to be understood. Above all men were warned by them not to arrogate to themselves the divine prerogative of judging opinions from which they differed.[3] The wit of men and even the zeal of religion necessarily produced divergences of opinion. Opinions might be right or wrong, but it did not matter which they were provided their foundation was the Gospel in its simplicity. The Parable of the Wheat and the Tares, which Falkland had used,[4] and which was often used by liberal writers of the period, was also resorted to by Hyde to illuminate the whole matter; 'unskilful and unlearned men may believe that to be an error which in truth is none, but enough consistent with the truth, and angry men will not enough consider, if it be in truth an error, what root it may have taken from some unquestionable truth, and how far it may have insinuated itself into the minds of good and pious men, which ought to be undeceived by application and gentle remedies, and by time, but will violently tear it from the hold it had, and make a greater wound than they found'.[5]

The trouble had come in, Hyde showed, when the settlement of these differences about inessential matters had become

[1] Ibid. pp. 116, 117.
[2] Ibid. p. 124.
[3] Ibid. p. 125.
[4] *Falkland*, for example, p. 216.
[5] *Animadversions*, p. 121.

the interest of professional ecclesiastics. He pointed, as those whom he now defended had pointed, to what had happened: there had first been the settlement or the attempted settlement, for final agreement was not possible, of unnecessary points with the consequent accumulation of doctrines. Buttressing clerical power, these in their turn had made possible the attempted suppression of inquiry in the name of unity.[1] The distinction between 'spiritual' and 'temporal', integral to this ascendancy, had produced a 'high and dismal confusion'. In reaction from a situation which made the logic of Christianity a socially disruptive logic, Hyde, following those whom he championed, and with the same relatively favourable view of human nature and the same refusal to emphasize its depravity, argued that since it must be the essence of religion to be socially creative, the present logic must be anti-Christian and must therefore be broken. It was a view which transferred the stress from doctrine to conduct, and which regarded the clergy as the men chiefly responsible for the ills complained of. The anti-clericalism of Tew runs through Hyde's pamphlet in answer to Cressy. Hyde was quite willing to accept a passing remark of Cressy's: 'that there is a horrible depravation in the minds especially of ecclesiastics...'.[2]

Animadversions on Cressy's reply to Stillingfleet is not the only piece of writing in which Hyde showed the persisting influence of Tew. Two of the *Essays* are very relevant in this respect: *Against the multiplying controversies by insisting upon particulars that are not necessary to the point in debate*, and *Of the reverence due to antiquity*. The former, which is dated 1672, seems to have been written at about the same time as *Animadversions*. To a considerable extent it is the elaboration of the points made in that pamphlet. In that it differs, and in places it runs word for word with the pamphlet, it contains a more explicit account of Hyde's conception of authority in religion which must be left for discussion to a later stage. It differs

---

[1] *Animadversions*, pp. 125, 126, 130, 179.   [2] Ibid. p. 225.

also in a way which is indicated by the title. This strikes the predominating note. Hyde begins by dilating upon the futile insuccess of religious disputes and proposes to explain and to remedy it. Such disputes, he said, engendered more heat than light, and even when this did not happen deadlocks were no less complete. He explains, as he had done in the pamphlet, that men failed to distinguish essentials, and in consequence unchurched one another. Provided unity in essentials was admitted, it ought to be possible to state differences with a greater precision. It ought, also, to be possible to agree to differ when these could not be resolved. Viewing the matter with greater breadth than had been open to him in the pamphlet, and with freedom to choose perspective, he pointed out that the Roman Church was taken by surprise at the Reformation, and that the indiscriminate violence of that movement provoked on the part of Rome an equally violent and undiscriminating reaction. The interplay of wholesale condemnations was intensified when the men of the Reformation settled down to habitual abuse and reviling of their opponents. 'Time, observation, and experience', however, 'with the event of things',[1] working chiefly upon the lay power and in the lay mind, served to lessen the tension and to introduce a more moderate tone. Before long the clergy, and even the court of Rome, were affected by the change of atmosphere. But this, unfortunately, was only temporary. Of late, he said, the Roman party in England had renewed the spirit of bitterness and reproach, and once again the situation had been aggravated by the Protestant divines retorting with opprobrious epithets. It is obvious that Hyde was referring to the dispute between Stillingfleet and Cressy. He referred to the changed tactics of the Romanists, and thus may be presumed to have been thinking of Cressy. What is striking is that he clearly condemns not only Cressy but Stillingfleet, also.

[1] *Essays*, II, p. 170.

269

The second essay—*Of the reverence due to Antiquity*—is dated 1670, and this fact, in view of its contents, shows that Hyde's Chillingworthian opinions were not rediscovered merely in connexion with the dispute between Cressy and Stillingfleet. The view of Scripture is expounded which has already been described; it contains the plain essentials of belief, but 'whatsoever is too hard for us there to understand, is in no degree necessary for us to know; and yet we may lawfully endeavour to inform ourselves of what is difficult there, though we may be deceived in our inquiry, because there is no penalty upon being deceived'.[1] It was evident, he said,[2] 'that no one controversy that is at present in the Christian Church, can receive a determination, or procure a submission, by anything contained in scripture; each party alleging the same, or some other part of scripture, for the support and defence of their different, and sometimes contradictory opinions...'. It had been so from the beginning, and the Apostles had 'rather endeavoured to extinguish those disputes by introducing the severe practice of Christian duties, than by examining and explaining the matter of those disputes; foreseeing that the restlessness and curiosity of the nature of mankind, the pregnancy, and fancy, and invention of succeeding ages, would be always raising of doubts, and making new interpretations of whatsoever was or should be said'. But in this essay Hyde's opinions on this matter are set in a wider argument. In spite of the title or in accord with it, the reverence due to antiquity is to be understood in a limited sense, and is to be sharply distinguished from resignation to antiquity. Hyde's contention was that both in regard to 'the civil and politic actions of our lives' and also 'in matters of practice or opinion relating to religion', antiquity as distinct from Scripture was a false guide because so little was known about it.[3] The appeal to the distant past by ecclesiastical disputants was

---

[1] *Essays*, II, p. 79. [2] Ibid. pp. 86–7.
[3] Ibid. p. 78.

a universal practice, but it was, he said, an ignorant, uncritical and useless one.

The appeal to antiquity, Hyde declared, concealed a distinction and involved an ambiguity. Did the appellants mean 'the concurrent testimony and consent of those times, or the opinion and practice of some pious and learned men who lived in those times?'[1] If it was the former which was meant, even the age of the Apostles considered as a whole was dark, wicked and disputatious. The age which followed was worse, a fact which was proved because we knew so little about it. Indeed, assuming that it was the character of an age as a whole which was considered important, it would be necessary to restrict ourselves 'to the age that was near three hundred years after our Saviour'.[2] For between this latter age and that of the Gospel there 'is a very great *hiatus* in history', and this same fact governed the reliability to be attributed to the Fathers of that period. These Fathers, 'to whom we pretend to give most credit',[3] claimed no special revelation or inspiration. They had the Bible. But so had all subsequent ages. On account of the *hiatus* they had no better sources of information about the age of Christ than the men of Hyde's own day had about the England of the fifteenth century, which, as he pointed out, were poor enough. That the knowledge, furthermore, of primitive Christianity possessed by these Fathers was as defective as the nature of the case would lead one to expect, was proved by the fact that they contradicted one another. Where all the Fathers and all the Councils agreed, no modest man would refuse to follow them. But even so, there were points on which the whole primitive Church was agreed, but which no modern Church held. Hyde's contention was that the appeal to antiquity should be discontinued. He urged that men should recognize and act upon what was in fact true; that the criterion was not the verdict of antiquity

[1] Ibid. p. 79. [2] Ibid. p. 88.
[3] Ibid. p. 89.

but the minds of those who examined it. 'Religion and truth have suffered much more prejudice by the too supine submission and resignation to antiquity, and the too much modesty and bashfulness that restrained men from contradicting the ancients, than they have or are like to do by our swerving from those rules and dictates which they have prescribed to us.'[1]

Hyde admitted the excellence of particular men in antiquity as in all ages. But recognizing that the ecclesiastical appeal to antiquity usually meant more than this, he set out to develop the implications of an argument which considered the age of the Fathers in the wider sense viewing its character as a whole. Falkland, it will be recalled, had been struck by the superiority of contemporary doctors in critical method to those of earlier times, including the early Fathers, and had spoken of the modern time having more helps from arts and no fewer from nature than its predecessors. Hyde was much more positive. Running over the histories of Italy, of Spain, Germany, France and England, he declared that 'they who take the best survey of them, will hardly find a time in which he would wish rather to have been born, or persons with whom he could more usefully and happily have conversed, than in this very time in which he hath been born, how vicious and wicked soever; or those worthy persons with whom he hath or might have lived, how depraved soever the greater number is, as it hath always been'.[2] He declared that the men of his day 'by the improvement of all kinds of learning, by the knowledge of languages, and by the communication of all that was known, or was thought to be known, by those who lived before, had many advantages towards the perfection of any science, above those times to which they [the clerical apologists for antiquity] would have us to resort for information'. 'And if wisdom and understanding be to be found with the ancient, and in length of days, that time is the

[1] *Essays*, II, pp. 100, 101.   [2] Ibid. p. 102.

oldest from which men appeal to the infancy of the world.'[1] 'For if', Hobbes had written, 'we will reverence the age, the present is the oldest.' The true antiquity, said Hyde in one of his rare points of agreement with that writer, was not the past but the present, and this was as true of theology as of the other sciences. He did, he said, in truth believe, though with all respect to the writers of the third, fourth and fifth ages, that there had been many books written in the last hundred years 'in which much more useful learning is not only communicated to the world, than was known to any of those ancients, but in which the most difficult and important points which have been handled by the Fathers, are more clearly stated, and more solidly illustrated, than in the original treatises and discourses of the ancients themselves....'.[2]

The science, the recent improvement of which had made possible the investigation of the past condition of all other sciences, was nothing less than the science of history, and much of that improvement consisted in the discovery that all previous historical science had been of very poor quality. The very paucity of reliable historical knowledge, the inferior quality of the historians upon whom it was necessary to rely, told against the possibility of imitating antiquity. What was known was enough to indicate that the darkness, distemper and faction of the ages in which the Fathers lived had affected and misled them. Furthermore, the basic assumptions of historical science, with or without detailed information of past ages, taught that, and also explained why a man who wished to profess the religion of the Fathers, or wished to apply the 'politic maxims of antiquity' would find himself at a loss in his own time. For different climates and different nations produced peculiarities which could not be transplanted elsewhere. Conjunctures of time, the results of trade and foreign intercourse, the rise and fall of arts and sciences, and the vicissitudes of peace and war, gave rise to conditions which

[1] Ibid. p. 85.　　　　　　[2] Ibid. p. 132.

were unique and which must therefore provide their own criteria for the settlement of ecclesiastical questions. The Apostles themselves, Hyde believed, were well aware of this and assumed that succeeding generations of the faithful, 'observing the foundations laid and prescribed by them in the Scriptures, would raise such superstructures for the exercise and practice of religion, as would be most agreeable to the nature, temper, and inclinations of the people....'. Their own experience had taught even the Apostles 'that though the substance must be the same in all, the forms and circumstances must be different in several climates and regions'.[1]

Modern learning according to Hyde's view required that men should no longer look submissively and resignedly to antiquity for instruction in religion and politics. Instead, they should look critically 'without restraining...inquiry or rational conjectures'. Men should resort to the past, however venerable, merely in order to discover 'matter of fact'.[2] They should 'consider the improbability of this matter of fact, and so doubt the veracity of it, the prudence and fitness of another, and think it might have been better done'.[3] Historical knowledge was to be used to countermine that appeal to antiquity which was so often made by the ecclesiastical partisans, and to regard the ancients as fallible, constituted in his opinion precisely that 'extraordinary improvement that divine and human learning hath attained to', in the most recent age.[4] There was no reason why sacred learning should be more traditionalist than secular. There was no difference of principle between them. He held that there was sound evidence for thinking that the men of his own time in the realms both of knowledge and of conduct, whether sacred or profane, 'will buoy [themselves] up from this abyss of servitude [to the past], and by their avowed endeavours to know more than

[1] *Essays*, II, p. 88.   [2] Ibid. p. 133.
[3] Ibid. p. 95.   [4] Ibid. p. 131.

the former have done, will teach the next to labour that they may know more than we do'.[1]

Hyde and the theologians of Tew were in agreement in holding that where the essentials of Christianity were concerned the circumstance of time was merely impertinent, although they did not hold that this was the case in respect of the arts and sciences. There were two points here with both Hyde and the theologians with whom he alined himself. The distinction between learning and religion was drawn, but enthusiasm for the learning of their own day worked to blur it again. Hyde wrote that it did not seem a natural thing 'that religion should arrive at its perfection in its infancy',[2] and Falkland, at least, made statements as optimistic. This is hardly the spirit of ecclesiastical authoritarianism. The High Anglican school, it is true, would have agreed that learning and religion were not the same thing, and their traditionalism was for this reason a critical one. Nevertheless, they were traditionalists and their tenets conspired to suggest a sentiment the reverse of that which has been described. They seemed to suggest that religion had reached its perfection in its late infancy. With Hyde, it may almost be said that the question of the right use of the Fathers, which was answered to the disadvantage of the Fathers by his Tew colleagues, has broadened out into the question of the Ancients versus the Moderns, with the answer given in favour of the Moderns, and largely because the latter had discovered or rediscovered historical science.

Hyde is so emphatic about this that he has, at least in this essay if not elsewhere, stumbled upon something resembling a doctrine of human progress. This progress was not a steady or an ineluctable thing. It manifested itself in the advance of the arts and sciences, but it was subject to vicissitudes. It appears to have been one of Hyde's general assumptions that the advance of the arts and sciences was closely connected

[1] Ibid. p. 137.　　　　　[2] Ibid. p. 94.

with the security of property, not only of course from subversive movements on the part of the lower orders, but also from the depredations of government. This was a point which he urged against Hobbes, whose absolutist doctrine of politics appeared to him to threaten that security.[1] Advance was thus dependent upon the art and state of government, a matter which, in its turn, depended upon human wisdom and conduct. It was here that history supervened as the coping stone of knowledge, and, on the human side, the guarantee of progress. For history, by recounting the deeds of notable men, provided that storehouse of good examples, by resorting to which wisdom might be extended and conduct improved.[2] In the performance of this function Hyde filled his own historical work with minute and systematic portraiture of character. A reason, he considered, why the ecclesiastical world was in such a lamentable condition was that ecclesiastical historiography was in a similar state.[3] His 'history' of Falkland would be of assistance in this respect.

The fact which emerges from the above account is that at the precise period at which he was painting himself as the High Anglican stalwart, *par excellence*, and comparing himself in this respect with Falkland to the latter's disadvantage, Hyde was also expressing his adherence though in a new and historical dimension to the latitudinarian tenets of the school of Tew. It is important, moreover, to appreciate that this seeming discrepancy is not of such a character that it can be employed for the purpose of sharply distinguishing the occasional writings which have been discussed in this section from the better known *History* and *Life*. In the *Life*, it is true, Hyde told the story of the debate on the first Bishops' Exclusion Bill on 10 March 1641, of his own opposition to it, and

[1] *Survey*, p. 111.
[2] *Essays*, II, p. 134; Clarendon, *History*, III, p. 178 (from the *Life*); S.P. Clar. II, p. 386.   [3] *Essays*, II, p. 135.

of Falkland's support of it, explaining that the latter 'had in his own judgement such a latitude in opinion, that he did not believe any part of the order or government of it [the Church] to be so essentially necessary to religion, but that it might be parted with, and altered, for a notable public benefit or convenience'.[1] But that is not all. If Falkland's speech of February 1641 be compared with the *Life* and later *History*, it will be seen that on nearly every count on which Falkland had indicted the Laudian regime in 1641, Hyde had something similar to say.

Falkland declared that[2] 'some bishops and their adherents' had destroyed unity under pretence of uniformity, and having procured from the King an order silencing disputes about Predestination and Free-will, made use of it 'to tie up one side and let the other loose: whereas they ought either in discretion to have been equally restrained, or in justice to have been equally tolerated'. Hyde said in the final *History* that he thought the equilibrium of the Church had been unjustifiably upset. When Laud became Primate, 'it may be', he wrote, 'he retained too keen a memory' of what he had suffered under the Calvinist party; 'and, I doubt, was so far transported with the same passions he had reason to complain of in his adversaries, that, as they accused him of popery because he had some doctrinal opinions which they liked not, though they were nothing allied to popery, so he entertained too much prejudice to some persons as if they were enemies to the discipline of the Church, because they concurred with Calvin in some doctrinal points; when they abhorred his discipline and reverenced the government of the Church'.[3] 'Some doctrinal points in controversy', the high points of Predestination and Free-will, he went on, 'had been in the late years agitated in the pulpits with more warmth and reflections, than had used to be; and thence the heat and animosity increased

---

[1] *Life*, II, p. 85.   [2] J. Rushworth, pt. III, vol. I, p. 184.
[3] Clarendon, *History*, I, p. 121 (from the *Life*).

in books *pro* and *con* upon the same arguments', the Calvinist party hotly urging Calvin and the other group 'the Fathers, the Councils and the ecclesiastical histories, with the same heat and passion'.[1] Hyde explained that the party of antiquity had nothing to do with popery, or even with Arminianism, but neither had the other party, he considered, anything to do with the church system of Geneva. Its opinions were entirely compatible with loyalty to the English Church. Hyde's attitude towards the party of antiquity is, thus, critical in retrospect, and he thought Laud was to blame in the matter. Falkland had declared that the Laudians had brought in superstition and scandal under the titles of reverence and decency, and that the conforming to ceremonies had been more exacted than the conforming to Christianity. Hyde said nothing about superstition. Moreover, he thought that something should have been done, as it was done, to make the churches more seemly and the services better ordered, sentiments from which, it may be supposed, Falkland would not have dissented. But Hyde thought that the way the matter was managed, the disputes and the lawsuits, for instance, caused something not far short of scandal. As for ceremonial, the point was prosecuted, he said, 'with the same earnestness and contention for victory as if the life of Christianity had been at stake'. The matter was not 'in itself of that important value to be either entered upon with that resolution or to be carried on with that passion'.[2] The main body of Anglican opinion was allowed to become disturbed and apprehensive. And this, even allowing for the unco-ordinated actions of the other bishops and the indiscretions of inferior clergy, was, Hyde said, Laud's fault. The archbishop 'prosecuted this affair more passionately than was fit for the season'.[3]

This solidarity is apparent on other points. Falkland said

[1] Clarendon, *History*, I, p. 123 (from the *Life*).
[2] Ibid. p. 129 (from the *Life*).
[3] Ibid. p. 128 (from the *Life*).

that the Laudians had dissolved the bond with Protestants beyond the sea. Hyde also referred to this matter, declaring that the ruling party in the Church had in this affair contracted 'their considerations in too narrow a compass'.[1] Falkland referred with disapprobation to the support which divines like Manwaring had given in their preaching to Absolutist doctrines. Hyde expressed equal disapproval and for a similar reason of the political philosophy of the Court preachers.[2] Falkland denounced the clerical opposition to the Common Law and 'the hindering of prohibitions'. Hyde went out of his way to analyse the relations of common lawyers and clergy and, while blaming the lawyers, blamed also the clergy and their jealous policy towards the Common Law. Why, he asked, should they have preferred the Civil to the Common Law? From that misguided preference, he wrote, arose 'their bold and unwarrantable opposing and protesting against prohibitions and other proceedings at law...'.[3] Falkland thought the Laudians had kindled and blown the fire between England and Scotland in the matter of the liturgy for the northern kingdom. Hyde, in his accounts of that affair, leaves us in little doubt that he considered the management of it by the clergy to have been very unwise.[4]

There is a further fact which enhances the significance of such agreement. Hyde, unlike Falkland, had been on friendly terms with Laud, and in some respects an admirer of the archbishop. Moreover, he was inclined to date the troubled condition of the Church not from Laud's appointment as primate, but from that of Abbott, for whom he would have preferred to substitute a man of the stature of Andrewes or Overall. Archbishop Abbott, he thought, had been distinctively illiberal and had 'considered Christian religion no otherwise than as it abhorred and reviled popery, and valued

[1] Ibid. II, p. 419.
[2] Clarendon, *Survey*, p. 55; and *History*, I, p. 96.
[3] Clarendon, *History*, I, p. 405.   [4] Ibid. p. 98.

those men most who did that the most furiously'.[1] But friendly as Hyde was with Laud, he was strikingly candid in his criticism not only of the policy of the archbishop but also of his character, even, if the account in the *Life*[2] is to be credited, criticizing him on one occasion to his face. He deplored the primate's 'unpopular natural infirmities', his rough, indiscreet and inconsiderate methods. The archbishop never made a friend, he said, and contrived instead to make an increasing number of enemies.

Hyde was too attached to Falkland's memory for it to be conceivable that he should in retrospect have manufactured a difference where none had existed. It will be necessary, therefore, to assume that Hyde indeed differed from Falkland, and the nature of that difference must be established, but it will be impossible to establish it unless it first be understood that even if we omit the story of his political career, Hyde's own statements of principle and many of his historical judgements point to the fact that in a decisive sense his own presuppositions and those of Falkland were identical and remained so to the end. Nor does the story of his political career from 1641 to 1646 suggest otherwise. It suggests the application in practice of the principles which not only Falkland but he himself expounded, though long years after Falkland was dead. In fact those principles provide the key to a more thorough elucidation of the story which has been told in the first part of this book. In 1641 and 1642 Hyde's object had been not to gain the King a side for a forthcoming war, whatever the King himself may have been doing, but instead to promote a settlement and with that object he was not concerned to oppose concessions in the ecclesiastical realm, and indeed, as has been shown, in the answer to the Grand Remonstrance propounded a 'wholesome accommodation'. Thereafter, 'ease for tender consciences in matters indifferent' had remained a part, and, in the personal *apologia* of May 1642 and

---

[1] Clarendon, *History*, I, p. 119.   [2] *Life*, I, p. 58.

in the *apologia* of March 1644 which he drew up on behalf of the entire non-violent party, a self-confessed part of a peace settlement as he envisaged it. Such a settlement on its ecclesiastical side was defined in concrete terms in the extensive proposals for liberalizing the Church put forward at Uxbridge. The definition was not Hyde's, but it was completely in the logic of his own approach to the matter.

If there be independent reason to hold that the intrinsic immutability of the ecclesiastical order other than the essentials of religion was no part of Hyde's intellectual constitution when he became a member of the Long Parliament, or even at the period when the final *History* was put together, it will be no matter for surprise that the story itself shows that he never affirmed or denied, never did or refrained from doing anything in that realm in 1641 or later which was not in accordance with the anglicanism of Falkland and Chillingworth, the distinctive feature of which was that in all save the essentials it was to be looked upon as flexible. 'This particular', a point of Church government, 'was not worth a war', he had declared in 1648. 'No reformation is worth the charge of a civil war', he wrote more than twenty years later.[1] Not only Falkland but Hyde himself had in his judgement such a latitude in opinion that he did not believe any part of the order of the Church to be so necessary to religion but that it might be altered for a notable public benefit or convenience. The fact is that even in retrospect Hyde's inflexibility was not so·much ecclesiastical in the strict sense, as constitutional. He claimed in his self-portrait in the *Life* that he 'always opposed, upon the impulsion of conscience, all mutations in the Church; and did always believe, let the season or the circumstance be what it would, that any compliance was pernicious; and that a peremptory and obstinate refusal' would reconcile more men to government than a policy of concession. We have a picture of a sensitive conscience reinforced even from the

[1] *Animadversions*, p. 136.

start with worldly wisdom. But this remark follows immediately upon the statement that the removal of the bishops from the House of Peers 'was a violation of justice; the removing a landmark, and the shaking the very foundation of government'.[1] Even in making his observation in 1648 about the part played by episcopacy in drawing men to the King he spoke of episcopacy not as an ecclesiastical principle but 'as it was a part of the Government of England'.[2]

§ 2. *Historical Religion*

What was the true character of the difference between Hyde and Falkland in matters of the Church? The fact that Hyde in 1641 opposed the first Bishops' Exclusion Bill and that Falkland supported it, and Hyde's account many years afterwards of the affair create the impression that he had been a stauncher and less compromising supporter of the Church, simply as such, than his friend. His opposition to the Exclusion is made to imply a devotion to the institution of episcopacy so vehement that he was foremost in vigilant defence of its outworks. The facts will the more easily support the opposite view.

In every important ecclesiastical debate, Falkland, in spite of his radical criticisms of it in the earlier ones, seems to have made a bigger impression than Hyde in defence of the traditional system of the Church. In the debate on the Root-and-Branch Petition on 8 February 1641, Falkland and Digby made a name for themselves by supporting, albeit with bitter attacks on the existing bishops, the retention of episcopacy. But at this juncture, when the question of the Church stood out for the first time from the general reformation of the abuses of Charles's government, and when for the first time the Church found defenders who would go to the length of

---

[1] *Life*, II, p. 89.   [2] *S.P. Clar.* III, p. 3.

breaching the reforming front, Hyde made no impression whatever. A diarist records nothing more than that, 'Mr Hyde not to have it [the Root-and-Branch Petition] committed, etc.'[1] Even in the *History*, Hyde makes little of the episode, referring only in passing to the petition and not even mentioning Falkland's speech. Hyde followed Culpepper and Bridgman in the debate, and, so far as can be discovered, contributed with them a less positive and explicit defence of the Church than even Selden did. There is not on this occasion a defence by Hyde of even a moderate and reformed episcopacy in the manner of Falkland. In his treatment of the church question in the *History* it is only on the matter of excluding the bishops from the House of Peers that he gives the substance of one of his speeches in the House, and he proceeds to record Falkland's spectacular disagreement with him on 10 March, when the latter expressed himself in favour of the Bill. The House was surprised, he said, and so was he,[2] though he need hardly have been since in his February speech Falkland had said that he was content to take away the civil attributes of the clergy including the bishops' votes in the Lords. However, an independent and contemporary source confirms this disagreement. Hyde is reported[3] as saying: 'this privilege enjoyed many hundreds of years this no usurped right neither the inconveniency so great but in better hands it may stand.' This report does not coincide with his own version of the speech, and suggests that what he said was in the vein customary with Falkland, admitting by implication that the bishops' power in the Lords might be an inconvenience, but that the inconvenience would be mitigated if bishops better than the present ones exercised it. Moreover, it seems to have been Selden and not Hyde who

---

[1] [*The Diary of Sir Simonds*] *D'Ewes* [*from the beginning of the Long Parliament to the opening of the trial of the Earl of Strafford*, edited by Wallace] Notestein, [1923,] p. 337.

[2] Clarendon, *History*, i, p. 312 (from the *Life*).

[3] *D'Ewes*, Notestein, p. 467.

impressed the House by arguing that the exclusion of the bishops would raise a constitutional problem of the first order. It is Selden, not Hyde, who in this debate is the most notable upholder of the episcopal rights under the constitution, and it is possible that the difference between Hyde's own version of his speech on this occasion and the contemporary one is to be accounted for by the fact that Hyde's subsequent thoughts on the matter were embellished through contact with the mind of Selden. Selden spoke after Hyde in the debate.

Hyde says[1] that throughout the spring of 1641 Falkland was tricked by the Puritans into supporting the first Exclusion Bill with the argument that the Church would be left in peace if it were carried, and that Falkland only came over to his own view in the autumn. If Falkland indeed fell into such a trap it would seem to show his solicitude for the Church, and that such solicitude was the mainspring of his conduct. The trick was planned for persons precisely like Falkland, persons with a predominant concern for religious matters. Hyde would have us believe that his own concern for the Church was such that he saw through the trick. But it may be that he evaded the trap because his concern at the time was so much less than Falkland's, and that his objection to the exclusion of the bishops was of the same type as Selden's.

It is important in this connexion to distinguish between the circumstances of the first Bishops' Exclusion Bill and those of the second. It was the second Bill which was the more obviously formidable from the ecclesiastical point of view. Between the first and the second Bill a majority of the Lower House had accepted the policy of Root-and-Branch. Even though Pym had now abandoned the radical policy in favour of a second Exclusion Bill in the autumn session in face of the strength of the episcopalian party, the harm was done, Root-and-Branch having once been entertained. That fact, together with the increasing disorder in the Church, sharpened and

[1] Clarendon, *History*, III, p. 186.

clarified the ecclesiastical issue in the House of Commons. 'Episcopical men' with Falkland pre-eminent amongst them were ranged more distinctly than before against a party of ecclesiastical innovation. The King himself was increasingly disposed to make his public policy turn upon the defence of the Church. In the autumn he had proceeded to fill up the vacant bishoprics with men of the moderate type, men who had not been associated with Laud's policy. The second Bill would have seemed a more serious attack on the Church than the first. The first Bill came at a time when the Commons were still redressing the constitutional exorbitances, exorbitances to which they all, including Hyde, admitted the bishops had been a party. The Commons were determined to destroy clerical ascendancy in the State and to prevent such ascendancy in the future. The exclusion of the bishops was a natural and an obvious expedient, and wide in its appeal, meeting the need both to reform the State and also the Church. Hyde attributes the trick to Hampden, but if it was a trick (and it should be remembered that we have only Hyde's word for it that there was a trick: it was a theory that would easily follow from his later doctrine that the violent party had planned a destructive policy from the start), it succeeded because its victims would not have seen the point or the necessity of it had it been disclosed to them. To vote for the exclusion of the bishops was in the circumstances of the early spring the natural course for those with ecclesiastical preoccupations to adopt. On 10 March, therefore, Hyde would not have stood out as an Anglican stalwart; Falkland's dissent from him on that day was a more significant action in this respect. Even if we accept Hyde's contentions, it was, as we have seen, Selden, and not he, who was the outstanding supporter of the constitutional rights of the clergy, and Selden, unfortunately for Hyde's interpretation of the story, had by the summer come out in favour of lay commissioners to take the place of bishops.

The ecclesiastical issue became sharper after the summer recess. Not only was it sharper in itself. It now held the centre of the political stage in a way it had not held it before. The second Exclusion Bill was not only a clear threat to the Church, it was now the crux of the struggle between Pym and Charles to capture the House of Lords. But even now Hyde played a minor part in the purely ecclesiastical debates. It is true that the episcopal men were a useful basis for the non-violent policy towards the King, but even so he refrained from emphasizing the ecclesiastical division in the House, since to do so would lose the non-episcopalians whom he might otherwise mobilize in support of his objective. Hyde's policy towards the opponents of episcopacy seems to have been similar to Pym's policy towards the episcopalians in dropping Root-and-Branch. The question of exclusion loomed largest with Hyde and that question now had a political significance it did not possess before. To oppose the second Bill was a line to exploit against Pym, who, through dallying with Root-and-Branch, had now lost the episcopalian ex-clusionists. Pym managed to carry it, though this time with a smaller majority. Its obstruction in the Lords, however, served Hyde's purpose. That purpose even now was not ecclesiastical defence for its own sake, nor constitutional defence for the sake of a political objective in the sense of the late spring and summer of 1642. His purpose was the achieve-ment of settlement, and in that connexion the containing function fulfilled in the winter of 1641 by the Lords in their refusal to pass this second Bishops' Exclusion Bill was what was important for him.

Falkland's change of front regarding exclusion in the second session and Hyde's leadership of a non-violent party, a great part of which was made up of more or less convinced sup-porters of episcopacy, must not be allowed to conceal the difference between them which it is now possible to state.

Though Falkland took part in the reform of the State and attacked Strafford, his main concern in the Long Parliament and onwards was to see that religion as he understood it did not suffer. His charge against Archbishop Laud and his party was that the interests of true religion had been overlaid in the interests of their own power in Church and State. So much can be gathered from his speech in February 1641. In that speech he declared that the clergy had been neither as innocent as doves, nor as wise as serpents. But it was their delinquencies under the former head which worried him. They had proved themselves serpentine enough in their own interests. They were children of darkness, he said, and, as was to be expected, had been wiser in their generation than the children of light; 'I may guess not without some eye upon the most politic action of the most politic church', the Church of Rome. His judgement upon the Church of Rome had been, as we have seen, that it was an edifice of ecclesiastical might which in its own interests accumulated spurious essentials in the spheres of doctrine and of observance, and he was troubled that the Church of England under Archbishop Laud seemed to have moved in the same direction. This concern drove him into the reforming party and carried him along with it. In relation to this fundamental preoccupation, his attack on the Laudian regime in February 1641 was more significant than his adherence at that time to the principle of episcopacy. This concern brought him to support the first Exclusion Bill and it brought him to oppose the second, when in the autumn it was apparent to him that the Puritan attack was growing rather than lessening as time went on. A system which at all approached the Scottish model would be at least as bad as and probably worse than Laudianism, since it was no less clericalist and much more theologically dogmatic than the latter. Such considerations made of him in the autumn and winter of 1641 the leader of the 'episcopals'.

Though his attitude in theological and ecclesiastical matters had a common background with that of Falkland, Hyde from the time that they both entered Parliament had an angle of vision which distinguished him from Falkland. He was not primarily interested in religion in the way that Falkland was. He was interested in politics: first, in the achievement, and then in the consolidation of the great reformation of the State. This predominating interest was to involve him in a concern for the Church, but not in the same sense as Falkland had been and continued to be concerned with it. So long as it was a question of religion as a thing in itself, of its immediate ecclesiastical environment, and of its pure essentials considered apart from politics, of the two, Falkland was pre-eminent in action. But when, with the second session, it became a question of political action which would preserve peace and continuity, ends which were involved in and demanded by religion and the interest of the Church, the parts were reversed and Hyde came to the fore. Falkland followed him now, taking second place; whereas, before, Hyde had followed Falkland and taken second place. Hyde quickly found that he was as concerned with religion as Falkland was, but under another aspect, under that of politics. Increased ecclesiastical disorder in 1641 was one of the danger signals which prompted Hyde's course in the second session, whereas Falkland, on the other hand, was concerned at the prospect not of disorder but of a new and more objectionable ecclesiastical order. It was Hyde's association with Falkland in matters of the Church which gave a man with so high a repute as a parliamentarian and as a political reformer his chance with the King, and which provided a liberal anglicanism for the building if possible of a bridge between the King and the House of Commons. Falkland, on the other hand, held to liberal Anglicanism as an end in itself, and, as will be seen, dragged it in where it was not wanted, annoying the King by doing so. It was a position taken up in March 1641 on an important aspect of the constitutional relations of the Church, namely the bishops' votes in Parliament, which, as reflected upon, wove itself into a doctrine of the relations between Church and State, while Falkland was interested only in the relations of the Church with religion. It was the determination of the Scots to erect if they could their own church order in England which brought Hyde to expand the position which he had taken in parliamentary debate and to formulate views which he held for the rest of his life.

Hyde, like everyone else, knew from the early days of the Long Parliament that the Scots desired to introduce presbyterianism into England and he, in common with the majority, opposed this. Early in 1643 Loudon and Henderson brought to Oxford a petition from the General Assembly of the Kirk, imploring the King to assent to the reduction of England to ecclesiastical conformity with Scotland. The King and the Council could not agree on a reply. The King wished to argue the point about church government and to assert in the reply the divine right, the theological indispensability of bishops. The Council favoured a curt rejection of the Scottish request without explanation. The problem was aggravated by Falkland who contested the King's theology. The King turned to Hyde, expecting an opinion which would coincide with his own. What Hyde proposed was different from them all. He proposed a rejection which should contain an explanation, but an explanation ostensibly of a political rather than a theological character; namely, that the Scots had no right to meddle with the legal constitution of another country. Under cover of the King's conviction that he thought as he did in matters of the Church,[1] he was able to steer clear of a 'brawl in religion' and to answer the Scots in a conclusive manner.

But whatever he might say, his answer enunciated theological principles, and they are the liberal principles already described as having distinguished the Tew circle though expounded now in a context and consequently with an emphasis different from

---

[1] *Life*, III, p. 163.

what those principles would have received when put forward by Falkland. It was, so ran his paper,[1] a scandal to interpret, as the Scots had done, 'all the differences in ceremony, government, or indifferent opinions...to be differences in religion'. Such things were naturally changeable, and, in the circumstances, it was assumed that changes would be made and that they would be part of the settlement which would emerge from the negotiations at Oxford. But

the government here established by the laws hath so near a relation and intermixture with the civil state...that till a composed, digested form be presented to us in a parliamentary way, whereby the consent and approbation of this whole kingdom may be had, and we and all our subjects may discern what is to be left [in] or brought in, as well as what is to be taken away, we know not how to consent to any alteration, otherwise than to such an Act for the ease of tender consciences in the matter of ceremonies as we have often offered; and that this, and anything else that may concern the peace of the Church and the advancement of God's true religion, may be soberly discussed and happily effected, we have formerly offered, and are still willing, that debates of that nature may be entered into by a synod of godly and learned divines...to which we shall be willing that some learned divines of our Church of Scotland be likewise sent, to be present, and offer and debate their reasons.

And

we cannot believe the intermixture[2] of the present ecclesiastical government with the civil state to be other than a very good reason, and that the government of the church should be by the rules of human policy to be other than a very good rule....

Nor are you a little mistaken, if either you believe the generality of this nation to desire a change of church-government, or that most of those who desire it desire by it to introduce that which you will only esteem a reformation.

[1] Clarendon, *History*, II, p. 510.
[2] In an outline of the discourse on the constitution originally planned for the *History* (*vide supra*, pp. 164, 222), Hyde included the head: 'intermixture and relation between the ecclesiastical and civil state.'

Reformation was

best to be in a common and ordinary way, where the passion or interest of particular men may not impose upon the public; but alteration be then only made, when, upon calm debates, and evident and clear reason and convenience, the same shall be generally consented to for the peace and security of the people; and those who are trusted by the law with such debates, are not divested of that trust upon a general charge of corruptions, pretended [by the Scots] to have entered by that way, and of being the persons to be reformed, and so unfit to be reformers.

Such a logic, Hyde pointed out, would rule out the possibility of any kind of parliamentary reformation including a reformation in the State.

Hyde denied the Scots' contention that the present juncture was an ideal one for change. The King had offered a measure of liberty to be secured by statute and had agreed that, later, a synod should follow. A true settlement was impossible till things were calmer. For following the complication which had been brought in by the party of antiquity amongst the clergy, there was now the counter-complication introduced by the extreme Puritan divines, egging on Parliamentarians who, apart from reasons which Hyde held were irrelevant to the ecclesiastical issue, would not have heeded such attentions or been eager for large structural alterations. It was not so much, as has sometimes been urged, that Hyde failed to appreciate the quality of Puritan conviction; it was rather that he sensed the relationship of the Church question with the political situation as a whole. That question had played its part in producing the original crisis, but, thereafter, its exacerbation was at least as much a result as a cause of a situation the essence of which was less the confrontation of fundamentally irreconcilable principles than a lack of confidence. Hyde would probably have been happily content to respect the religious opinions of a Pym or of a Hampden.

What he almost certainly doubted was whether the course which they had come to pursue could have had much to do with religion. If it were religion which produced such a policy as theirs, it would, in his judgement, have difficulty in qualifying as such.

Such were the views behind the reply which was drafted by Hyde to be tendered to the General Assembly of the Church of Scotland. Whatever the King might think or Hyde might say, theological principles were involved in that document, and they were more like Falkland's than the King's. But they diverged, also, in an important respect from those of Falkland. If it be said that the motive of Falkland's conduct remained the consideration that clerical politics produced and were producing bad religion, Hyde's was, it seems, the consideration that if politics whether clerical or lay were bad politics, they were for that very reason bad for religion.

Hyde's ultimate comments on Falkland's character and conduct bring out the difference between them in a way which his account of their disagreement on ecclesiastical policy in the Long Parliament fails to do. He emphasized his purity and detachment: 'he was of a temper and composition fitter to live in *re publica Platonis*, than in *faece Romuli*.'[1] But it seems clear that Hyde thought, and had ground for thinking, that this rare quality in Falkland was a disadvantage, since he not only had to contrive to live in a far from ideal world, but was also actually called upon to take political action in it. Not only did he belong to the Country, as Hyde himself did, and not to the Court, but 'he was fatally unacquainted with business and the forms of it'. He did not possess or develop the qualities of mind necessary for the conduct of affairs, either as parliamentarian or minister of state. He was and remained 'too much a contemner of those arts, which must be indulged in the transactions of human affairs'.[2] From the outset of his political career he acted upon a perfectionism

---

[1] *Life*, I, pp. 41–2.   [2] Clarendon, *History*, III, p. 181 (from the *Life*).

of outlook which was dangerous both to himself and to others. He was too trustful and too idealistic. He hoped for too much both from Parliament and from King. He thought that the intentions of parliaments need not be questioned,[1] and did not learn to question them until it was nearly too late. He thought that kings existed to concede the demands of their subjects and that it was only necessary for them to do so for all to be well. But a settlement depended not upon a universal conformity to an ideal pattern, but upon a compromise which both took into account the least upon which each party to the dispute was actually insisting, and also assuaged intelligible fears and suspicions entertained on either hand. It was only with the utmost difficulty[2] that Hyde persuaded Falkland to become a minister of the Crown: a responsibility which involved an attempt to see things from the King's point of view. Falkland was afraid that the office would impede his liberty of conscience.[3] Hyde indicated[4] that this attitude in a minister qualified the usefulness of his advice to the King. Then, in regard to the King's acceptance in February 1642 of the Bill to exclude the bishops, though Hyde does not mention Falkland as having pressed that acceptance, he does not say that he opposed it. It is possible that Falkland was reverting again to the doctrine of the intrinsic merit of concession by the King divorced from all consideration of the circumstances. When it came to the outbreak of war, there was more than a tinge of pacifism in his attitude to it. He was so anxious for peace that his tendency was to neglect to ask the question whether conditions existed indispensable for its establishment. He could hardly bring himself to approve the routine functions of his office, espionage and censorship.

Such an attitude in Falkland was not purely personal. It seems to have been part of the very atmosphere of Tew. At

---

[1] Clarendon, *History*, III, p. 181 (from the *Life*).
[2] Ibid. p. 183 (from the *Life*).
[3] Ibid.   [4] *Life*, II, p. 86.

least, it seems to have been shared by Chillingworth. Chillingworth, wrote Hyde, 'did really believe all war to be unlawful'.[1]
Further, he seems to have had the same uncritical parliamentarism, or, at least, to have declined to believe that the
Parliament 'did in truth intend to involve the nation in a
civil war, till after the battle of Edgehill'.[2] He placed an
enthusiasm for mechanical devices at the disposal of his desire
to stop hostilities as quickly as possible by inventing military
engines. The impressive sermon in which he described the
war as a war between Scribes and Pharisees on the one hand
and Publicans and Sinners on the other, suggests a detachment which was perhaps excessive. It seems, in fact, that the
men of the Tew circle having discovered how tarnished the
cause of true religion had become in the rough and tumble of
history, displayed a certain squeamishness when confronted
with the urgencies and dilemmas of politics: or else that their
humanism was too rationalistic and too optimistic. They felt
that if politics touched religion the latter forthwith became
contaminated. Chillingworth in *The Religion of Protestants* no
sooner touched upon the subject of religion and politics than
he thought of St Paul's words—'the weapons of the Christian
warfare are not carnal'—and hurried on to speak of 'human
power and Machiavellian policy'.[3] He was hypersensitive in
regard to the likelihood that 'the temporal benefit and tran-
quillity of temporal states and kingdoms' would conflict with
the interest of true religion. The same thing is evident in
Hales's sermons. Tew seems to have been obsessed by the
extent to which religion had suffered by the interposition of
'interest' whether clerical or lay. For the Chillingworthians,
religion and politics were contrary not complementary to
each other.

After the summer of 1641 Falkland seems to have become
a disillusioned man and to have made political decisions in

[1] *Life*, I, p. 54. [2] Ibid.
[2] Chillingworth, *The Religion of Protestants*, pp. 381, 382.

accord with the principle of the lesser evil. That would have been unimpeachable from Hyde's point of view had not his surprise that such a thing should have been necessary expressed itself in a sense of the evil of the lesser evil, so acute as to be almost paralysing. It is to be suspected, indeed, that, as in the matter of theological principle, Hyde in describing Falkland's attitude to politics is at the same time describing himself to an extent which the method of his writing obscures. It is probably necessary to picture Hyde as having been less realistic and Falkland as having been more realistic than Hyde's own picture suggests. Falkland did much political work, and Hyde was always a man of letters as much as a political lawyer. They were both, as Philip Warwick points out, 'great masters of reason, yet could not pretend unto experience'.[1] Hyde's words and actions in the Long Parliament reveal sufficiently clearly the intellectual background of Tew, and he had caught, also, its theological manners. Indeed, his sober and rational bearing in face of the torrent of anti-Romanist passion worked perhaps to the disadvantage of his policy, since in the last weeks of 1641 men whom it is accurate to describe as Royalists seem to have been infected by that fever as much as the violent party of the Parliamentarians, and he might, in the cause of reconciliation, have exploited the fact more than he did, for instance in the answer to the Grand Remonstrance. He cared as much as Falkland did for reconciliation, and thought of it as involving an accommodation between divergent ecclesiastical viewpoints. If Falkland assumed for too long that there was no 'design against the peace of the kingdom',[2] in the breasts of the parliamentary leaders, and 'believed long their purposes were honest', that was a view which was more like Hyde's own than the doctrine of the *History*, and the same must be said of Falkland's fear, as an adviser of the King, that in the exercise of his parlia-

[1] *Memoirs of the Reign of King Charles I*, 1702, p. 198.
[2] Clarendon, *History*, III, p. 182.

20-2

mentary duties he should display any bias towards the Court. If in describing Falkland's religious position, he was describing his own, we must be prepared to admit that to some extent he was doing the same with reference to politics.

It was, however, precisely the pursuit of an end which was so thoroughly in accord with Chillingworthian ideals but in terms of the concrete situation and by the whole-hearted application of the necessary methods of politics which distinguished Hyde from Falkland, from the opening of the second session onwards. As a lawyer, he had been more interested in the reformation of the State than of the Church and in the saving of that reformation from the dangers which threatened it. That fact explains why from the outset he was a political Chillingworthian. But if it was possible for him to separate the ecclesiastical from the civil side of affairs in order that the one might be related to the other in a way which would avert the collapse of all parliamentary aims, religion and policy were all of a piece with him from the start. His policy was not as unscrupulous in regard to means as Pym's was, and it may be assumed that Falkland's political moralism was by no means foreign to him. Pym, viewed from the line along which Hyde moved, allowed the interests of religion and civil politics to get athwart one another, and consequently brought himself to frustration in both respects. But, compared with Falkland, Hyde was a politician in the same sense as Pym was. He dwelt squarely amidst the facts as they presented themselves, transcending them only to make the best of them. If he shared Falkland's 'presaging spirit that the King would fall into great misfortune', and was numbered amongst the 'too many' who shared Falkland's belief that 'the King would in the end be prevailed with to yield to what was pressed', that fact sprang from his very parliamentarism and was a factor in a constructive policy rather than merely a melancholy and dispiriting reflexion. And when war could not be avoided, that circumstance did not cripple his resolution, or present itself as necessarily incompatible with a continuing purpose of peace.

Hyde was a political Chillingworthian: the proponent of an idea which was, in a sense, a contradiction in terms. But there is no call to interpose too quickly with the conclusion that if he shared in the latitudinarianism of Tew, the significance of the fact is that it enabled him to subordinate religion to immediate political needs as they arose. Such action is possible without any distinctive ecclesiastical tenets, and if such action on his part proceeded from the Tew platform, it would merely have constituted an abandonment of it. It appears that he accepted without question the proposition that ecclesiastical changes were necessary to consolidate the Revolution, rather than that he shared Falkland's positive desire for such changes. But it is possible to doubt whether this implied a point of view which was political in the sense of excluding any concern for religion. If, as would appear, parliamentarism in a narrow sense came first with Hyde, it was not unnatural that it should do so, since everything else depended upon its survival. That Hyde's outlook was not so exceptional as to be consciously secularist, is a thesis which his own explicit contentions already noted and discussed in the preceding section may be allowed to disprove. Even the assertion in the *Life* that he was motivated by devotion to the Church, if rejected as it has been in one sense, may justifiably be admitted in another. The Revolution, as part of itself, embodied a programme of ecclesiastical changes which were profounder and of a more lasting character than the programmes of the Puritans. The power of the clergy in the state and in society was to be curtailed, the government of the Church was to be subjected to Parliament, and the law of the Church adjusted to the supremacy of the Common Law. Puritanism was one way of clothing these purposes with the decencies of a sincere theological outlook. But puritanism's tempestuous course and character obscured an alternative way which was in the long run to be of greater consequence than itself, namely latitudinarian individualism. Hyde was not a Puritan. It is difficult to see that he was not a sincere latitudinarian. He said of himself in his second exile that those who seriously consider the political aspects of religion must be wary 'to escape the censure of being without religion'.[1] Hyde expounded at that time a position which was a religious one, but a religious one in which the politics of religion had priority. It was a view, it is true, which was expounded in opposition to Roman Catholics. But it is not for that reason to be dismissed as standing in no relation with his experience of other antagonists. The fact that his doctrine is basically nothing but the doctrine originally expounded to the Scots in 1643, elaborated now in a fuller and more comprehensive form, indicates that such a dismissal is not called for.

Hyde at the end of his life wrote a book called *Religion and Policy and the Countenance and Assistance each should give to the other*. In this book he failed to discuss his chosen subject in general terms. In spite of the title, he preferred to devote himself to the elucidation of the sub-title, *A Survey of the Power and Jurisdiction of the Pope in the Dominions of other Princes*. It is, however, clear from his works as a whole what he meant by the countenance and assistance which religion and policy should afford one another. The English Reformation was to him an as nearly perfect example of such mutual relations as could be desired or described. It was an operation in the realm of policy undertaken in respect of the countenance and assistance which it should give to religion. Hyde described[2] errors and corruptions under three heads: those introduced by connivance and improved and carried on by faction for the advancement of particular interests: those innocent in their first institution, but now harmful to religion 'in tract of time and ill manners of the age'; and, third, those 'so incorporated into the customs and natures and humours of

---

[1] *Essays*, II, p. 179.   [2] Ibid. p. 202.

the nation, that they can hardly be examined, much less reformed, without producing more inconveniences and mischiefs
than it would remove'. Not only was the hasty eradication
of errors contrary to the divine teaching, in that, as was explained in the Parable of the Wheat and the Tares, such action
was prejudicial to the wheat—the minds of simple men could
be undeceived, only 'by application and gentle remedies',
but, also, Hyde contended, 'a conformity in humours and in
manners, is a great introduction to conformity in religion'.[1]
Violent action not only assaulted individual stability and
assurance, it also tore into the fabric of habit and disrupted
religion in its social manifestations. Clearly, for Hyde, the
crucial point was not the theological delineation of errors, but
the question: what errors could safely be treated as such? The
clergy must be consulted in the definition of errors and corruptions, but they could be relied upon to have and to express
views on such matters at all times. It was the lay judgement
which was primarily required because the wider and more
decisive question was not a theological but a political one,
even though it was the interest of religion which was at stake.
Action so discriminating was possible only after long experience of the beliefs and practices in question and involved the
patient resisting of precipitate measures. 'No one *classis* of
men will dispassionately weigh all necessary consideration in
this matter',[2] least of all the clergy. Every moment was the
right moment in their view, if the interest of religion as they
conceived it was at stake. They lacked the sense of 'pious
wariness'[3] which was necessary in human affairs, and the
sense of the 'just season': they acted as if they believed that
matters of the Church ought to proceed in accord with a logic
of their own. 'We never had anything to do with Luther',[4]
Hyde declared: 'it was long after his time, and not at all by
his model'[3] that the English Church was reformed.

[1] *Animadversions*, p. 136.   [2] Ibid. p. 138.
[3] *Essays*, II, p. 147.   [4] *Animadversions*, p. 257.

But the excellence of the English Reformation was not exhausted when it had been explained that it exemplified the countenance and assistance which policy ought to render to religion. It was a demonstration, also, of the support which religion was obliged to render to policy. If it was true that religion must have suffered if handled by policy in any ways less circumspect than those employed in the English Reformation, it was equally true that the peace of the civil State would at once have been compromised by any indiscriminate presentation of religious issues. Not only did the plucking out of tares wound religion in the sense of imperilling the harvest of souls, whether considered individually or socially, it also jeopardized the security of the State. The Church of England was 'a Church, that chose rather for a long time to endure many errors and corruptions in the exercise and worship of the religion that had been established, and which were for many ages discovered to be so by many learned men of that and other nations, than precipitately to enter upon any alteration, which might have been attended with such a concussion in the State, as might have destroyed the peace and security thereof'.[1] 'No reformation is worth the charge of a civil war.' After the Reformation, those who adhered to the old forms were left in peace so far as was possible. No other attitude was compatible with political security. Furthermore, it was no part of the doctrine of the English Reformation either to condemn countries which remained unreformed or to commend 'all those who desire to be thought to have followed our example'.[2] Hence that event had no implications in the realm of diplomacy, and need not complicate the relations of the English government with its neighbours.

Hyde's anti-clericalism is thus different from that of Falkland, a fact which is apparent, if they are scrutinized more closely, even in those passages from the *Life* and the *History*

[1] *Essays*, ii, p. 147.
[2] Ibid. p. 207.

which have been adduced as running parallel with Falkland's
speech of 1641. They show that Hyde's deepest complaint
against the clergy when he came to reflect upon the matter
was the political harm which they did. Falkland indeed
pointed this out in his speech, but it was not his main complaint. Hyde, on the other hand, stressed this aspect of the
matter. He exposed the mischief done by the clerical attitude
to the Common Law, and dilated upon the fact that the papal
missions and Laud's administration of the Church had caused
political disturbance. Moreover, he held that the civil State
had suffered from clerical predominance in it.[1] Even in the
question of relations with French Protestants this difference is
apparent. Falkland abused the clergy in the 1641 speech for
a breach of charitable union with foreign Christians. Hyde
in the *History* criticized them for disrupting a tradition of high
national policy dating back to the Reformation. Falkland
only made a speech in 1641, and Hyde, writing history at a
later date, was able to continue the story of the clergy's
propensity to neglect the political implications of their
actions. The Bishops' Protest at the end of December 1641
was in his view the culminating and fatal error of the English
clergy, the action which their enemies hailed as *digitus Dei*. It
has been seen that it was this step which, when combined with
the activities of Digby, precipitated the avalanche which had
so fatally compromised the opening phase of Hyde's second
endeavour towards settlement. Archbishop Williams, a leader
in the affair of the Protest, was a politician as disastrous in
Hyde's eyes as Laud. Like Laud, he failed to consider 'as
well what was fit as what was right'.[2] 'Clergymen', wrote
Hyde, 'understand the least, and take the worst measure of
human affairs of all mankind that can write and read.'[3]

If Hyde had agreed with Falkland in starting out with the
proposition that the clergy were bad for religion, considered

---

[1] Clarendon, *History*, III, p. 417.
[2] Ibid. I, p. 471.   [3] *Life*, pt. I, p. 61.

as distinct from civil politics, and though he made statements in later life to that effect,[1] it would appear that at the end he was chiefly concerned to say that they were primarily bad for politics both civil and ecclesiastical, and bad for religion chiefly for that reason. People like the Emperor Constantine and Henri IV and Queen Elizabeth had done most service to religion in the past precisely because they were laymen and precisely because they combined ecclesiastical with civil politics. Even the English Civil War itself had had a partially ecclesiastical origin only in that laymen had failed to keep the clergy in order through their faculties having become 'dull, lazy, and unactive', and in that the laymen of the violent party had exploited the activities of the Puritan preachers.

It will be observed that when co-operation between religion and policy was as complete as in Hyde's exposition of the English Reformation, it was strictly speaking not possible to separate the two or to show in what respects each was helping the other. It was rather the case of a single operation possessing a double aspect. The transaction which was 'so blessed as to abolish nothing that was necessary or fit to be retained, and retained nothing but what was held decent by the most venerable antiquity',[2] was, when considered under the aspect of religion, a punctilious observance of the teaching of the Parable of the Wheat and the Tares, and a scrupulous exercise of the virtues of forbearance and patience. There seemed no better way of emulating the harmlessness of doves and the wisdom of serpents at one and the same time. Under the aspect of policy, however, it was an act of the highest state-craft, a consummate operation of State surgery. The leniency

[1] 'If Christianity were deposited with one Churchman, or any body of Churchmen, we have too much reason to apprehend what would become of it...'. (*Animadversions*, p. 135.)
'It must not therefore be the ecclesiastical persons, who have given each other too ill words to be of one mind, who can procure this unity of faith and doctrine, that must constitute this peace.' (Ibid. p. 108.)
[2] *Essays*, II, p. 147.

in regard to the opinions of those who would not accept the change was, simultaneously, both religious toleration and conformity to political necessity. The refusal to blame the absence of reformation elsewhere, or positively to commend all other reformations regardless of the way in which they might have been achieved, was both the following out of what was required in respect of the suspension of judgement upon the failings of others and the reservation of indignation for one's own shortcomings, and, at the same time, the pursuit of the neatest diplomatic convenience.

Hyde was explicit about this identification. He made it when he expounded the difference between religion and what he called Religion of State. The former alone constituted religion proper. The latter was the politics of religion; religious indeed, but emphatically politics. The former was by definition unalterable. The founder of Christianity

prescribed the essential principles himself of that religion which he intended should be established, and left persons trusted by him who not only knew his mind, but knew all things which are necessary to be known for the accomplishment of it. And no temporal or spiritual authority under heaven hath power to alter anything that was settled by him or his Apostles... and they performed their parts with that plainness in what is necessary, that there remains no difficulty to men of very competent understandings.[1]

... The body and substance of religion (as is said) is enjoined and determined in Scripture, which must not be altered.[2]

Religion of State, on the other hand, was by definition alterable. It was everything which comprised the superstructure upon the original body and substance, all the forms which doctrine, government, discipline and worship had taken at different times and in different places. All these it was permitted to alter because they were inessential. Either they were not in Scripture at all, or else they were in it but not

[1] *Animadversions*, p. 111.   [2] *Religion and Policy*, 1811, p. 3.

303

plainly so. It was impossible, indeed, but that they should alter, for the reason that times and places differed, and the superstructures differed with them. They differed in accordance with 'the nature and the humour of the people', and 'the custom and disposition of the time'.[1] In accordance with such circumstances, they were altered or improved or abolished by the State, preferably in the non-violent, co-operative and parliamentary manner of the English Reformation, and 'in order to the better advancement of those ends which are essential, and which no power on earth can make alteration in'.

Religion of State was law and politics, not religion. The power of the prince in the ecclesiastical sphere was not spiritual power in the sense claimed by the clergy. Indeed Hyde hardly ever called it spiritual power: it was ecclesiastical, and ecclesiastical was a department or subdivision of temporal, not something in principle different from and over against it. 'There may be alterations made by, and according to the wisdom of the government, and as the good order and peace of the nation requires, and with the same gravity, and deliberation as all other mutations and provisions are made.'[2] As a subdivision of the temporal, the ecclesiastical realm rightfully belonged to the prince. When outside the prince's control and in the hands of the clergy, it was equally political, but wrongful. It is remarkable that heartily as Hyde disapproved of Hobbes, his praise for the thirty-ninth chapter of *Leviathan*, where the distinction between spiritual and temporal is castigated as an invention of the clergy to make men 'see double', was unqualified. 'I would', he said, 'have been very glad, he would have enlarged upon [this theme] so proper for his excellent way of reasoning; and I cannot avoid saying, that it is great pity that the most faultless chapter in the book, for aught is evident, should be the shortest.'[3]

[1] *Religion and Policy*, p. 3; *Essays*, II, p. 88; *Animadversions*, pp. 136, 137.
[2] *Animadversions*, p. 138.   [3] *Survey*, p. 233.

Religion of State was political in the sense that its content was made up of inessentials, of beliefs and practices which in themselves were not necessary to salvation. Their primary reference was not to the relationship of man with his Maker, but to the relationships of society—the nature and humour of the people. Religion of State, moreover, was political not only in that it was comprised of things inessential to salvation, but also in that it did not exclude beliefs and practices also inessential, but other than those prescribed by Religion of State: it did not exclude them provided, that is, that they themselves proved capable of co-existing with Religion of State, that they were combined, in those who held them, with a right political attitude. In short, the aim of ecclesiastical laws was unity and not uniformity, and they could only achieve the former because they did not aim at achieving the latter. Hyde spoke of the civil magistrate as the person who had pre-eminently secured 'this unity of faith and doctrine that must constitute this peace', but he added the qualification, such unity as was necessary.[1] 'Nothing is more mistaken, or more misapplied, than this precious word unity.'[2] Uniformity of belief was neither desirable nor possible, save in a sense which was self-defeating. It was enough that there should be a unity in diversity, a unity in fundamentals, underlying and emerging from and expressing itself in a diversity of inessentials. Anything else was prostration to the dictates of the clergy. If uniformity were attempted by Religion of State, as it was, Hyde said, in Spain, the result would be disastrous. 'The acuteness and vigour of that nation' was 'totally decayed, and their spirits broken.'[3] Hyde, when ambassador in that country, and later, at the time of the attempted alliance to overthrow Cromwell, had plenty of opportunity to observe 'a general failing in all their affairs'.

These rounded definitions of the final exile, when considered

---

[1] *Animadversions*, p. 108.   [2] Ibid. p. 109.
[3] *Religion and Policy*, p. 373.

in relation with Hyde's own political career, are clearly directly continuous with the experience which that career afforded him. In the Revolution's programme for the Church there was envisaged a reform of those things which had been introduced by connivance and carried on by faction, namely the Laudian distempers. But there were to be modifications only, and no abolition of the episcopal government, since the latter had proved its worth in the past. This view, the moderate programme, was held, and Hyde knew it was held, by most of the laity; by a majority, in fact, of those who cared for such things. The Root-and-Branch programme was the programme of a minority. A change of this character, moreover, apart from its inherent merits, was demanded by the political circumstances in their inescapable actuality. King and Parliament, if they were to be brought together at all, could have been brought together by no other. The impact of the Scots served only to make explicit the kind of reformation which was desired, and Hyde had proceeded to outline the very views of which the writings described above are the elaboration. From the time of the impact of the Scots till the end of his political phase, Hyde is seen on the one hand, and in respect of the English, admitting the desirability of a change, and on the other, and in the face of the Scots, stressing the necessity for it to be a conservative one.

In the second or historical phase, and with the collapse of the institutional presuppositions of his former policy, he proceeded to stress, as in the matter of the civil State, what he had previously assumed. England, he urged, was fundamentally wedded to the old ecclesiastical order. The King had gained more men in that he had stood for the bishops than on any other account. The violent party had opposed episcopacy only in the logic of their political line and were not wedded positively to any other system. Episcopacy was part of the nature and humour of the English people, and facts must prove it so, especially if the King adopted the policy

now recommended by Hyde. The King's obstinate ecclesiastical attitude, which in the first phase had been in one sense
a term of settlement, and in another sense an obstacle to it,
could now be approved as an example of that intransigence
which Hyde advised as the best and only method of restoring
a situation which was temporarily dissolved.

The King, however, failed him. Precisely at the point
when Hyde could at last endorse as supremely appropriate
to the situation methods which in his view had been wrong
before and during the war, Charles, on the face of things,
proceeded to conduct himself with something of the flexibility
Hyde had before so much desired. Unyielding at heart,
Charles nevertheless embraced negotiations which seemed
to imply the possibility even of ecclesiastical concessions. It
was only in his death that he allowed his heart's convictions
in the matter of the Church to play that passive but em-
inently creative part which Hyde would have had them
play since the military defeat. The new King's mind in
Church matters was different from what his father's had been.
Charles II lacked Charles I's specifically ecclesiastical convictions. He could see the force of the argument from Religion
of State, but was on the other hand often tempted by short-
sighted royalist projects which envisaged restoration at some
cost to the Anglican Church. In these circumstances, though
it was an ecclesiastical intransigence without strictly speaking
ecclesiastical roots, and though it had a bearing dictated by
a historical politics which the late King had only hit upon at
the precise moment when it was too late to implement it in
his own life, it was Hyde himself who in the period 1646–60
became the repository of Charles I's original uncompromising
churchmanship.

Religion and policy, as seen from Hyde's place in the
succession of events, and according to the series of his own
recommendations, had in truth been all of a piece throughout,
and the justice of the identification when in the end he came

explicitly to make it seemed to have been confirmed by experience. The constitution was so 'equally poised' that the people suffered when they diminished the prerogative of the King, and the King suffered when he diminished the rights of the people. In such a way Hyde embodied in a paradoxical formula the constitutional experience of both his political and his historical phase. An analogous paradox explains his doctrine of the relations of Church and State. Religion (a religious attitude and an ecclesiastical policy) which did not assist the civil State was bad religion. The religious outlook and the ecclesiastical policy both of the King and of the violent party had been a prime factor in promoting and extending the civil strife of the war. Hyde had only to reflect upon the anarchical ecclesiastical consequences of the failure of the King and the success of the violent party in the first phase. A civil policy which did not assist religion (one which was divorced from a religious spirit and ignored the tradition of Religion of State) was bad civil policy. That was demonstrated for Hyde in the ultimately transient character of the civil regime which the violent party, promoting its own divisions and incapable of transcending the dilemmas created by itself, had founded on the ruins of the Church. It was demonstrated even more unmistakably and triumphantly in the converse. Hyde had only to remember, what indeed he was not likely to forget, the sensational civil benefits which followed upon the success of that policy which, conceived in a faith that an authentic tradition could under Providence be brought to reassert itself, he himself had maintained in the second phase. Both the constitutional formula and the formula for Church and State were the outcome of experience, and could not have been the outcome of any experience more obviously than of his own.

The fact of the matter is that, whereas in respect of civil politics, apart from the historical presuppositions which were common amongst the men of 1640, it was only in the second phase that Hyde's policy came to be based on historical considerations and recent ones at that, in respect of ecclesiastical affairs, on the other hand, his policy seems to have sprung from a preoccupation with history from a much earlier period in his career. He assumed that ecclesiastical change was in principle always feasible, and sometimes, as in the Revolution of 1640, to be desired. In this he shared and followed the theology of his Chillingworthian colleagues, but his criterion, for instance, in the reply to the Scots commissioners in 1643, was to be found in the results of changes which had been made in the past, and these, assuming as he did the distinction between essentials and inessentials, were to be considered in a sense which drew no distinction between religion and politics. Starting in this way, it was inevitable that views which had indeed been truly his should prove to be ones which experience confirmed. The result is seen in the measured utterances of the post-Restoration exile. Even the declaration that he had always opposed all changes in the Church was an aspect of the truth, for he had always opposed a revolutionary change, but as a total explanation, it was contradicted by the facts. In the first phase, while stressing what was dictated explicitly by past history and implicitly by present politics in regard to method, his policy accepted and recommended change though most probably not with the enthusiasm of Falkland who exalted ecclesiastical reform into the prime purpose of the Revolution. In the second phase, historical considerations fill the stage completely and views connected with recent English experience were reinforced and generalized by foreign examples. The case of Spain has already been mentioned. He was interested also by the circumstances in France. 'What is the Religion of the State', Hyde asked a correspondent in France in 1647,[1] 'and how come they, who acknowledge neither the Pope's supremacy, nor his infallibility (for they neither receive the Council of Trent nor admit the Pope to be above

[1] Hyde to Creighton: 8 January 1647. Clar. MSS. 29, 50.

a council) to be accounted Roman Catholics? Are they not a politic church between the Roman and the Protestant, rejecting that of either which would prove inconvenient to their own greatness?'

In the second phase it was a matter of an increased stress upon the nature of change, a stress so great that it ruled out any admission of the need for it. But the Chillingworthian liberalism is still present. Bishops, he told Nicholas in 1646, were not of divine right any more than kings were.[1] On the other hand, their order was rooted in history and was part of the law of the land. In the 'last will and profession' drawn up in Jersey in expectation of an end which did not come, Hyde distinguished in his directions for the education of his children between the essence of Christianity and those desirable embellishments which had formed the English superstructure and which were at that time in abeyance. He was, he admitted, devoted to the latter, 'yet I am not sure, that it is so essential to the soul's health, that no other may be complied with. And therefore, if it shall be with the consent of the Sovereign Power, changed, I would not have their tender years perplexed with any odious impressions, which may make them inclined to disturb the peace of their country'.[2] In the conditions of the second phase the question of the possibility or desirability of ecclesiastical changes of the type which Hyde's criteria might have allowed or promoted obviously could not arise as a practical one, and it is of singular interest to observe the shift of emphasis as between the first and second phase expressing itself in terms of the controverted question whether exiled Anglicans should enter into communion with the Huguenots. At the end of 1646 and the beginning of 1647, Hyde was telling Nicholas, as we have said, that bishops were not *jure divino* and that he must join in communion with the French Protestants. He would not himself, he said, have been opposed in principle to worshipping with the parliamentary

[1] *S.P. Clar.* ii, p. 308.   [2] Ibid. p. 359.

commissioners at Uxbridge in one of their own churches, nor would he be opposed to attending service at that very moment in London if for any reason he were suddenly to find himself there. To Hopton in the middle of 1647[1] he expressed the same view: 'in truth there are very few simple opinions, the difference wherein ought to separate men from communion with one another, which I doubt was brought in, or let in, to the best Churches sooner than were to be wished; and one [? which] hath been the greatest occasion of making rents in the garment of Christ in that matter of communion'; Hopton, however, was much more inclined to do as Hyde recommended than Nicholas was, and by the summer of the following year, provoked apparently by the attitude of the Huguenots themselves to English affairs, Hyde had changed his mind. He now appears to go the whole way with the high anglican view, to concur at long last with his King and to unchurch the Huguenots on the ground that, lacking bishops, their ministrations were invalid.[2]

It is important to notice, however, that whether or not he continued to hold this view for the rest of his life, it did not constitute an intellectual revolution. It was a view which even if adhered to by Hyde from this time forward did not abrogate or alter the criteria of policy and the basic assumptions we have been describing. The general pardon which he twice in 1649 recommended the exiled Charles II to offer to his subjects was to cover the ecclesiastical as well as the civil deviations of the past years, and what he recommended in 1649, he was still recommending a decade later. Moreover, the suggestion of a synod to discuss church differences in the calmer circumstances which it was hoped would follow the healing of the political schism remained throughout one of Hyde's assumptions for dealing with ecclesiastical restoration when it came. As it drew near, there were preparatory negotiations with individual Presbyterian clergy and offers of

[1] Ibid. p. 367.　　　　[2] Ibid. p. 403.

preferment on a par with the transactions which in the civil sphere had always been advocated and practised in the case of individual members of insurrectionary parties in England. There was no difference in principle here between the treatment of ecclesiastical and civil affairs. It was assumed that individual clergymen were like laymen convertible, and that they were to be encouraged, if desirous to help, on the basis of an acceptance by them of the main structure of religion of State in England, namely the principle of the formal liturgy and an at least *de facto* episcopacy. But in Hyde's judgement the worst ecclesiastical troubles had been a function of civil troubles, and if laymen could agree in the settlement of the latter, the differences between clergymen would fall back into their proper place and significance. The synod was an admission that such differences existed. Its relatively late position in the strategical time-table of restoration is to be connected with the Chillingworthian idea that disputes were the offspring of passion and uncharitableness which delay would allow to cool; with Hyde's sense of the priority of civil over ecclesiastical causes of disturbance in the late troubles, and also with his conviction that lay action in matters of the relation of Church and State should predominate. At the Restoration, the Church policy of the first phase is brought out once more, and in a way which it is less easy for historians to ignore. The phase of intransigence with its high point in Hyde's adherence to the doctrine that episcopacy was theologically indispensable provides no retrospective clue, as has generally been assumed, to his earlier activity. But it is not true, either, that it represents a conversion from the ideas of the first phase, when properly understood, to a point of view which would make it unthinkable that the comprehensive policy pursued by him at the Restoration could have been deliberate or sincere. At the Restoration, comprehension, a widening of the boundaries of the Church and a softening of partisan rigidities, were in Hyde's judgement as much demanded and justified by the circumstances as such a policy had been from 1641 to the Treaty of Uxbridge.

The apostrophe in the final writings of the English Reformation, which had been achieved 'without the least appearance of force and compulsion, and with that regularity and solemnity that no alteration, with reference to Church or State, was ever made in any state or kingdom of Europe more warrantably',[1] was the offspring of Chillingworthian theology and non-violent parliamentarism, the two so closely bound together that it seems impossible to draw a line between them at any period of Hyde's life. In this sense Hyde's pretensions to a lifelong consistency and also his reputation with posterity for having achieved the consistency which he claimed are vindicated. It has been shown that in the case of his Chillingworthian colleagues there was no such merging of religion and politics. Their attitude was in some sort a bar to any whole-hearted political thought or action. Even Cressy, who, as a convert to the Church of Rome, exposed and confounded Chillingworth's utopianism, perpetuated his own earlier outlook when he expressed the opinion that the Church of England was 'the most free from corruptions in practices commanded, the most pure in doctrines decided and received, and the most moderately and charitably allowing a latitude to men's understandings of any under the sun', but only 'if considered as abstracted from the intrigues and interests of state'.[2] If this be compared with Hyde's judgement upon the same institution a genuine antithesis emerges. For Hyde, the English Church was 'the most exactly formed and framed for the encouragement and advancement of learning and piety, *and for the preservation of peace*,[3] of any church in the world'.[4] This difference between Hyde and his original circle, together with the circumstance that his ecclesiastical viewpoint, in contrast

[1] *Dialogue...concerning Education. The Miscellaneous Works of the Rt. Hon. Edward Earl of Clarendon,* 1751, p. 335.
[2] *Exomologesis,* pp. 34, 35.
[3] The present writer's italics.   [4] *Life,* II, p. 89.

with his viewpoint in civil politics, seems to have been a historical one from the outset, produced in the end a distinction between them which is complementary to the one described in the present section, and which ultimately placed him in a position from which he was able actually to out-Chillingworth Chillingworth.

Hyde would never have charged Chillingworth and Falkland with the ill-temper and bitterness of mind which lay behind so much religious controversy. On the contrary, it was their distinctive merit in his eyes that their condemnation of such evils was surpassed only by the moderation which they themselves displayed in their handling of controverted points, and he blamed Cressy for the lack of that objectivity and courtesy in regard to his late mistress, the English Church, which he expected 'from his natural genius, and from the conversation he frequented [namely at Tew] where bitterness of words was never allowable towards men whose opinions were very different'.[1] But it is clear that he meant more by 'ill-temper of mind' than the passionate manner in which controversy was conducted. The ill-temper of mind which he deplored was consequent upon, or even identifiable with, 'the want of knowledge or of consideration, how much of the religion in all national Churches [and all churches in his view were national churches] is of the religion of State, nor hath any other foundation than in reason of State'.[2] This statement is the culmination of an argument directed against the use of such terms as 'anti-Christ' and 'idolater' in controversy. In the original *History*, in the course of describing the benefits enjoyed by the country in the period before the Civil War, Hyde mentioned the learning which had in a pre-eminent degree flourished in the Church: 'and the Protestant religion [was] more advanced against the Church of Rome by writing, especially (without prejudice to other useful and godly labours)

[1] *Animadversions*, p. 239.   [2] *Essays*, II, p. 198.

by those two books of the late lord archbishop of Canterbury his grace, and of Mr Chillingworth, than it had been from the Reformation'.[1] It is illuminating to compare the reference here to *The Conference with Fisher*, the Jesuit, and *The Religion of Protestants* with Hyde's remarks in the *Essays* written at a much later date, where he explained what he held to be the root cause of religious dissensions. 'Learned men look upon it only as a contest in religion.' 'It may be', he went on, 'some learned men of the present age...have handled and enlarged upon those particulars, with much more clearness and evidence, than hath been done before;...yet, I say, let what is urged be true or not true, it is not the method....'[2] It was not the method because it involved an attack upon Religion of State in other countries.

The criticism of the use of such terms as 'anti-Christ' and 'idolater' obviously fell most directly upon Stillingfleet, the leading anti-Roman and indeed the leading Chillingworthian divine of the period in which Hyde was writing, who belaboured Roman Catholicism with epithets of this character, and indeed, as has been seen, provoked that book of Cressy's which Hyde answered. Nor did Hyde ever expressly criticize on this head the theological works either of Laud or of Chillingworth. But even though these abusive terms were not used by Laud and Chillingworth in their books, none the less *The Conference with Fisher*,[3] *The Religion of Protestants*, and even Falkland's *Discourse of Infallibility* were, equally, frontal attacks on Catholicism as a religion and, as such, were wide of the mark from the point of view of a correct understanding of Religion of State. There was little to choose, here, between the party of antiquity and the Chillingworthians. Indeed, in that the latter could be held to have conducted the more effective polemic, to the extent of forcing their opponents to

[1] Clarendon, *History*, I, p. 95.   [2] *Essays*, II, pp. 177, 178.
[3] A commonplace book of Hyde's contains some extracts from Laud's book under the date December 1646. Clar. MSS. 126.

change their ground, they might be said to be the worse offenders. There is, moreover, another point. Unlike Hyde, Falkland had spoken bitterly and abusively in his parliamentary criticism of the Laudians in 1641, and in the answer to the Grand Remonstrance Hyde had refrained from speaking abusively of the Puritans. Should it have occurred to him, and should he have wished to do so, he was now in a position to make a virtue for himself out of a detachment on his own part in 1641 which had been due less to disagreement with Falkland than to preoccupations of a more strictly political nature than those which Falkland had characteristically entertained.

Hyde said that the distinction between religion and Religion of State being well understood, and the understanding how much of what seemed to fall into the first category rightly fell into the second, would be the best expedient to reconcile many great controversies.[1] There ought, he said, to be more National Councils, and these should make contact with one another across the national boundaries,[2] a recommendation which, it may be noted, tallies with the project of afforcing an English synod with foreign divines which he had countenanced since 1643. But no doubt the upshot of such transactions was intended by Hyde to be the clarification of the fact that differences were mainly explicable in terms of the inevitable and historical differences between Religions of State. In that case, the reconciling many great controversies would have meant something not so immediately acceptable to churchmen. Argument in religious controversy normally proceeded not only upon the assumption that truth was at stake, and that in consequence it was an urgent matter that opponents should be converted, but also upon the assumption that opponents were convertible. Hyde was striking at these assumptions. If differences sprang mainly from varieties of social temper and of historical tradition, they could be resolved only if it

[1] *Essays*, ii, p. 179.   [2] Ibid. pp. 202–4.

were possible, as it was not possible, to iron out such varieties. Hyde was denying that most of the differences could ever be resolved. The reconciling many great controversies meant for Hyde, not an agreement arising from the successful termination of rational discourse on the points at issue, but, instead, an agreement which was to spring from the abandonment of discourse on the ground that it was necessarily futile. He wrote:[1] 'If I endeavoured to convert a French Catholic,' and began with an attack on the power of the Pope, using the customary Protestant arguments from Scripture and antiquity, he would reply that the Pope had no power in France beyond what was congruent with national interests and sentiments, and that he reverenced not the Pope but the laws of France. In regard to Purgatory, he would reply that he was not competent to judge, and that

'since the doctors differ so much in opinion of the place [of the departed souls], he thinks fit rather to conform (without farther inquiry) to the judgement of the Church and State under which he lives, than to perplex himself with the several disputes about it.... In the mean time he is well assured, that if he takes that care of his soul that he ought to do whilst it is in this world, God Almighty will provide for it sufficiently in the next, and to Him he will leave it'.

Hyde then described himself trying to shake the Frenchman on the points of Invocation of Saints, images, the denial of the Cup to the laity, and Transubstantiation. But the Frenchman was not daunted. It was possible the saints could not hear: on the other hand, it was possible that they could. As for images, he never worshipped one in his life: they were recommended by authority as a means of recollection. The Protestant argument for the restoration of the Cup was plausible, but no doubt there were reasons on the other side, and he was unable to believe that the Most Christian King and a learned and virtuous clergy could conceivably conspire

[1] Ibid. pp. 180 et seq.

to damn him. Similarly with Transubstantiation: for his part, his eyes were shut when the Host was placed on his tongue, and he swallowed it as soon as it was placed there. He had, therefore, nothing to say in regard to Hyde's point (which he frequently stressed in these writings) that the doctrine of Transubstantiation contravened the evidence of the senses. But many learned and good men upheld that doctrine, and he was the less inclined to abandon it, knowing that though the Protestants denied it they could not agree upon an alternative. With this, he took the offensive, and demanded to know whether it was not better to conform to the religion of his country, whether, indeed, it were not better to conform even if Hyde's arguments were unanswerable on the level of divinity.

Hyde confessed himself beaten, and held that the theologians who thought and acted in terms of a simple contest in religion ought to be taught to confess themselves beaten too. Men were convertible but only to their own history. They were convertible only to institutions which in the passage of time had been fitted to the specific characteristics which they, as a people, happened to represent. Moreover, it was their own history, the fact that they were inescapably the representatives of a given national type, which must be the chief agent of their conversion. Hyde was repelled by the use of the words 'heretic' and 'schismatic' and 'apostate' by the Popes and their partisans, and he would not allow the Protestants to use the words 'anti-Christ' and 'idolater'. It was not merely that such epithets were impolite. If that had been all, it would have been possible for a good man to use them advisedly. But they were technical terms, and Hyde implied that they were meaningless ones because the science to which they referred was one the validity of which he questioned. For it was a science which assumed that from the fount and essence of religion there was derivable a single and complete system of theological truth and a single orthodox church. 'All those choleric words, of heretic, schismatic, and apostate, are terms of art which need no definition, not terms of religion, which ought to be generally discussed and understood.'[1] The science which alone could help forward the discussion and the understanding of religion was not theology of the traditional type but the science of history.

Hyde said that 'that may be a truth and fit to be retained in France, where it hath the approbation of church and state, which is a great error in England, where it is rejected and condemned by both'.[2] With Chillingworth, and Chillingworth may perhaps have differed from Falkland in this respect, rationalism had worked itself through the full circle. It is on record[3] that Chillingworth held that 'there was not any certainty in matter of religion', and Hyde, in the *Life*, stressed his scepticism.[4] Between this scepticism and the view that a proposition could be true in France but false in England there might appear to be little to choose. But at least it may be said that Chillingworth's scepticism was a result of the operations of rationalism in the field of philosophical and theological speculation. It was the final term of such a rationalism. It was not the product of political experience and historical reflexion. The latter might produce, as it did in Hyde's case, an element of relativism. But in that instance, it was precisely politics translated into history which was responsible for a robustness of faith which could disregard any dangerous implications in the relativism. Hyde was happy to emphasize with the rest of the Tew circle the part of reason in religion, but with him it was in the last resort a historical reason which prevailed, a reason which allowed to rationalism no place at all either in politics or in religion.

It was, first, the political, and, at a later stage, the historical point of view in Hyde which qualified his assimilation of the

[1] *Essays*, II, p. 171. [2] Ibid. p. 204.
[3] *The Lady Falkland: her life, from a MS in the Imperial Archives at Lille*, 1861, p. 81. [4] *Life*, I, p. 52.

radical individualism of Tew. In practice, he was identified with it but once only; on the occasion late in 1641 when he had stood for a right of protestation on behalf of members of the House of Commons. Chillingworth also, strangely enough, was involved in this episode, gratuitously supporting such a right, and doing so at the bar of the House whither he was summoned.[1] An abstract right of protestation did indeed flow directly from the principles of the Tew circle. 'He had given his opinion', so ran Chillingworth's confession at the bar, 'that he thought a Protestation lawful in all cases; wherein any vote was to pass against the conscience of those who were the minor number...if a parliament would bring in the mass, a man might protest against it for the discharge of his own conscience...'. What had chiefly aroused the House of Commons, however, and the offence which led to his imprisonment for a time in the Tower, was his report that 'we had sides and parts in the house which has but one body, so to set a division amongst us...'. Hyde would never have agreed that the House of Commons could be regarded as other than 'but one body'. It had been an active orthodox parliamentarism which had driven him into a position in which parliamentary principles and the principles of Tew happened to conflict, and there is no reason to believe that he rejoiced, for the occasion, that he could choose the latter.

Chillingworth, in dedicating *The Religion of Protestants* to King Charles I,[2] distinguished himself from all those whose beliefs were governed 'by the prejudice and prepossession of their country, education and such like inducements, which, if they lead to truth in one place, perhaps lead to error in a hundred'. Both he and Falkland and Hales stressed, as a universal procedure, the necessity of every man working out and directly apprehending the truth for himself. But though Hyde, as against Rome, stressed the duty of criticizing

[1] *D'Ewes*, Coates, pp. 232-4.   [2] *The Religion of Protestants*, p. 1.

religious opinion, he also said that 'education and laws constitute Religion of State'.[1] 'I will not say, that which a great doctor of the Church of Rome affirms, and says it is very plain, that it belongeth truly to the nature of religion to be propagated in mankind by discipline, and delivery over from father to son, and to be embraced in the mere virtue of such a reception, through the natural credulity of children to their parents and teachers.' But he would very willingly say that impressions were and ought to be made by education which would not easily be removed. Some beliefs, indeed, should give way before 'the improvement of natural science', and some notions would be 'contradicted by those faculties which God hath made superior to such infusions'. But 'all other things which do not carry in themselves a visible disapprovement, are insensibly inculcated by education, and innocently retained, without obliging the thousandth part of Christians to make any further inquiry into the truth of them, having neither faculties to judge, nor reason to believe, that they can be better informed, than they have been by those who bred them'.[2] Hyde, whatever he may have said in other contexts about the duty of the rational man to be critical in matters of religion, accepted education and laws as a matter of course, and it did not occur to him that the sifting and refining process by conscience and reason which was so insistently commended in the Chillingworthian circle was either possible or desirable on the scale which was implied. Hyde's views in the end were more in keeping with traditional estimates of the limitations of the human reason than those of his colleagues had been, and he learned to attach more importance than they seem to have done to the guarantees which were afforded in a doctrine of Providence.

Granted that institutions were not predominantly clerical, and provided laymen were firmly in control, Hyde embraced

---

[1] *Essays*, II, p. 190.
[2] Ibid. pp. 238, 239, 240.

them without question as a patriot, and as a historian described them with enthusiasm. Humanly speaking, and therefore by divine Providence, there could be no religion without Religion of State, and 'education and laws constitute religion of State'. In the later part of the *Contemplations* on the Psalms, the part written in the last exile,[1] he discoursed exactly as Chillingworth might have done in a sermon on the superiority of a true and individual 'religion of the heart' over 'religion of the brain' which was doctrinal and institutional, but at a later point in the same exercise he went on to point out that the religion of the heart, the authentic spiritual and moral life of the individual, could not stand alone. Christ had not made 'all things so entirely lay and secular' that he had not countenanced religious institutions, and indeed it was clear that they had always been 'thought an essential prop and support of sanctity and religion itself',[2] and this was a point which Hyde had argued and maintained with a correspondent as far back as 1647.[3] If this were so, it is clear that in Hyde's view of the matter there was a very important sense in which the term 'religion of the heart' could and should be applied to the religion which in the Chillingworthian scheme was merely religion of the brain. Religion of State, the product of education and laws, rightly merited the attachment of the heart as much as the intelligent concurrence of the mind, and indeed depended for its existence with all which that implied in Church and State more particularly upon such an attachment than upon anything else.

True religion could not exist without ecclesiastical institutions and the loyalty they engendered in the people to whose characteristics they had become adapted. These institutions in their turn had depended and therefore would continue to depend for the sweetness of their condition upon the institutions of the civil State and the policy of civil statesmanship

---

[1] *Contemplations*, p. 424.   [2] Ibid. pp. 489–90.
[3] Hyde to Hopton. *S.P.Clar.* II, pp. 368–9.

which, while necessarily conservative, ought also in Hyde's view always to be liberal. Without such policy these institutions would in the logic of the activities of ecclesiastics usurp the place of true religion and injure both true religion and also, at one and the same time, the State. Thus while Chillingworth and Falkland, academically ignorant and suspicious of politics, relied excessively upon the enlightenment of private men to break the yoke of the churchmen, in Hyde's case in an active life of politics, the interests of true religion and those of the State came to be inextricably woven together. Politics with him were all-important and in his case the measure of scepticism which should be sufficient to abate clerical pretensions without sacrificing Christianity itself was nourished in political rather than in academic experience. Hyde was thus enabled to leave behind traditional theological rationalisms, both ancient and modern, and at the same time to escape the dilemma which was to confront the line of thought which had been pursued in the Tew circle. For it seemed that men in such a tradition must either sacrifice too much wisdom in the process of building up a new atheological rationalism, or else be caught in a pessimism born of a self-accumulating scepticism. Chillingworth, as Cressy said of him, 'had managed his sword much more dextrously than his buckler'.[1]

But if politics played this all-important part in Hyde's mind, it was because they were not all-in-all and self-sufficing as they were in the mind of Hobbes. It was possible indeed, looking back, to say that politics had created Religion of State; but it was not possible to say that politics had created religion. For not only did Christianity in its essentials trace itself to a divine interposition to which Hyde had much less difficulty than Hobbes in attributing an existence in its own right and therefore a self-authorized domination over Religion of State, but events themselves, the results of politics, revealed in the

[1] *Exomologesis*, p. 140.

last resort not the minds of men, but the action of that reality of which belief in the essentials of Christianity was the recognition, and of which, therefore, the political man as much as all private men in the recesses of their souls must take account. The knowledge of what was thus revealed in events Hyde knew as history. History was the knowledge of political actions in the past and of their deposit in the shape of temporal institutions, whether civil or ecclesiastical. But since there was organic, providential connexion between religion and Religion of State, meaning could be attached to the movement of events only if it was studied in a profoundly religious spirit which was humble enough but also confident enough to trace therein the action of Providence.

There can be nothing strange in the discovery that Hyde shared the robust faith of the English gentry, who made the Revolution of 1640, that history—the march of events under the generalship of Providence—was on their side: the belief that success was guaranteed by the moral structure of the universe. But it will at once be evident that Hyde differed for instance from Cromwell. Cromwell, with many others of the party which was in Hyde's eyes the violent party, saw political necessities as they presented themselves as imperatives from Heaven. Cromwell identified himself with those imperatives as Heaven's chosen agent, and in his success read the proof that he had been and would continue to be right. But with Hyde 'prosperity was never yet thought a good argument of men's piety, or being in the right'.[1] He evaded such irresistible identifications as Cromwell's and reached something more profound because in the phase of his greatest political activity he himself had continuously failed. At that time, as the pupil of Tew, and as against the 'mere moral man', he had struggled in the face of all the obvious political necessities and all the obvious ecclesiastical fanaticisms from the platform of conscience and reason. Because he failed he became

[1] *A full Answer.*

324

a historian, and to that fact, as we have seen, he owed a political success which for all the qualification which it is necessary to make when the post-Restoration period is studied, especially in the ecclesiastical field, was in itself sufficiently distinguished and indeed spectacular.

What proved decisive for Hyde was not the mere belief that events revealed the government of Providence, a belief which was subscribed to by many in the seventeenth century, especially amongst the Puritans, but the fact that the achievement of such a belief in the form of an operating conviction coincided with and found its expression in the actual study and writing of the history of the events in which he had been recently engaged. And because it was this which proved decisive for Hyde, the same fact was decisive also for the vindication in 1660 of the revolutionary achievement of the Long Parliament both in the civil and in the ecclesiastical sphere.

INDEX

327

HYDE, EDWARD, Earl of Clarendon
(*cont.*)
Independents, 193, 195, 198–9,
216–17
on aims and methods of Cromwell,
194, 198–203, 208–10
on the platform to be adopted by
the King in defeat, 195–8
on possibility of Spanish intervention, 207–8, 305
*A letter from a true and lawful
member*, 208–10
his case against opportunism, 212–
15, but is sympathetic to negotiation, 218–20, 226–8
Survey, 222, 224, 304
Restoration a vindication of his
views, 238–9
Religion:
dispute of 1641, 2–4, 18–20
opposition to Grand Remonstrance,
22–9, 181–2
ecclesiastical aspects of answer to
the Grand Remonstrance, 37–
40
opposition to Bishops' Exclusion
Bills, 60–3, 233, 240–1, 276,
282–6
Contemplations and Reflections, 165–70,
175–7, 183, 322
Restoration an 'Anglican miracle',
238–9
nature of his Anglicanism discussed, 240–3
influenced by Tew circle, 261–2
defends Tew theology: (*Animadversions*) 264–8; (*Essays*) 268–76;
but at variance with some Tew
ideas, 313–16, 319–23
agreement with Falkland in criticism of Laud, 277–80
latitude of opinion in all save
essentials, 280–2
on reformation of the English
Church, 281–2, 298–300, 302
contrasted with Falkland: in religion, 287–9, 292, 300–1, 323;
in politics, 296–7
reply to the Kirk, 289–92

comments on Falkland's character,
292–3, 295
Religion and Policy, 298
political anti-clericalism, 300–2
Religion of State, 303–5, and its
relation with policy, 306–13,
316, 321–4
on religious controversy, 317–19

Instrument of Government, 209
Irish rebellion, 21–2, 80, 91, 94;
Impressment Bill, 58–9

Jermyn, Sir Henry, 78, 84, 147, 172
Juxon, Bishop, 5

Kentish petition, 84
Kirk, General Assembly, 289–92

Laud, Archbishop, 5, 16, 89, 183,
240, 247, 254–5
criticized by Hyde and Falkland,
277–80, 287, 315
The Conference with Fisher, 315
Levellers, 187–8, 201, 205–7, 210,
216–18
Lilburne, John, 201
Lister, T. H., 10–13, 114–15
Littleton, Lord (Lord Keeper), 101,
107–9, 111, 116
Loudon, 1st Earl of, 289
Lunsford, Sir Thomas, 50, 84
Luther, Martin, 245, 248, 252, 255,
299

Machiavelli, Niccolo, 192, 194
Discorsi, 194, n. 3
Prince, 194
Manchester, Earl of, 112, 194
Manwaring, Bishop, 222, 279
May, Thomas, 22, 116–17, 148
Maynard, Sir John, 20
Melanchthon, Philip, Falkland on,
259
Mixarchy, 12–13, 152, 223–4
Monk, General, 219–20, 236
Morley, Bishop, 244, 262

Newcastle, Earl of, 49, 59, 84